CONTRA DANCE CALLING
A Basic Text

Also by Tony Parkes
>Shadrack's Delight and Other Dances
>Son of Shadrack and Other Dances

Recordings featuring Tony Parkes
>Kitchen Junket (with Yankee Ingenuity)
>Maritime Dance Party (with Gerry Robichaud)
>Heatin' Up the Hall (with Yankee Ingenuity)
>More Down East Fiddling (with Gerry Robichaud)
>Shadrack's Delight and Other Dances

CONTRA DANCE CALLING

A Basic Text

SECOND EDITION

Tony Parkes

Hands Four Books

Bedford, Massachusetts

Printed on acid-free paper

ISBN 978-0-9632880-3-5

Library of Congress Control Number: 2010938633

Library of Congress subject headings:

> Country-dance – United States
> Folk dancing – Study and teaching
> Folk dancing – United States
> Square dancing
> Square dancing – Study and teaching
> Square dancing – United States

Copyright © 1992, 2010 by Tony Parkes. All rights reserved. No part of this book may be reproduced in any form or by any means now known or to be invented without written permission of the author, except as provided under the Copyright Act. For information address Hands Four Productions, P.O. Box 641, Bedford, Massachusetts 01730. **www.hands4.com**

Cover art © 1992 by Karen Brown

Back cover photo of author by Doug Plummer **www.dougplummer.com**

Because of the dynamic nature of the Internet, any Web addresses or links contained in this book may have changed since publication and may no longer be valid.

The mention of a product, trademarked or otherwise, in this book does not constitute an endorsement. The description of a product does not necessarily apply to other products from the same manufacturer.

Printed in the United States of America

Second edition

*To the glory of God
and the memory of Ralph Page
(1903–1985)
this book is gratefully dedicated*

Contents

Acknowledgments	ix
Preface	xi
Preface to the Second Edition	xiii

Part One: The Theory and Practice of Calling — 1

1: Getting Started	3
2: What Is a Contra Dance?	13
3: Music – the Cornerstone	25
4: Delivering the Calls	33
5: Teaching and Walkthroughs	49
6: Choosing Your Material	63
7: Working with Music	79
8: Sound Equipment	95
9: Calling for Special Groups	113
10: Reaching Your Community	125

Part Two: Basic Moves and Dance Routines — 141

11: Before the Basics	143
12: The Basic Moves for Two People	149
13: The Basic Moves for More than Two People	167
14: Circle Dances	193
15: Whole-Set Dances	205
16: Contra Dances	215
17: Yes, We Do Squares Too	231

Glossary	253
Resources	275
Index	301

Acknowledgments

Many people made this book possible. A few helped directly in its birthing; most helped by fostering my growth as a caller. I owe them all a debt that I can never repay except by passing on the knowledge they have given me.

First of all, my undying gratitude to my parents for telling me that in the matter of my career choice, what made me happy would make them happy, and for convincing me that they meant it.

Thanks to the callers and other leaders who convinced me to take up calling and encouraged me in my early efforts: Jonathan Lurie, John Melish, Jack Bailey, and Dave Fuller at the Farm and Wilderness Camps in Vermont; Dudley Laufman in Vermont and New Hampshire; Dick Kraus, Michael and Mary Ann Herman, the late Betty McDermid, and the late Don Durlacher in the New York City area; Cindy Green and everyone at the Eastern Cooperative Recreation School; Ted Sannella, Louise Winston, Roger Whynot, and all the members of the North of Boston Callers' Association; Don Armstrong and the entire Lloyd Shaw Foundation and Fellowship; and always the presence of Ralph Page, in New York, in Maine, in New Hampshire, in Boston, and now in memory.

The speaking and writing of Cal Howard, Walter Lenk, and the late Jim Hilton influenced my thinking on the subject of sound.

For good times and many insights into the musician's point of view, I am indebted to the members of Yankee Ingenuity, past and present: Peter Barnes, Henry Chapin, Joyce Desmarais Isen, Donna Hébert, Cal Howard, Mary Lea, and Jack O'Connor.

Nearly all the people whose names appear in the Resources section inspired me in some significant way. Some of them I am privileged to call friends; others are friendly acquaintances; some I know only by reputation.

The Country Dance and Song Society generously allowed the use of material from their publications in the Resources section.

Jerry Helt, Dudley Laufman, and Ted Sannella graciously gave permission to include their original or adapted dance material.

Larry Jennings and Jack Sloanaker read and criticized the manuscript from the respective viewpoints of a caller and a non-caller. Many of their suggestions are incorporated in the book.

Karen Brown managed to capture the flavor of contemporary New England contra dancing in her cover design.

Apologies to ace financial writer Andrew Tobias for stealing one of his best gags.

Finally, my wife Beth applauded my decision to write the book, initiated me into the mysteries of PageMaker software, encouraged me to keep going when the going was tough, let me know when a sentence or a chapter wasn't good enough (and just as important, when it was), and believed in me throughout the project. Thank you, my love.

Acknowledgments to the Second Edition

Nearly two decades after this book was first published, all but a handful of my mentors have passed from this life, but their actions and words continue to inspire me.

In producing the second edition, I am indebted to the members of the Trad-Dance-Callers mailing list for suggesting additions to the Resources section; to Amy Cann for exchanging ideas on the social aspects of the dance; to Chris Ricciotti for sharing his thoughts on gender-free dancing; and to David Millstone for helping convert the book's computer files from an obsolete format and for assuring me, time and again, that the book was worth revising and re-publishing. Beth was once again invaluable, for her computer expertise and her willingness to use and share it, and for her encouragement in general and her belief in the book and its author.

Preface

Contra dancing is an enjoyable social activity that almost anyone can join in. It can serve as an icebreaker, an exercise medium, and a means of building community spirit. With a very small investment of time and money, people of all ages and conditions can learn a skill that will pay huge dividends of happiness for a lifetime.

But not every community has the knowledgeable leadership that an effective contra dance program requires. Even where willing leaders have emerged, information on teaching and calling techniques is often hard to locate. This book is, to the best of my knowledge, the first comprehensive entry-level guide to the subject. It is aimed primarily at readers who presently enjoy contra dancing and want to learn to call, but it should also be helpful to potential callers who are not yet dancers: school and college instructors, camp counselors, and various recreation leaders.

What this book is, and does, can be readily seen by a glance at the table of contents. It attempts to deal with every aspect of the dance caller's work. It is not primarily a collection of dance material; many fine collections already exist. It does not make all other books in the field obsolete; each writer looks at the subject in a unique way. And it is certainly no substitute for listening to actual callers and practicing in private and in public. But it should give the new caller a place to start, both by covering the elements of calling and by pointing the way to other resources.

The particular viewpoint of this book is that of an active caller and musician who loves country dancing of all kinds but identifies most closely with square and contra dancing as it has evolved in New England and, more specifically, in the Boston area. Ted Sannella and Larry Jennings have documented the Boston style thoroughly and well in their respective books *Balance and Swing* and *Zesty Contras*. While many of my biases are similar to theirs, I recognize that other communities, geographic and social, do some things differently, and I have tried to allow for varying styles in my descriptions.

Until about 1970, the term "square dancing" was used universally to mean whatever style and formation of Anglo-American group dance was familiar to the speaker or writer. Since then, the style common in New England, and characterized by vigorous dancing and loose organization, has become known as "contra dancing" even though it frequently embraces squares and circles. As a long-time devotee of squares, I am sorry to see them divorced from contras in the public consciousness, but certainly gladdened by the interest shown today in all forms of country dancing. In response to the current demand for information about contras, I have written primarily of them and of the circle dances that resemble them. For readers who want to broaden their outlook, Chapter 17 and several entries in the Resources section deal specifically with New England squares.

More than a quarter century of experience, ten years of active research, and two years of writing have gone into the making of this book. If you, the developing caller, find it useful, I will feel amply rewarded. May you enjoy acquiring and using the skills of a caller!

Preface to the Second Edition

It is hard for me to believe that nearly two decades have gone by since *Contra Dance Calling* first saw the light of day. The book was well received, but when the initial print run was exhausted, I was not at all sure that there would be enough continuing demand to justify a second printing. The economics of book publishing have recently undergone a radical change, and it is no longer necessary to estimate the demand for a book in order to have it printed at a reasonable cost.

Any living thing must grow in order to survive, and with growth comes change. As it is with plants and animals, so it is with human institutions. Contra dancing has evolved since the early 1990s, in its choreography and its music. A few new movements have been added to the basic list, and hundreds upon hundreds of new dances written – some merely slight variations on one another, but some innovative, interesting, and rewarding to dance. Musicians have worked long and hard to improve their technique; they have learned new tunes and written their own. As a result, contra dance music has reached a level of sophistication not encountered since the turn of the twentieth century – and perhaps not even then.

The fundamentals of calling, however, have not changed. Contra dancing is as closely wedded to its music as ever, and the caller's task remains the same: to enable the dancers to move with the music by prompting ahead of the phrase – and in most cases, to teach the basic movements quickly and clearly, as separate classes are not part of the contra dance tradition. The core of this book is as timely in 2010 as it was in 1992.

What *has* changed is technology. When this book was first published, the Internet was still in its infancy; the World Wide Web had just been created, and browsers as we know them did not yet exist. Now the majority of information – including contra dance information – is transmitted using websites and e-mail. Search engines such as Google make it easy to find out when and where dances are held. Specialized websites enable musicians to post audio samples and offer their music for sale, on CDs or as downloadable computer files. Dances are advertised on social networking sites such as Facebook. Young people arrive at a dance and send text messages to their friends, urging them to come (or stay away). Auction sites like eBay have made secondhand dance books and recordings easier to find and obtain than ever.

Although electronic books – to be read on a computer or a specialized portable device – are now commonplace, I believe that the average person in need of a how-to manual will prefer a paper copy for some time to come. I see printed books and the Web as complementing each other, not competing. With that in mind, I have updated the Resources section, realizing that the reader is likely to turn to the Web to make a purchase or to seek additional information, rather than drop an order form in the mail or visit a library in person.

In addition, I have reread and reconsidered every word of the book, asking myself whether it is still what I want to say and how I want to say it. I have added a few new points, clarified others, and updated all references to technology. The result, I trust, is a work that will prove useful to a new generation of dance leaders.

PART ONE
The Theory and Practice of Calling

1
Getting Started

If you're reading this book, it's a pretty safe bet that you've at least considered learning to call country dances. You may not be sure, though, if you have what it takes. This chapter is designed to help you decide that question, and to give you some pointers on how to begin to turn that goal into a reality.

What Is a Caller?

A caller is a curious mixture of teacher and entertainer. He or she must give clear directions to the dancers, but must blend those directions with the music in a pleasing way. Like a singer or a stand-up comic, a caller must keep a crowd of people feeling that they're having fun. But unlike other performers, a caller also teaches people a valuable skill which they can enjoy using for the rest of their lives.

Never forget that a caller's purpose is to make people happy. Technical skills are important, but they're only a means to an end. No matter how much you learn about material and delivery, from this book or elsewhere, remember that you're there to give the dancers a good time.

Soul-Searching

Before you get started as a caller, you'll need to do a bit of soul-searching. What kind of caller do you want to be? One who travels all over the country and can handle any kind of group? Someone who knows a few dances and can liven up a party if there's no one else around to do it? Or somewhere in between?

The amount of time and effort you put into learning to call will determine the amount of skill you'll develop. Think about how much time and energy you're willing to divert from other interests – family, work, school, other hobbies, spiritual life – to your study of calling. It's nothing to be ashamed of if you choose to stop short of the top of the pyramid.

Another important question to ask yourself is: Why do you want to call? There is no right or wrong answer; there are many legitimate reasons for calling. Some of these are:

- A desire to see people enjoy themselves
- Love of dancing and music and a desire to do more with them
- Ego gratification
- A wish to ensure the future of enjoyable dancing
- Willingness to take the initiative if there are no callers in your area
- The need to add calling to your repertoire if you're a teacher, camp counselor, or recreation leader

Money is not a good reason for becoming a caller. It is possible to come out ahead financially from calling, but like any other honest occupation, it takes a deal of time and energy. If calling is right for you, even as a sideline, the money may well be there; if you go into it expecting to get rich, you're sure to be disappointed.

There are three general requirements for success as a caller: talent, technical knowledge, and a sense of historical and cultural perspective. Given a bit of talent to start with, all three can be developed with time and practice.

Talent

Your talent is a gift from God. It's appropriate to be thankful for it, but you don't need to be apologetic about it. A caller needs a moderate amount of many different talents, rather than a great deal of just one (see the list below). We're given talents in varying amounts, but we have the ability to develop them. It's important to be honest with yourself about your talents. Then you can be thankful for the ones you have in greater measure, and willing to work on your weak spots.

Don't get discouraged just because you have those weak spots. No one, not even your favorite caller, has a full measure of every possible talent. One of the finest callers I've ever known had what some people might think an insurmountable handicap: he was not at all musical. He compensated for this by learning everything he could about the structure of dance tunes and by making careful notes on what tunes worked well with each dance that he used.

Another caller suffered from near-terminal shyness when he began his career. He dealt with it by treating his calling as an act, in which he could relate to people under a different persona from the one he used offstage. Little by little the act became a genuine part of his personality, and now he is only moderately shy.

Here is a list of talents or qualities that are helpful to the caller. Some of these apply more to the professional than to the casual caller; others will come in handy in any calling situation.

- Self-confidence
- Patience
- Good judgment
- Emotional balance
- A sense of rhythm and timing
- A pleasant speaking and/or singing voice
- Good diction
- Musical ability
- Good memory
- Spatial sense (ability to see what's happening in the set)
- A love of people and a desire to see them happy
- A delight in bringing order out of chaos
- Perseverance in the face of disappointment and frustration

Remember, no one has all of these to the same degree. If you're lacking in some, you're just as well off as anyone else who's starting out. If you feel you lack nearly all of them, though, you might reconsider your decision to be a caller.

Above all, you must enjoy what you're doing. If you do, your dancers will too.

Technical Knowledge

There aren't many rules or principles involved in traditional dance calling, but the few that exist are extremely important. To become a caller, you'll need to learn the mechanics of calling thoroughly. At the outset you'll be in for a great deal of practice and drill. Eventually the responses you need will become second nature, like turning on the water in the morning. When you've reached that point, you can "fly on autopilot" from a technical standpoint and use your conscious mind to deal with the variables – the things having to do with the people present rather than your dance material.

It may be that you're a teacher, camp counselor, or other professional working with people in groups, and that you've been ordered to become proficient as a caller in two months. This is hard to do well; like any other skill, calling takes time and practice. But you can shorten the learning period by disciplining yourself to do some work every day, and by acquiring and listening to a variety of recordings with calls (see the Resources section). If the time allowed you for preparation is extremely short, you may be better off if you use called recordings with your group and focus on learning the basics of country dancing and how to teach them.

A Sense of Perspective

Country dancing wasn't invented yesterday. Many callers make classic mistakes – such as using inferior material or doing an inadequate job of teaching – that could have been avoided if the callers had done a little digging into recent history. Older callers and some libraries have dance books, recordings, and perhaps most valuable, magazines. Books and recordings are increasingly available through online dealers and auction sites, too. Learn as much as you can about what's been done so far, what's worked and what hasn't. Studying dance history will not only provide a wealth of practical information, it will give you a sense of the dedication that leaders of the past have had, and heighten your feeling that the dance is worth preserving.

All this, of course, takes time and effort. All the good things in life do – there's no shortcut to success. But think of the sense of accomplishment you'll have when you've mastered the skills of calling – not to mention the fun you'll have along the way!

The First Steps

The initial stage of learning to call can be divided into several parts. Some things need to be done before you ever try calling to live dancers; others can only be done after you've tried a few times. Many of the habits you develop at this stage should be kept up as long as you continue calling.

Dance

First, make sure you know how to dance. You shouldn't even think about trying to call until you can react automatically to all the calls you're going to use. You should also be familiar enough with the calls that even if you couldn't list them all from memory, you could tell whether or not a given set of words was a legitimate call. Many years ago a fellow camp counselor with little dancing experience persuaded me to try to teach him to call some simple squares. He had a good voice and a good sense of timing, but he didn't know the calls. In a dance that began "First lady to the right, circle three hands around," he persistently called "Circle three *times* around." If he had been dancing longer, he would have seen what was wrong.

I generally recommend two years of dancing, or one year of extremely intensive dancing, as a minimum before anyone tries to call. The only exception to this rule would be someone who is thrust into the caller's role by circumstances. Perhaps you're a schoolteacher who is ordered to teach a unit on square or contra dancing. Or you've just moved to an area that has no regular dancing and you want to start some. Or the only caller in town has moved away and no one else wants to take on the job. It is possible to start calling with very little experience on the dance floor; you'll just have to work that much harder.

Keep Dancing

Regardless of your experience level, you should keep dancing even after you've begun to think of yourself as a caller. You'll remember more easily how much fun it is, and you'll continue to get valuable insights into the dancers' viewpoint. Visit dances other than your favorite local ones whenever you get a chance. Eventually you'll be able to size up the callers and compare your progress with what they're doing. If you're not sure you have enough knowledge to judge, ask some of the experienced dancers if they think the caller that night is good. You might even ask why or why not.

As you dance, practice being aware of what's happening in the set. What does each movement accomplish? Does it give you a new partner? Does it change the direction you face? Does it alter the shape of the set? Notice, too, how the figures fit the music. Try to pick out the first beat of each eight-beat phrase, and the beginning of the tune as it comes around again. (Don't worry if you're confused by some of this language; the rest of this book should answer most of your questions.)

Listen

Listen to other callers, at dances and on recordings. Find as many different ones as you can. Make your own recordings of callers at dances – never without permission, but most callers will be flattered that you asked. The older ones, especially, will be glad to know that someone is interested in keeping the tradition alive. Listen till it comes out your ears. (But ask yourself or a trusted friend whether the callers are good or not. Don't assume that a famous caller is strong in the areas you're focusing on. Often, though, you can glean one or two good things from a caller who is otherwise undistinguished.)

Buy a few recordings of dance music without calls. You'll need them for your practicing, and they'll help give you the feel of country dance tunes. Away from the distractions of a live dance, you can listen again for the phrases and subphrases of the typical 64-beat tune. You'll hear the difference between reels and jigs, marches and hornpipes, smooth tunes and bouncy ones, in a way that no book can tell you.

In addition to commercial recordings, you may want to record some local dances if there are any near you (and if the band doesn't mind). "Live" recordings will give you more of the feel of an actual dance than recordings made in the studio. If you're allowed to plug your recorder into the sound system, you may be able to record the music without the calls – it depends on the system. If this is impossible, you can try to ignore the recorded calls when you practice, or use only the portion of each dance after the caller has stopped calling.

Practice

Now that you have some music, it's time to start practicing. If some of your called recordings have dances you like, try calling along with them. Do it several times, until you think you know the dance by heart. Then put on the same or similar music without calls and try calling the same dance on your own. Like training wheels on a bike, recordings with calls can give you the extra confidence you need at first. But like training wheels, they can become a crutch; make sure you do at least part of your practicing without them, making up your own wording.

You might try dancing with an imaginary set while you call. Some people find it helps, others think it's confusing. Try standing still and visualizing a set of dancers in front of you, too. As you gain experience, they'll act more and more like real dancers.

Record yourself as you call. Play the recording back and listen as critically as you would to any other caller. You don't have a sound recorder? Get one right away. It's an indispensable tool of the caller's trade. Even an inexpensive machine will tell you what you need to know.

At the outset, concentrate on learning a few dances well. It's better to know three dances thoroughly than to be acquainted with ten dances but not really sure of them. The same principle holds later: it's better to know ten dances well than two dozen poorly, and so on.

Be prepared to give a lot of time to practice and planning, both now and later. Experienced callers often spend more time programming a dance than calling it. Even occasional calling is going to make demands on your time; only you can decide if it's worth it.

Breaking In

So far we've talked about the things you can do by yourself. Most of them should be kept up even after you start calling to real people. But now it's time to think about how you're going to find those people.

In some cities, like Boston, it's become hard to break into the calling scene, precisely because dancing has become so popular that it's attracted a large number of callers. But in many places the field is wide open.

There are two ways you can start calling to live dancers. One is to seek out and accept guest slots on other people's programs. The other is to gather some friends and call to them privately. You can, of course, proceed along both roads at once.

Guest Sets

Guest sets are the accepted way of developing new talent in some localities. In other areas you may have to approach the subject delicately. Many callers will be sympathetic and quite helpful. If there are older callers near you, talk to them about opportunities to call. As with the question of recording, older callers will often be delighted to help you because they're concerned about the future of country dancing. They may even be looking for new blood, thinking of the day when they'll die or retire. Ask their advice, and listen to their answers – even if you think their best years are behind them and they should be getting advice from you!

If you do a guest set, of course, remember your manners. Thank the dancers, the band, and anyone involved in letting you call. Choose a dance you're sure you could call in your sleep; try it and your delivery out on a friend to make sure. The dance should be easy enough for everyone there – when you're a new caller, it's better to underestimate the crowd slightly than to risk "stopping the floor." Think beforehand about how you're going to teach it, what words you're going to use. Have a second dance ready, but don't offer to call it unless you're asked to in so many words. If there's a stated time limit, as there often is at festivals, observe it slavishly; make sure your walkthrough doesn't consume most of your allotted time.

Then take a few deep breaths, relax as best you can, and try to enjoy yourself. Remember how much fun the dancers are having. Remember, too, that most of them don't care how good or bad your calling is as long as they can get through the dance – that's one reason for picking an easy one. If you do happen to do a good job, the sponsors of the dance will take note, and you'll quite likely be asked to do more guest sets. In an area with few regular callers, you may be offered an entire evening quite soon, possibly before you feel ready. You should accept if at all possible – the only way to get good at calling is to call.

Calling for Friends

The private method of starting to call requires three things: enough people to form a set, enough space to dance comfortably, and absolute candor on your part. You must level with the group about your lack of experience. Don't try to pass yourself off as an expert; they'll discover the truth as soon as they go out into the dance world and compare you with other callers. Instead, emphasize the positive aspects of being "all in this together." It's often easier for people to share a good time if they feel they're equals, with no pecking order to worry about.

The dancing space can be someone's basement or spare room, a classroom, or a conference room at work. If you can get the use of a small gym rent-free (at a school, church, or club you belong to), so much the better. But a space many times larger than you need can work against you – the acoustics are often poor, and your group will start to feel like a handful of people waiting for something to happen, instead of a cozy party.

The informal set of dancers can be helpful even before you're ready to try calling. You can dance to called recordings at first, doing only the walkthroughs yourself, then switch over to your live calls as you build confidence. This approach works particularly well if none of you has had much experience with country dancing. If you're a schoolteacher assigned to do a dance unit, for instance, you'd do well to try yourself and the dances out on a group of peers before you take on an entire class of children or adolescents.

Starting a Series

Almost every budding caller dreams of having a dance series to call home. In Chapter 10 we'll talk about some of the factors involved in running a successful series. Here we'll just discuss the question of when and how to start a series.

A Shared Series

If there are other callers or would-be callers in your area, try setting up an "open mike" dance – one at which anyone is welcome to call a single number, with a second one later if time allows. Dancers will support such a dance if admission fees are reasonable. You can keep costs down by using recorded music or, better, making the band "open mike" too. The dancing space doesn't have to be large, so rental costs can be low.

If there are only a few callers around, you may want to get together and organize a multi-caller dance. This differs from an open mike dance in that the number of callers is fixed beforehand. How much calling you each get to do, of course, will depend on how many of you there are. A multi-caller dance can mean anything from two callers splitting the program, either in halves or one or two numbers at a time, to half a dozen callers each appearing once or twice during the evening.

Your Own Series

Maybe you can't find enough support in your area for an open mike dance, and no one wants to share a multi-caller dance. In that case, you'll have to use your judgment about when (or even whether) to start a series of your own. As a rule, a series will succeed only if it has a solid core of people who will come regularly and share the work of making it happen. This core can be your friends, perhaps the ones you've trained in your basement. Or it can be an existing affinity group – a school, church, or club. One of the longest-running dance series in the Boston area began as a church party, the kind that callers term a one-night stand (see Chapter 10). The group had such a good time that they scheduled another dance soon afterward. In a short time the dance had become a monthly series, which ultimately ran more than fifty years.

But don't just hang out your shingle and assume that people will come. I made that mistake once, back when I lived in New York City. A dancer asked me to call at an event she was planning in her hometown, a New York suburb. She had rented a church hall and advertised a square dance with the idea of turning it into a series if there was enough interest. I agreed to do it on a volunteer basis; I was pretty new at calling, and I've always believed in supporting new local series. It was a good thing I hadn't asked for any money – we got to the hall and set up the sound, and *one* person showed up.

Speaking of affinity groups, seize every opportunity to call to non-dancers, even if there's little or no money in it. I'm talking about cases where a church or club presents you with a ready-made audience, not situations like my New York fiasco. As with your basement set, don't misrepresent yourself. Make sure everyone understands that you're new at this. But if the group can accept that, everyone can have a lot of fun while you get some welcome practice. If it's your own school, church, or social group, there's the added appeal of having the leader be someone everybody knows.

Hang In There

You'll almost certainly get discouraged at some point during your startup period. Many new callers get acute stage fright the first time they call in public, even if their "public" is just a handful of friends. Other people make it through that first time on adrenaline, but begin to fall apart a bit later, when the initial thrill has worn off and they realize how vulnerable they feel up there in front of the group. Mastering the skills needed for effective calling begins to feel like keeping half a dozen plates spinning on poles.

If this happens to you, remember that it's normal. Don't give up now – the worst part of learning to call is nearly over. Things will seem much easier once you've passed through the initial stage of practicing at home. Likewise, the first few times you call in public are the hardest. The confidence you build in yourself through experience is something you couldn't get in any other way.

Mistakes are normal too. Like bee stings, they hurt, but they'll hurt ten times as much if you spend all your time dreading the ones that might happen. Once you've made a mistake, admit it and try to learn from it. Ralph Page, one of the most influential callers of all time, said, "The person who never makes a mistake is a person who never does anything."

If you've read this far, chances are you've got the will to succeed. Welcome to the world of calling – I wish you all the best!

2

What Is a Contra Dance?

If you're interested in calling contra dances, you probably have a good idea of what they are. But different people notice different things when they dance, and your idea may be accurate as far as it goes, but not comprehensive enough. So in this chapter we'll take a look at the history of contras and at their fundamental concepts. Please keep reading, even if this material looks familiar; the information given here will help you understand the rest of the book.

A Basic Definition

A contra dance is a North American social dance done in sets made up of two lines of facing partners. Originally the men danced in one line, women in the other; now men and women usually alternate in each line. The number of couples is flexible, ranging from five or six to as many as the dancing space will accommodate. In a true contra, every other couple is active, not just the first couple as in the *Virginia Reel*. The latter is a "whole-set longways," whereas a contra is a "progressive longways." Half the couples in a contra are moving down the set while the other half move up, dancing with each couple they meet. This keeps everyone dancing most of the time, one of the most appealing aspects of contras.

Contras are similar to square dances, and indeed are closely related to squares. (Squares and contras together are sometimes referred to as "country dances.") A square set is limited to four couples, who dance a variety of figures together. Conversely, dancers in a contra perform the same figure over and over, but with a different couple each time. All retain their partners throughout the dance, but usually spend a good deal of time with their neighbors, too. (Your neighbor is the person of opposite sex in the couple you are dancing with.)

Contra dancing is closely wedded to its music. Almost every contra dance routine is exactly the same length as the tune it is danced to. In other words, once through the dance equals once through the tune. Further, each part of the routine has its own part of the tune, so that the dancers' movements are always synchronized with the musical phrase. This is not only an important aid to learning contras, but a tremendous source of dancer satisfaction. (Phrasing will be discussed in detail in Chapter 3.)

A Little History

Many people first encountered the contra dance in the 1970s, when it seemed to appear out of nowhere in some parts of North America. But the contra is really much older (during the 1980s we had to explain that it had no connection with the Central American insurgents known as *contras*). It is a direct descendant of the English "longways for as many as will," which dates back at least four centuries. The name "contra dance" is a corruption of the French *contredanse*. Many older books will tell you that this French term was coined because partners stand opposite each other to begin the dance, but it seems more likely that it was itself a corruption of the English "country dance." (Ironically, the dictionary tells us that the word "country" is derived from the Latin *contra*, meaning "on the opposite side.")

The Early Days

The earliest danceable descriptions of longways are in a book entitled *The English Dancing Master,* first published in London by John Playford in 1650. The book went through seventeen printings, growing each time until it contained over 900 dances. (Some of these were in square formation; squares and contras have been close cousins ever since.) The dances in the first edition were too well developed, and presented too casually, to have been brand new in 1650, and there are passing references to some of them in earlier books. Presumably, these circles, squares, and longways were based on dances of the English villagers, modified somewhat to suit the taste of London society.

Contras and squares came to North America with the English settlers, and were enjoyed by people of all social classes throughout the Colonial period. (The Puritans approved of them as a way for young people to socialize and develop grace and good posture.) After the Revolution, the dance titles took on a different hue (*British Sorrow, Jefferson and Liberty, Lady Washington's Reel*), but the dances themselves changed little.

The First Big Changes

By the late 1800s, some innovations had occurred. Contra dances were now done in "improper" sets, with men and women intermingling in the same line. The two-hand turn with partner or neighbor evolved into an energetic "buzz-step" swing, often in a waltz position or something equally intimate. On the musical side, immigrants from Scotland and Ireland brought their jigs and reels to the New World. Their steps had little impact on contras (though they did influence African-American dance), but their tunes practically swept the English melodies into oblivion. To this day, almost any tune used for contra dancing is either a Scottish or Irish jig or reel, or a frank imitation of one.

At some point in the nineteenth century it became the custom for a teacher or musician to remind the dancers of the next figure. These prompts sounded better if they were given in time with the music; this led to the practice of rhyming the directions and even harmonizing with the orchestra, and the prompter became a caller. In the twentieth century, calling developed into an art in itself, especially in the squares, where the caller could actually determine the pattern of the dance "on the fly." But even in the contras, with their repetitive figures, a master caller could liven things up with outlandish rhymes and teasing comments on members of the group. The caller is now an integral part of square and contra dance tradition.

The Low Point

From 1850 to the early 1900s, contras suffered a decline. Dancing masters encouraged the urban upper and middle classes to learn fancy squares and couple dances, which required more teaching and practice. Everyone knew how to dance contras; they put no money in the pockets of the masters, who therefore dismissed them as old-fashioned. They survived chiefly among country folk – where Elizabeth Burchenal collected a few contras in the early 1900s for use in schools and Ys – and disappeared altogether in many areas.

Even the squares and waltzes were shoved aside around World War I by a new breed of couple dance, of Latin and African influence. Many of these dances were named for animals (the Bunny Hug, the Grizzly Bear); the sole survivor of the period is the Fox Trot. Henry Ford railed against these "immoral" dances and spent a good deal of time and money promoting "the dances of our northern peoples" (i.e., waltzes, squares, and contras). Although he failed to kill off the new dances, Ford's efforts encouraged a number of groups to work at preserving the older dance forms.

The First Revival

The square dance revival began in earnest in the 1930s. Its time had come; groups in many parts of North America sprang up independently. Depression and war spurred people to look to their roots and to band together for inexpensive, homespun recreation. At that time "square dancing" meant whatever the local style of group dancing happened to be, whether it was done in circles, squares, or long lines. Even in Maine, where country folk did the classic contras *Haymakers' Jig* and *Lady of the Lake* alternating with foxtrots and waltzes all night, they called it a "square dance."

A few strong leaders were in the right place at the right time to promote the activity to the public and to guide it along healthy lines. In the Northeast the mantle of leadership fell on Ralph Page of Keene, New Hampshire, a dance musician who learned to call from his uncle in 1930. Page's dry humor and his style of half-singing, half-chanting the calls, along with his insistence on clean and liquor-free parties, attracted dancers from all over central New England.

By 1950, square dancing had reached the status of a national fad. Contra dances found favor along with the squares, especially in New England, where they had survived in many towns. City dwellers who skied in Vermont and New Hampshire discovered the local dances and soon began to hire callers like Ralph Page for their own parties. Some of the city folk learned to call the figures themselves, and contra dancing became a part of the urban scene once more. A few new contras were written, the first in nearly a century.

During and after the fad years, a new style of square dancing emerged, known as "modern Western" (because it evolved from traditional Western figures) or "club style" (because its devotees usually organized themselves into formal clubs). In the 1950s it became highly stylized and regimented, with a great emphasis on correct costuming and etiquette. Old calls and movements were discarded as new ones were written; callers were expected to keep everyone in the set moving most of the time. Many of the new moves took odd numbers of beats to execute, and the historic connection between the dance and its music was lost to a great extent. But even here, contras gained a foothold, with prominent traveling callers like Al Brundage and Ed Gilmore spreading them across the continent. One Massachusetts caller, Herbie Gaudreau, took up the challenge of writing "modern contras" in which everyone was equally active, and became the most prolific contra choreographer of his time. His influence on present-day contra dancing, in both the modern square dance movement and the traditional network, has been greater than many people realize.

The Second Revival

By the 1960s, interest in squares and contras had declined somewhat from the "fad" levels of 1950. A few leaders had quit the modern square dance movement in disgust and joined forces with those who had remained outside it under the name of "traditionalists." Devotees in both camps had banded into close-knit groups, and little new blood was coming in. Then Dudley Laufman entered the scene. A Bostonian who moved to New Hampshire to become a subsistence farmer and caller, Laufman anticipated the widespread "back to the land" movement. His informal approach to dancing caught the attention of college students throughout the Northeast and sparked the second great group-dance explosion in modern times. (This time most people called it "contra dancing," partly because Laufman emphasized the contras and possibly because the term "square dancing" had become linked in too many minds with the modern square dance movement.) Laufman revived interest in the old jigs and reels, which had been neglected in the previous revival; hundreds of young people learned to play contra dance music. In the 1970s, young callers appeared across the continent to join the young musicians, assuring the survival and growth of contra dancing for another generation.

Present and Future Trends

Contra dance choreography has undergone radical changes during the current revival. The "equal" dance, in which couples moving up the set do the same things as couples moving down, has become the norm. Older dances with their active and inactive couples are done less and less often; many new dancers have never seen or done some of the classic routines like *Lady Walpole's Reel* or *Money Musk*. Balances and swings are more vigorous than a generation ago; twirls are replacing courtesy turns in some communities. Change in anything is inevitable with the passage of time, but contra dance leaders would do well to maintain a sense of perspective and to think about which changes will improve the activity and which will do more harm than good.

Since the 1970s, contra dancing has become a hobby for thousands of people, much as modern square dancing has done since around 1950. Some of the recent contra dance trends are reminiscent of the growth years of the modern square dance movement, including:

- The shift from actives and inactives to all-moving choreography.
- The fascination of callers and long-time dancers with complicated material.

- The growing gap between what a newcomer understands and what a dancer must know in order to be completely comfortable.
- The increasing standardization of style and terminology as dancers migrate from one area to another and visit between regions.
- A growing tendency among callers to play with their dancers by using material – such as contra medleys, no-walkthrough dances, and even outright hash – that keeps dancers more dependent on the caller than they would be in a traditional dance.

Many if not most contra dancers have a casual attitude toward organization and are wary of manifold rules and regulations. This, combined with the close traditional ties between the contra dance and its music, makes it likely that New England style dancing will avoid the worst excesses of the modern square dance movement. But thoughtful contra leaders can learn from square dance history and try to maintain a place for beginning dancers, in the face of pressure to cater to the "hotshots."

Plusses and Pitfalls

Contra dancing is an ideal recreation for almost any kind of group. Among its many advantages are these:

- It combines the benefits of moderate exercise with the joy of moving to music.
- It requires very little footwork to be learned, but consists primarily of walking toward and with other dancers and joining hands with them – skills that most people already possess and enjoy using.
- It follows consistent rules, and the sequence of each dance is predictable. Once the dancers understand a few basic terms and concepts, they can enjoy hundreds of different dances with almost no further teaching.
- It is a social recreation in itself, and also encourages socializing off the dance floor, whether the group is composed of singles, couples, or a mixture of both.
- It allows the dancers to relate not only to their partners, but to everyone in the room. In today's society, there are few opportunities for adults to socialize with both sexes in a non-threatening way. Contra dancing provides such an opportunity.
- It does not require participants to buy expensive equipment or special clothing. Comfortable shoes are the chief essential, and almost everyone has a suitable pair. The only investment is on the part of the leader or sponsoring group, for a small public address system.

Chapter 2: What Is a Contra Dance?

However, the contra dance can be intimidating to the beginner. The leader can do much to smooth the road for new dancers, but must remain aware of these pitfalls:

- There is no "home position" in a contra dance. The correct spot on the floor for each dancer is constantly changing, moving up and down the room.
- The timing in a contra dance is unforgiving. Because one round of the dance coincides with one repetition of the tune, the caller and the other dancers cannot wait for anyone who is behind time.
- Because the groupings of couples change every thirty seconds, one lost dancer can throw a whole line into chaos.

These points of caution are not meant to discourage you from using contras with new dancers. On the contrary, because they use so little footwork, they are one of the easiest dance forms for beginners to learn. But it is important to proceed slowly, making sure the group understands the basic concepts of contra dancing, particularly the idea of progression.

The Formation

Most contra dances employ the same starting formation, although there are minor variations. Nearly all contras use the same couple progression and the same length of sequence. This is good news to leaders who want to add contra dances to their repertoire. Once you understand the basic contra formation and progression, you can teach and call dozens of different contras with minimal preparation.

Almost any number of couples may join a single contra set. (This is one great advantage that contras have over four-couple squares; no couple ever needs to sit out because the numbers come out wrong.) The smallest practical number is five; with fewer couples, too high a percentage of the set will be waiting at the ends during each round. There is no arbitrary upper limit to the number of couples. In an "equal" dance (all the couples doing the same thing), the size of the set is limited only by the length of the hall. Twenty, thirty, or a hundred couples can dance a contra with equal ease. In the case of certain older dances in which half the couples stand still much of the time, it's best to limit each set to ten or a dozen couples.

To form a contra dance set, the dancers stand in two lines extending from the caller's end of the room to the opposite end. Experienced dancers face their partners immediately, forming a line of ladies facing a line of gentlemen. With beginners, it's often more effective to have couples face the caller and line up in a column, each couple behind the next, the lady on the gent's right. After lining up, dancers can turn to face their partners. (From the caller's point of view, the ladies are on the left, the gentlemen on the right, but telling the dancers this will merely confuse them.)

The two lines should be close enough that partners can almost touch each other's fingertips; for adults this will be five or six feet apart. Adjoining dancers in the same line should be far enough apart that one person could fit in between them, standing shoulder to shoulder. You'll probably have to caution your dancers repeatedly to keep their sets small; sets tend to spread out to fit the available space. The larger the set becomes, the more trouble the dancers will have staying in time with the music.

The long set is divided into "minor sets," usually consisting of two couples, who will work together for one "round" or sequence of the dance. The easiest way to designate the minor sets is to have the first four dancers join hands in a circle, followed by each adjoining group of four in turn. The traditional call for this is "Hands four from the top."

In each minor set, the couple nearest the head of the line will generally lead the figure. This couple is often referred to as "active" and the other couple as "inactive." However, the "inactives" frequently have as much to do as the "actives," and at any rate should not think of themselves as passive; if they do, their attention may wander when their time comes to dance. For these reasons, I prefer to call the couples "ones" and "twos," as is done in England. These terms have the added advantage of being short and easy for callers to fit into their wording. (In many newer contras, the couples' parts are identical, and it may seem that there is no need to number the couples. But many dancers welcome the security of knowing which way they're going, and will appreciate having the couples numbered.)

A contra made up of two-couple subsets is sometimes referred to as a "duple minor" dance. In the "duple proper" formation, all the ladies start in one line and all the gents in the other. In a "duple improper" contra, the "ones" or active couples cross over before the dance begins. Most contras written since the 1940s are duple improper.

While the beginning leader will need to master only the standard duple formation, other contra types exist. Many older dances, and a few new ones, are "triple minor," with subsets of three couples ("Hands six from the top"). Triples may be proper or improper. The "mescolanze" consists of lines of two couples facing each other, up

Chapter 2: What Is a Contra Dance?

Some Common Country Dance Formations

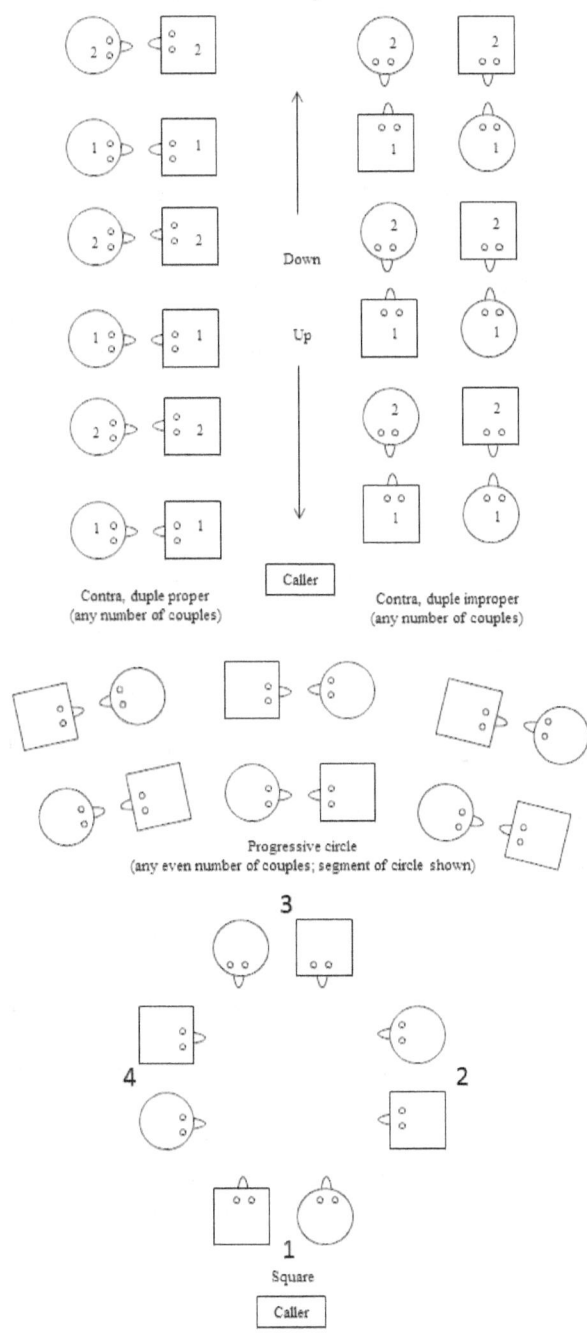

and down the hall or around a circle. A recent addition to the duple family is the "Becket formation" (named for Herbie Gaudreau's *Becket Reel*, the first dance to use it), in which partners stand side by side facing another couple in the opposite line.

The Progression

The most difficult idea for new contra dancers to grasp is the concept of progression, with its related concept, the change of roles. You must be prepared to teach the progression slowly and patiently, spending as much time as necessary, but as always saving new information until the dancers are in a position to use it. If you explain contra dance progression while your group is standing still, you'll probably find that no one has absorbed the idea when it comes time to practice it.

The couples in a contra dance have no fixed home position. Instead, each couple moves up or down the line, dancing with each other couple in turn. The "ones" or "actives" move one place down the set (away from the music) during each repetition of the dance. At the same time, the "twos" (and, in triple minor dances, the "threes") move one place up the set (toward the music).

This exchange of places is the all-important "progression," and is not always obvious. In many older contras, it's readily visible in the "cast off," with each active person dancing around an inactive one and ending below him or her. In modern contra dances, it often occurs during a swing, as contra choreographers have adopted the square dance rule that swings always end with the lady at the gent's right side. It may also take place during an excursion down and back by four dancers, when each pair turns as a couple in order to reverse direction. In this case, the progression is not at all obvious, since the dancers are neither above nor below each other when the move takes place. It's helpful to point out the progression in each dance, especially when the group is unfamiliar with contra dancing.

In Becket formation, just as in normal duple formation, half the couples are progressing in each direction, but each couple perceives itself as moving to its own left (or, in some dances, right) along its side of the set.

A relatively new type of contra is the "double progression" dance, in which couples move two places up or down the set in each round. Most such dances are duple minor; many dances in Becket formation have a double progression.

Neutral Couples and the Change of Roles

Two effects of contra dance progression are (1) the presence of neutral couples at the ends of the set, and (2) the change in each couple's role as it re-enters the dance.

Neutral couples are the couples that have progressed to the head or the foot of the set, and have no one to do the dance with. They simply wait through one sequence (about 30 seconds) and, if the dance is improper, exchange places during that time. (In a double progression dance, couples reaching the ends of the set wait out only part of a sequence.) When the next sequence begins, the neutral couple at the head becomes a "number one" or "active" couple, and the one at the foot becomes a "number two" or "inactive" couple.

All the dancers must understand that they *keep their numbers* while they progress up or down the set, changing roles only when they reach either end. They must also realize that they are to keep progressing in the same direction, dancing with a new couple in each round. A common error is for two couples to try to reverse roles and dance together a second time.

Couples suddenly finding themselves neutral can make one of several mistakes: they may leave the set, thinking their part in the dance is finished, or run to the other end of the line to dance with the other neutral couple. They may also try to re-enter the dance too soon, before the next round begins. This last mistake is the hardest to detect and to deal with. If you offer a word of extra direction to the erring couple, the rest of the dancers will hear it and may try to follow it, further confusing the set. One leader actually stands between the neutral lady and gent during their time at the head, then steps back from the set and sweeps his arms together to encourage them to cross over.

How often will a neutral couple appear at each end of the set? In a duple minor dance (every other couple active), it will happen every other time through the routine. If the set contains an even number of couples, everyone will be dancing the first round, while the second round will see neutral couples at the head and the foot. The third round will have everyone dancing, the fourth will have new neutral couples, and so on. If the set contains an odd number of couples, the sequence at the head will be the same as before, but the foot will be "out of sync" with the head: the foot couple will be neutral for the first round, only a couple at the head will be neutral in the second round, and so on.

If your dancers need to be reminded to cross over, it will be easiest to call to sets containing an even number of couples. The most challenging situation for the caller is that of two or more sets, some with an even number of couples and some with an odd number. In this case, the only sane procedure is to prompt the neutral couples at the head and let the foot couples figure out when to cross.

In a triple minor dance, there may be one or two couples left over at each end of the set. Couples at the head should simply stand still until there is a new group of three. A group of two couples at the foot, however, should continue to dance the routine, modifying it if necessary, so that a progression takes place. Otherwise, the last couple in line will never get back into the dance!

The principles given in this chapter apply to most dances and most teaching situations. More specific guidelines will be found in the following chapters.

3
Music – the Cornerstone

Although you don't need to be a musician in order to be an effective caller, you should know something about the structure of dance music. Country dancing, like other dance forms, is closely tied to and dependent on its music. This is particularly true of contras.

Tune Structure

Nearly all contra dances, and contra dance tunes, are the same length: 64 beats. At a tempo of 128 beats per minute, this means that one sequence of a contra dance lasts 30 seconds. (Actual tempo is often a few beats slower, but 30 seconds per round is still a good rule of thumb.) The dance movements and the tune coincide exactly; that is, they both begin on beat number 1 and end on beat number 64. Many New England squares also follow this rule, but squares from other regions often don't.

Contra dance tunes fall into one of several types: jigs, reels, hornpipes, marches, songs. Tune types will be discussed in Chapter 7. For now, it should be noted that although the various types of tune feel slightly different to the dancers, they're all the same length and calling to any of them involves the same skills.

The 64-beat tune is divided into four sections of 16 beats each. Most tunes have two musical strains, called the "A" part and the "B" part. The "B" part is usually higher in pitch, and often more complex harmonically, than the "A" part. Normally each part is 16 beats long, and each is repeated to provide the necessary 64 beats. The standard notation for such a tune is AABB, and the parts are A.1, A.2, B.1, and B.2. Even if you're not at all musical, you should memorize this notation, as these names are often used for the parts of the dance as well as the tune.

A good example of the structure of a contra dance tune is the familiar song "Jingle Bells." The verse music corresponds to the "A" part, and the chorus music to the "B" part. As in dance music, both the verse and the chorus music are repeated. The main difference between "Jingle Bells" and most contra dance tunes is that in the song, the end of the first "A" is slightly different from the end of the second "A" (this is also true of the "B" parts), while in most dance tunes the two

"A" (or "B") parts are identical. But this is a minor difference compared to the similarities. Each "A" or "B" part in "Jingle Bells" is 16 beats long, and the whole song contains 64 beats. In fact, any contra routine of standard length can easily be danced to "Jingle Bells."

Rhythm

Rhythm is the fundamental pulse or beat of the music; it's the basis of tune structure, timing, phrasing, and all the other niceties of dance composition and analysis. Its steady rhythm is what distinguishes dance music from other kinds of music.

When we talk of "beats" in a contra dance tune, we are referring to strong beats or *downbeats*. In the following example from "Jingle Bells," the downbeats fall on the underlined words or syllables:

<u>Dash</u>ing <u>through</u> the <u>snow</u> — in a <u>one</u>-horse <u>open</u> <u>sleigh</u> —

<u>O'er</u> the <u>fields</u> we <u>go</u> — <u>laugh</u>ing <u>all</u> the <u>way</u> —

Notice that some of the downbeats fall where no word is sung (these are indicated by dashes). In calling as well as singing, the voice will be silent during some beats.

Contra dancers take one step on each downbeat, so that after one playing of a 64-beat tune, the dancers will have taken 64 steps. Most people can easily hear and respond to the downbeat, which is generally played in the low or bass notes: the pianist's left hand, the guitarist's thumb, or the string bass, tuba, or bass guitar. With an average group, you probably won't need to mention that one beat equals one step. If your group has trouble finding the downbeat, you may need to talk a little about it, and also make sure that your music (live or recorded) has a downbeat that's easy to hear. (But beware of music with too much downbeat and not enough upbeat; the music needs to lift the dancers, not hammer them into the ground like tent pegs.)

Calling in rhythm with the music will help the dancers find the beat, as well as making your calls more pleasing to the ear. See Chapter 4 for an explanation of how it's done.

Timing

Each basic dance movement requires a certain number of steps to perform comfortably. The movements that have stood the test of time can be danced in multiples of four steps, making them easy to fit to music. Timing is the art of allowing dancers the right number of musical beats for each movement.

It's important to know the number of steps required for the most common basic movements. If you try to call a dance without this knowledge, you run the risk of telling the dancers to do the impossible by giving the calls in too-quick succession. Of course you can memorize an exact set of words and pauses, but if you skip a call by accident, you won't know how to recover. And because there are so few basic movements in contra dancing, it's just as easy to memorize their timing as it would be to memorize words for one or two dances. A little extra effort now will pay off later. To paraphrase the proverb, learning one dance by rote is like buying a fish; learning the timing of the basics is like learning to fish.

If you've danced for a year or two before starting to call, as recommended in Chapter 1, you've probably begun to develop a feel for timing. As you study the timing of the basics, you may find that you know a lot of this information even though you've never consciously thought about it.

Note that timing has nothing to do with the speed, or *tempo,* of the music. The tempo could be quite slow, and the timing of a dance would still be too fast if you weren't allowing people the full number of beats to dance each movement. Conversely, a fast tempo can be quite comfortable if you use proper timing (assuming the dancers are physically fit and can adjust their stride to the speed of the music).

The table on the next two pages lists the basic movements you're likely to encounter in contra dances and New England style square dances (not all of them are used in this book), with the generally accepted number of steps required to do each one. (See the Glossary in the back of the book for definitions of any terms that may be unfamiliar to you.)

Timing of Contra and Square Dance Movements

		Beats
Allemande	*See* Hand turn	
Balance	Once	4
	Repeated or double	8
Bend the line		4*
Box the gnat		4
Break to a line	(including circle half)	8†
California twirl		4
Cast off		4*
Chain	*See* Ladies chain	
Chassez		Varies; often 8
Circle	Four people halfway	4
	Four people 3/4 around	6–8
	Four people once around	8
	Six people halfway	6–8
	Six people 3/4 around	8†
	Six people once around	12–16
	Eight people halfway	8
	Eight people 3/4 around	12
	Eight people once around	16
Circle to a line		8†
Contra corners	*See* Turn contra corners	
Courtesy turn		4
Cross trail (through)		4
Dip and dive		Varies; usually 16
Do-si-do	New England style	6–8
	Southern & Western styles	12–24 (often 16)
Down and back		16
Down and back, cast off		16†
Ends close (or turn) in		4*
Figure eight	Half	8
	Full	16
Forward and back		8
Four ladies chain	One way	8†
	Round trip	16†
Gents chain	*Same as* Ladies chain	
Grand right and left	Four people once around	12–16
	Six people once around	16
	Eight people halfway	10–12
	Eight people once around	20–24

		Beats
Grand square	(including reverse)	32
Gypsy		6–8
Half figure eight		8
Half promenade		8
Half right and left		8
Half sashay		2–4*
Hand turn	Halfway	4
	3/4 around	4–8
	Once around	4–8
	Once and a quarter	8
	Once and a half	8
	Twice around	8–12
Hey	For three	12–16
	For four	16
Honor		4–8
Ladies chain	One way	8
	Round trip	16
Ladies grand chain	*See* Four ladies chain	
Ladies half chain		8
Pass through		4
Pass through and on to the next		4–8
Promenade	Across a contra set	8
	Up or down a line and return	16
	Halfway around a square	8
	Once around a square	16
Right and left (through)	One way	8
	Round trip	16
Rights and lefts	Four changes	12–16
Roll to swap		2–4*
Sashay or **Slide**		Varies; often 8
Square through	Four hands	12–16
Star	Four people once around	8
Star through		4
Strip the willow	Per turn	4–6
Swing		Flexible; 8–16
Turn contra corners	Until actives meet in center	16
	To starting position	16†
Twirl to swap		4*
Wheel around		4*

*Often "stolen" from the time allotted to other movements.
†This timing is considered demanding.

Phrasing

Phrasing is closely related to timing, but it's not the same thing. As noted above, timing is the art of allowing the dancers enough time (measured in musical beats) to execute each movement. Phrasing is the art of letting the steps of each movement coincide with the beats of a corresponding part of the music.

Contra dances are written to fit the AABB tune structure described earlier in this chapter. Not only are both dance and tune 64 beats long; the dance is divided, like the tune, into four parts of 16 beats each. Each part of the dance is always done to its own part of the tune. Therefore, the dance parts, as well as the tune parts, are known as A.1, A.2, B.1, and B.2.

Because most contra dance movements are done in 8 beats, there are usually two dance movements in each "A" or "B" part. In the simpler dances, these two movements are closely related. They may be two things done with the same person, such as do-si-do and swing. Or they may be opposing halves of a whole, such as circle (or star) first one way and then the other. This kind of simple, well-constructed dance is ideal for teaching beginners that contras and their tunes are written in distinct parts.

The following notation illustrates how the parts of a dance and its tune correspond:

Essex Reel

Contra dance, duple improper

A.1	Do-si-do neighbor	8 beats
	Swing neighbor	8 beats
A.2	Down the hall go four in line	4 beats
	Turn as couples	4 beats
	Come back to place and ends close in	8 beats
B.1	Circle left	8 beats
	Circle right	8 beats
B.2	Right-hand star	8 beats
	Left-hand star	8 beats

If we set this dance to our old friend "Jingle Bells," the do-si-do, which takes 8 beats, would be done to the music of "Dashing through the snow, in a one-horse open sleigh," which contains 8 beats. The swing, another 8-beat movement, would be done to "O'er the fields we go, laughing all the way," and so on. The following notation shows when each movement would be danced (*not* when the calls would be given; see the next chapter).

Essex Reel
(The Dance Movements, if done to "Jingle Bells")

A.1 *Dashing through the snow, in a one-horse open sleigh*
Do-si-do neighbor

O'er the fields we go, laughing all the way
Swing neighbor

A.2 *Bells on bobtails ring, making spirits bright*
Down the hall go four in line; turn as couples

What fun it is to ride and sing a sleighing song tonight
Come back to place and ends close in

B.1 *Jingle bells, jingle bells, jingle all the way*
Circle left

Oh, what fun it is to ride in a one-horse open sleigh
Circle right

B.2 *Jingle bells, jingle bells, jingle all the way*
Right-hand star

Oh, what fun it is to ride in a one-horse open sleigh
Left-hand star

4
Delivering the Calls

Once you thoroughly understand the structure of contra dance tunes and the timing and phrasing of the dance movements, you can begin practicing with recorded music, trying to deliver the calls at the right time. (A list of all-purpose recordings is given in the Resources section at the end of the book; any 64-beat tune can be used for practice.)

The Prompted Call

Contra dance calls are given not at the beginning of the musical phrase, as with some forms of square dancing, but at the end of the phrase. Each call is a prompt to the dancers, who perform the movement during the next phrase. For example, to get the dancers to circle left during the first half of the B.1 music, you need to call "Circle left" during the last few beats of the A.2 music. The chart on the next two pages shows when each call of *Essex Reel* would be given if the dance were set to the tune of "Jingle Bells."

Introductory Calls

The first call in the dance sequence must be given before the A.1 music; that is, before the tune begins. Once the dance is under way, this will be during the last few beats of B.2 in the preceding sequence. The first round of the dance presents a special challenge. The very first call must be given either during the musical introduction or, if there is no introduction, before the music starts.

With an eight-beat introduction, you can wait four beats and give the first call on the next four. Most bands, however, prefer to play four-beat introductions, making it difficult to fit in the first call. One solution is to say, before starting the music, "Get ready to do-si-do your neighbor," and then, during the last two beats of the introduction, "[One, two,] Ready, go."

A few older recordings have no introduction at all. In the past, if you used such a recording, you would have to say, "When you hear the

Essex Reel
(The Calls, if done to "Jingle Bells")

Beats:	1	2	3	4	5	6	7	8
Intro:	<u>Oh</u>, what	<u>fun</u> it	<u>is</u> to	<u>ride</u> in a	<u>one-horse</u>	<u>open</u>	<u>sleigh</u>	—
	—	—	—	—	With your	neighbor	<u>do</u>- si-	<u>do</u>
A.1:	<u>Dashing</u>	<u>through</u> the	<u>snow</u>,	— in a	<u>one-horse</u>	<u>open</u>	<u>sleigh</u>	—
	—	—	—	—	—	—	Swing that	<u>one</u>
	O'er the	<u>fields</u> we	<u>go</u>,	—	<u>laughing</u>	<u>all</u> the	<u>way</u>	—
	—	—	—	—	Down the	hall, go	four in	<u>line</u>
A.2:	<u>Bells</u> on	<u>bobtails</u>	<u>ring</u>,	—	<u>making</u>	<u>spirits</u>	<u>bright</u>	—*What*
	—	—	—	— As	couples,	turn and	come on	back
	<u>fun</u> it	<u>is</u> to	<u>ride</u> and	<u>sing</u> a	<u>sleighing</u>	<u>song</u> to-	<u>night</u>	—
	—	—	—	—	Ends close	in and	circle	<u>left</u>

B.1:

Jingle	bells,	jingle	bells,	jingle	all the	way
—	—	—	—	—	Circle	right
Oh, what	fun it	is to	ride in a	one-horse	open	sleigh
—	—	—	—	Same	four,	right-hand star

B.2:

Jingle	bells,	jingle	bells,	jingle	all the	way
—	—	—	—	Change	hands,	left hand back
Oh, what	fun it	is to	ride in a	one-horse	open	sleigh
—	—	Leave the	star,	on to the	next and	do-si-do

music, do-si-do your neighbor." (This didn't work well if the dance started with a balance, as balances must begin precisely with the musical phrase to be effective.) Happily, digital technology now lets the user control exactly when the music starts; see Chapter 7 for details.

Voice Technique

The actual calling of the dance – the physical speaking of words to your dancers – might seem to be the part of your job requiring the least forethought. After all, you talk to people every day. But there are a few aspects of vocal technique that almost everyone can improve, and attention paid to them will make your calling much more effective. One of the fastest ways to learn is to record yourself (and other callers, if possible) and listen with a critical ear.

Calling in Rhythm

For best results, contra dance calls should be given in rhythm: that is, they should be spoken in time with the beat of the music, just as the words of a song are sung. This is true even if you don't rhyme your calls:

> <u>Down</u> the <u>hall</u> go <u>four</u> in <u>line</u>
>
> <u>Turn</u> a - <u>lone</u> and the <u>same</u> way <u>back</u>

It may feel stilted at first; simply speaking as you would in normal conversation will probably feel more natural. But because the rhythmical calls blend with the music instead of clashing with it, they'll actually sound more natural and appealing to your dancers.

Similarly, keep the pitch of your voice up as you speak the last few words of each call. In everyday speech, most people drop their voices at the end of a normal sentence. Like calling in rhythm, keeping your voice up will feel unnatural at first. But it's necessary in order to emphasize both the call itself and the fact that the call ends on the eighth and last beat of the musical phrase (see "Timing the Call," below).

Projection

Learn to take a full breath before each line of the call (professional singers refer to this as "support"). It will give your voice more resonance and make it carry farther. It will also be more physically satisfying and put less strain on your voice. In addition, particularly if you're speaking loudly or pitching your calls on definite musical notes, learn to produce your tone in your chest and head, avoiding any tension in your throat. A few lessons from a voice teacher may prove helpful.

New callers often make one of two mistakes: either they speak too quietly, as if they were confiding a secret to a close friend, or they shout their calls, usually ending up with a sore throat or laryngitis. To avoid these extremes, pretend you're talking to someone about ten feet away. Often the dancers nearest you will be about that distance from you; just aim at them. If you're using a sound system, trust it to carry your voice to the back of the hall. (Note that you need to stand where you can hear yourself, or you'll end up straining no matter what!)

Care of the Voice

This deserves a chapter to itself. Your voice is your instrument, and unlike fiddlers and pianists, you only get one. Never force your voice; for instance, avoid long conversations in noisy places where you can't really hear yourself and so have no clear idea of how loud you're speaking. Drink lots of water – ideally every day, but especially during the day or two before a dance. Get in the habit of warming your voice up before using it, with lip rolls, humming, and vocalizing on "oo" and "ah" (again, a good voice teacher can help get you started).

Diction

Another important quality that needs to be cultivated is diction. You'll need to pronounce every letter in each word, giving special attention to consonants. As with calling in rhythm, you may think this sounds stilted. But diction is like stage makeup: it needs to be exaggerated in order to seem natural at a distance. With no makeup, an actor's face would appear washed out to the people in the last row; with less than perfect diction, your words will sound slurred to the dancers in the back of the hall. They'll enjoy dancing more if they can tell one call from another. Again, recording yourself will give you an idea of how you're doing.

Microphone Technique

Most present-day callers prefer to work with a microphone, except possibly with a very small group in a very small room. The proper use of a mike can enhance a caller's effectiveness while reducing the danger of straining the voice.

Some older books and magazine articles on calling say to keep the mike well away from you, while others will tell you to let it touch your lips. This contradictory advice stems not only from differences in calling style and philosophy but also from differences in microphone construction.

The ideal distance between your mouth and the mike is a compromise. In general, the closer the better because a mike's "gain" or volume of sound drops off quickly with distance. But getting too close will distort your voice, making it less pleasant and harder to understand. This is especially true of the bass tones, as unidirectional microphones (the best type for calling; see Chapter 8) have a quality known as "proximity effect": the closer you are to the mike, the more it exaggerates the low frequencies in your voice. With a typical unidirectional model, you should be able to insert two fingers between the mike and your mouth.

The angle at which you hold the mike is also important. A good unidirectional mike has a small "sweet spot" on the business end that picks up your voice the most strongly; if you hold the mike upright and talk over it, you'll miss that spot and will have to turn up the gain control, running the risk of feedback. But if you hold the mike straight out from your mouth, like a cigar, you'll hide your face from the dancers and may even block your view of them. I like to hold my mike at a 45-degree angle, which lets me talk into the sweet spot without losing the two-way visual contact with my dancers.

Note that I've been assuming you will hold the mike in your hand. I've found that using a mike stand forces me to focus some of my consciousness on keeping my head the right distance from the mike – an unnecessary use of energy and a potential cause of tension in the body. Some callers use a stand only as a handy place to park the mike when they're not using it.

Emphasizing the Key Words

Some of the words you'll be using in your calls are more essential than others. The key words are the words that the dancers have learned to react to – the "code words" that have a special country dance meaning, over and above their usual meaning in plain English. Other words may be "helping words"; they may clarify things for the dancers or reassure them that they're in the right place. Or they may be patter, added to fill out the meter of a line, to add color or humor to the call, or both. Common sense dictates that the key words be the easiest to hear, the helping words next, and the patter kept in the background. For example, in the call

Chapter 4: Delivering the Calls

<u>One</u>s <u>swing</u> in the <u>mid</u>dle of the <u>ring</u>

<u>Swing</u> with the <u>great</u> big <u>hand</u>some <u>thing</u>

the key words are the initial "Ones swing," which should be emphasized above the rest of the call. "Middle" is a helping word and can well get some secondary emphasis; it's not a key word because (1) it's plain English, not code, and (2) the context of the dance presumably dictates that the middle is the only convenient place for the ones to meet. The second line is pure patter and should be kept subordinate, with the possible exception of the word "Swing," which could be considered a helping word as it comes early enough to reassure the ones that they're doing the right thing. (Note that the underlines signify the musical downbeats, not the words to be emphasized.)

You can emphasize a key word or phrase in one of two ways: by raising your voice in pitch or by raising it in volume. (In reading aloud or public speaking, you can draw attention to a passage by lowering your voice as well; but this is impractical at a dance due to the music and the noise of the crowd.) Normally, you'll probably find yourself doing a little of both at once: raising both the pitch and the volume of your voice slightly. When you consciously decide to stress a key word more than usual, it's good to raise pitch sometimes and volume at other times, for variety's sake. Here, as in every aspect of calling, it helps to get the opinion of trusted friends and to listen to recordings of yourself.

Timing the Call

One of the most effective ways to help dancers find the musical phrase is by precise timing of the calls; that is, giving each call at the best possible moment to reach the dancers and allow them to react. There are two aspects of timing a call: placing the entire call so that it ends with a phrase of music, and placing the key words within the call to accommodate the dancers' reaction time.

Call within Music

Although the call could theoretically be given at any point during the preceding phrase, it's good practice to deliver it so that its last syllable falls on the last beat of that phrase. In this way, the call will "point to" the first beat of the following phrase, and allow the dancers to step out with confidence on that first beat.

Here's an example of some well-delivered calls:

Beats:	1	2	3	4	5	6	7	8
Intro:	—	—	—	—	Join	hands,	circle	left
A.1:	—	—	—	—	Circle	right, the	other way	back
	—	—	—	—	Same	four,	right hand	star
A.2:	—	—	—	—	—	—	Left hand	back
	—	—	—	—	Same	couples,	ladies	chain

Not only does each call end precisely on the eighth and last beat of a musical phrase, but most of the calls begin on the fifth beat. The sole exception, "left hand back," begins on the seventh beat. This is because the odd-numbered beats in country dance music are slightly stronger than the even-numbered beats. It's important to begin as many calls as possible on odd beats, as it gives a more pleasing effect. You'll be glad to know that it's actually easier to do it that way!

Key Words within Call

Even within the constraint of always ending the call phrase with the musical phrase, there are different ways to deliver the call. One significant point of difference is where the key words – the words that actually cause the dancers to react – are placed within the call.

The ideal placement of the key words will vary from one situation to the next, depending mainly on the reaction time of the dancers. This reaction time will itself change from session to session, and even during a session, based on the dancers' levels of experience, interest, and fatigue. For example, if a group of beginning dancers (whose reaction time is relatively slow) are circling to the left, and you want them to reverse direction, you may need to call:

>   Circle right, go the other way back

in order to give them an extra couple of beats to respond to the word "right." Experienced dancers, who have shortened their reaction time through long practice and who can often guess what call is coming next, may only need to hear:

>   — — Back to the right

If a sequence of calls is not easily guessed, even experienced dancers may need a couple of beats to react. Normally, this would be an effective wording:

> Same four, circle four

But in the contra dance *The Nova Scotian,* in which a ladies chain is followed by a circle when the dancers are expecting to chain back, you'll need to catch their attention by calling:

> Circle four, the same four

– at least the first few times through the dance.

(A review of emphasis: In the last two sample lines above, the key word to emphasize is "Circle." The expression "Circle four" also has a coded meaning, but the "four" is less critical, because the dancers in a contra expect to be working in groups of four unless they're instructed otherwise. "Circle" is the action word, the word that will get the dancers moving, and it's the crucial one to stress. "The same four" is a helping phrase; it should be audible but not quite as prominent as "Circle four.")

Occasionally a call line will contain two key phrases, and you'll need to think about which one should come first. Following is a common traditional call:

> Do-si-do with the one below

People who grew up dancing contras were able to follow that call without much trouble, as their reaction time was short and the call often came at the beginning of a sequence, when they were expecting to dance with "the one below." Today's routines, however, may include a neighbor do-si-do at any point. Because of this, and because most dance groups include inexperienced or hesitant dancers, it's better to call:

> With the one below, do-si-do

as this wording first tells the dancers whom to face or to move toward, then tells them what to do when they get there.

Currently, the following call would be even more readily understood and accepted by the average dancer:

> With your neighbor, do-si-do

as it is directed equally to the dancers facing up and to those facing down.

Diminishing Calls

Because the movements in each round of a contra dance are identical to those in the preceding round, most dancers memorize the movements after about half a dozen rounds. Once the dancers have reached that point, many callers prefer to let them enjoy dancing to the music alone, without any calls.

Rather than stop calling "cold turkey," a wise caller will first decrease the length and detail of each call, watching the dancers carefully to see if this causes any confusion. The next step is to omit some of the calls entirely, still watching for trouble. The calls to drop first are those that the dancers are most likely to follow without conscious thought. In a dance with a ladies chain (or right and left) over and back, the call to return may safely be omitted after a very few rounds. A call to circle right after a circle left is not quite as safe, because the dancers can erroneously extend the circle left into the next phrase of music; but many groups can soon do without it, especially if the music is well played and strongly phrased.

The final step in the process is to quit calling entirely. It's a good practice to stay alert and watch for any signs of confusion or hesitation. If you're using a microphone, hold it "at the ready" for at least one round after dropping out, in case you misjudged and many of the dancers still look uncertain.

Occasionally, you may find it necessary to resume calling after several rounds. Most often this will be when an inexperienced couple reaches the head or two such couples meet in mid-line; but sometimes a whole set will experience a kind of mental fatigue after a few minutes of dancing and will forget what comes next. It pays to watch the dancers carefully for signs of trouble; often you can see problems about to happen and forestall them with a few well-chosen words. Once the moment has passed, you can quit calling again.

You may also need to come back in with a few calls when the band changes tunes, particularly if the new tune is sharply different in character from the old. Dancers often subconsciously rely on the melody or chords of a tune, as well as the number of beats, for help in remembering the figures and their timing. A different tune may confuse them momentarily, but one called round will usually get them back on track. (Of course, if you're about to drop out and you become aware that the band is about to change tunes, you can simply keep calling for another round or two.)

How Long Should a Contra Run?

Contra dances have no special beginning and no fixed end. The figure of a contra is danced and called the same way each time, and may be done as many or as few times as the caller chooses. The question therefore arises: what is the optimum length of a contra?

The musicians and the dancers may have different opinions on this question. Musicians with long experience and sophisticated tastes will often plan medleys that raise the dancers' excitement level as the dance progresses, building to a climactic finish. Too long a dance will upset the band's carefully thought-out strategy. On the other hand, a musically satisfying medley can be too short for the dancers, leaving some of them with only one or two chances to be active.

My feeling is that ten minutes is about right for experienced dancers. For beginners or people beyond retirement age, you may want to reduce your sets to five or six minutes.

Traditionally, contras were danced "all the way down and all the way back"; that is, until the original head couple had worked their way to the foot of the line and then up to the head again. This was necessary in order to give everyone an equal amount of dancing, as until the 1950s most contra routines left at least half the couples standing still much of the time (hence the name "inactive couples"). It takes about one minute per couple to let everyone go "all the way." If the lines are short – six or eight couples – this old custom is still practical. But longer lines present a problem.

There are two things you can do:

- Limit the number of couples in each set. This can be done by creating several relatively short sets, or by dividing each long set in half and making a gap between the halves. The latter can be confusing unless you set up a physical barrier, such as a row of chairs. In a long, narrow room, it's better to call from one of the long sides if this is practical. If you're at the end of the hall, you can set up short lines across the hall for old-style contras.
- Run the dance all the way down and about halfway back, so that each couple gets to be active at least one-third of the time (inactive all the way up and active halfway down, at worst). Most dancers would rather have you operate this way than run twenty-minute sets and limit the number of partners they can have in an evening.

In extra large halls, these two approaches may be used at once.

With modern routines in which everyone is moving constantly, fatigue rather than fairness is the chief limiting factor. Running the dance "all the way down" but not back (letting the original head couple reach the foot) will give each person the chance to meet every possible neighbor without unduly tiring the dancers. With twenty couples in a set, this will take about ten minutes.

It's a good idea to select a "marker" couple at the beginning of each contra so you'll always know how far the original head couple has progressed. Before the music starts, look at the head couples in all the sets, and memorize the appearance of at least one. It's better to use two or even three couples; if you pick just one, you may be undone when that couple reaches the foot and decides to sit down!

No matter when you decide to end a contra, always let the top couple dance as an active or "number one" couple. Don't let them wait out the last round as a neutral couple and leave them stranded. True, they'll only get one turn as actives; but someone has to be in that fix – and one turn is better than none.

Ending Calls

Because a contra dance has no special ending figures, it's not essential to give any special calls as the music stops. But some callers like to end each contra with a little flourish (possibly to remind the crowd that they're still there). And if the dance begins with something like "balance and swing your neighbor," it's nice to let people know when they're at the end of the last round, so they won't leave their partner and try to balance someone new.

An ending call can be as simple as

— And bow to your partners all

This is especially effective if the routine comes to a natural resting place, or it can serve to forestall a neighbor balance. Or a call or two can be substituted for the calls in B.2; for instance, instead of "ladies chain over and back" you could use

Everybody forward and back

— — — —

Forward and swing your partners all

More elaborate ending calls can be devised, requiring one complete round of the tune. Ralph Page often used to call "Everybody forward and back . . . forward again and pass through, bow to the one you meet [coming from another set] . . . turn around" [all that again] "and swing your partners all . . . now promenade right off the floor; that's all there is, there is no more."

To Read or Not to Read

Many beginning callers despair of ever memorizing the amount of material they feel is necessary to their success. They read the calls of each dance from the index card they've prepared for it. Some callers do this with no qualms; others seem to feel guilty about it or at least assume that people will disapprove. "Why shouldn't I read?" they say. "It makes no difference to the dancers as long as I'm giving them a good time."

While there's nothing immoral about reading the calls, it's bound to get in the way of the rapport you're trying to build with your dancers, and it can rob you of the satisfaction that always comes with growth. If you rely on index cards or "cheat sheets," they will become a crutch that you'll never feel able to throw aside. If, instead, you work at memorizing one or two dance routines, you'll find that the next one or two will come more easily. (Part of the beginning callers' problem is that instead of taking small bites they tend to look at the whole amount of material they want to learn, and panic.) Memorization has been downplayed in schools for many years, but most people can learn short passages of prose or poetry by heart if they try.

Granted, contra dance sequences are similar enough to be confusing. Callers – even experienced ones – frequently begin one dance and find themselves in the middle of another, just as musicians do with dance tunes. Some callers find that the more dances they learn, the more trouble they have telling them apart. If this is a problem for you, I suggest looking at the card for each dance just before you have the dancers walk it through. Most people can put a single item the length of a dance routine into their short-term memory. Once you've reviewed the dance, hide the card and rely on memory for the walkthrough and the actual calls. If that doesn't work, try keeping the card in front of you for the walkthrough and hiding it when the music starts; reciting the movements during the walkthrough will help cement them in your short-term memory.

Notation – How to Use This and Other Books

While this is (I believe) the only comprehensive entry-level book on contra dance calling, there are many books that will be of great help once you get started. Most are collections of dance routines; some include music and/or explanatory matter. There are two things to notice about these books:

- Not all the routines in them will be equally useable. Some are intended for experienced dancers, some for beginners. Some flow

more smoothly than others (fashions change, and not all choreographers are equally skillful). Different dances will be appropriate under different conditions; for example, dancers in long sets will appreciate routines that keep everyone moving.
- There are several different systems of contra dance notation. You'll need to learn to decipher them – not during the dance, but in your study beforehand. It's important to remember that even though authors use different notations, they're talking about the same thing.

The biggest single difference in notation systems is between those that give the *dance movements* and those that give the *calls*. The difference has to do with how the writer relates the dance to the music. Dance-movement notation puts the description of each movement *within* its own part of the tune, because that's when the dancers do it. Call notation puts the call for each movement *before* its part of the tune, because that's when you must call it – in advance of the music.

This book uses both styles of notation for each dance, to show the difference and to get you used to reading and interpreting both kinds. Some callers find one system easier to use than the other; eventually you'll decide which you prefer. By then you'll be able to take dances you find in printed sources and convert them to your favorite notation.

Fine Points of Notation

Another difference in notation systems is in the way they label the parts of the 64-beat dance sequence. Most contemporary authors divide the sequence into the four parts of the typical contra dance tune: A.1, A.2, B.1, and B.2, with each part having 16 beats or steps. Some of these authors describe the length of each movement in beats or steps, while others prefer to think in musical measures or "bars." There are two beats to a bar (no matter what time signature is used for contra dance music, each bar is considered to have two strong beats). This means that each "A" or "B" part is 8 bars long. It's important to know which system is being used: one author's 8-bar phrase is another's 16-beat phrase, and has enough time for two 8-step movements. (This book uses beats or steps throughout.) Authors who write in terms of the tune's "A" and "B" parts usually use dance-movement notation.

A few authors avoid the AABB terminology altogether. Larry Jennings in *Zesty Contras* and *Give-and-Take* breaks each dance routine into eight 8-beat phrases, and numbers them 1 through 8.

Thus, his "1" phrase equals the first half of the A.1 music, his "2" phrase the second half of A.1, and so on. Jennings uses dance-movement notation. Don Armstrong also divides dance routines into eight parts, but numbers them according to the beats of music they use: "1–8," "9–16," and so on until "57–64." Armstrong uses call notation; his *Caller/Teacher Manual for Contras* was the first widely circulated source to do so (although the explanations in that book use an expanded form of dance-movement notation). Call notation is now almost standard for contras in the modern square dance field, which was the primary audience for Armstrong's *Manual*.

This book adheres to the AABB form in order to emphasize the connection of contra dance figures with their music. This requires you to see the two halves of each "A" or "B" part as a whole, not as two isolated 8-beat moves. In many contras, as noted above, these two movements are closely related, making it easier to think of them together. The call notation in this book is similar to Armstrong's, but with A.1, A.2, etc., replacing the 1-to-64 system.

5
Teaching and Walkthroughs

If you're calling to a group of friends with contra dance experience, and you've chosen a routine they all know, you don't need to do anything but call the dance. But in most situations you'll have to explain a few things first. You'll quickly discover that teaching and calling are two different skills.

A century and a half ago, callers didn't have to teach at their dances. In the city, people took lessons from a dancing master before attending a ball; in the country, folks learned to dance by watching and then muddling their way through the sets. Nowadays teaching is usually done during the evening's dancing, and every caller is expected to be an instructor as well.

Many good callers could stand to improve their teaching. This chapter deals with some of the skills involved.

Note that teaching only one contra dance to a group is an inefficient use of time. Contra structure takes a while for most beginners to grasp, but once it's understood, dozens of dances can be enjoyed, all following the same ground rules. It's better, therefore, to use contras only if you have time to do several, whether in one session or in a series.

Dances vs. Basics

Contra dances, in spite of their variety, are all constructed from a limited number of basic movements, or *basics*. Variety is produced by combining these basics in different ways.

Basics themselves vary in complexity, from the simple do-si-do to the bewildering hey. Naturally, beginning contra dancers should be presented with dances using the simpler basics. Some groups may want to explore the outer limits of contra dance choreography, not only using more complex basics but trying dances that use standard basics in unusual combinations. But the average group, treating contra dancing as a social activity rather than an all-consuming hobby, will be content with about a dozen basics, combined in fairly predictable ways.

In the past, there has been considerable debate about whether beginning square dancers should be taught complete dances or only drilled in the basics they will encounter. This debate has intensified as modern square dancing has evolved away from set routines toward "hash," or total improvisation by the caller. In contra dancing, fortunately, there is no conflict: Contra dances are all set routines (hash is done only as a novelty on rare occasions), but they are also all made up of standard basics. Dancers should definitely be taught the basics as separate entities, but this can well be done by presenting good, cohesive dances, teaching basics as they occur. There should normally be no need to concoct drills in order to teach basics; the repetitive nature of the contra dance will serve the same purpose.

Chapters 12 and 13 describe the basic contra dance movements in detail.

It's Not Just a Bunch of Basics

Square and contra dancing is too often taught as a series of isolated basics strung together, with no thought given either to how the dancers should move around the floor or to how they will get from one basic to the next. In the most extreme cases, this has led to a style of dancing that resembles a chess game with human pieces: when they hear a call, the dancers walk quickly to their new spots on the floor and wait there for the next call. Good timing and phrasing (see Chapters 3 and 4) will prevent this to some extent, but for best results you'll need to think about posture and transitions.

Posture

How to move is as important as when and where to move. For the most satisfying results, dancers should stand erect and lean very slightly forward, so that the weight is over the balls of the feet. If the knees are slightly bent, or at least unlocked, the dancers will become less tired. Steps should be taken with confidence, but dancers should avoid thinking of their feet as stepping out in front of them. Instead, they should push back with each foot as it touches the floor, keeping their weight forward.

The best way to visualize one's motion is to imagine the body as gliding smoothly forward, always on the same level, with the feet merely coming along for the ride. It may help to imagine a string attached to the chest, being pulled forward and upward at a 45-degree angle. As someone has said, "Lead with your heart and your feet will follow!"

Giving Weight

Closely related to posture is the idea of giving weight. The concept applies to movements in which dancers hold one another, such as hand turns, swings, and circles. To give weight, each dancer pulls away from the partner or group enough to let them feel his or her body mass acting against theirs. The resulting sensation in each person's body should be quite different from that of a dancer moving alone. If the holds were suddenly released, particularly in a swing, dancers giving weight would be in danger of falling. This means, of course, that tried and true holds must be used and that caller and dancers must be aware of the hazards. But giving weight is what makes traditional dancing so exhilarating, and the activity would be much poorer without it.

Transitions

Another aspect of country dancing that is often ignored is the transitions between movements. During a walkthrough or even a beginners' teaching session, the caller is likely to ask for a swing and then a promenade without explaining how to get from one to the other. Traditionally, dancers have discovered the easiest ways to combine movements by trial and error. But with so many of today's contra dances demanding split-second timing, a few people spending one or two beats figuring out a transition can throw a whole set off the musical phrase, lessening the enjoyment of the dance.

It behooves the caller, therefore, to spend a little time on transitions. When you're planning a program, think about the combinations of figures in the dances you're going to use: which ones are likely to cause trouble? Think about what you could say to smooth the transition in each case. It doesn't have to be lengthy; often a single sentence will do the job. The important thing is to acknowledge that some transitions are as much of a skill to be acquired as the movements themselves.

Transitions are dealt with in detail in Chapters 12 and 13. Under each basic movement, the most common transitions to and from other movements are discussed.

Anticipation

Closely related to transitions is the concept of anticipation. In contra dancing, the pattern of each dance is repeated many times, and the dancers always know what the next move will be, because the caller tells them in plenty of time or (after the caller has quit prompting) because they have memorized the sequence, at least for the short term.

Because the sequence is familiar and there are (ideally) no surprises, the dancers are able to anticipate each movement. Indeed, to get the most enjoyment from the dance, they should anticipate. This doesn't mean "jumping the gun" and starting each move before the music says to start. What it does mean is that the dancers, knowing how much time they have left and what kind of transition is coming, can adjust their timing of each move so that they finish comfortably on the last beat of the phrase, ready to start the next move with the new phrase.

Anticipation is carefully taught to English country dancers, who can be seen taking a little preparatory step just before they go into motion from a standing start. This is part of the English style, and doesn't need to be adopted by contra dancers. But the mental attitude should be the same; the dancers should be preparing in their minds for the new move, even if their bodies are still dancing the old move.

The Walkthrough

Ever since square and contra dancing became a popular recreation, it has been the custom to "walk through" each number before calling it. This means that the leader directs the dancers to perform the movements at walking speed, without music, one or two calls at a time. Calls that are new to the group are explained as they appear; calls already taught are simply referred to by name and the dancers are given time to complete them. Spots that are causing trouble can be repeated to smooth them out. When all seems well, the dancers return to starting positions, and the dance is done to music.

Before the Walkthrough

The time between the applause for one dance and the walkthrough for the next one is an opportunity for you to set the tone of the party, especially by controlling its pace. It's a good idea to announce the next dance right away, encouraging people to change partners. If the dancers form new sets immediately, you can let them socialize in their lines for a minute or two before calling for "hands four." If they do their socializing first, then amble onto the dance floor, you can afford to be quicker about starting the walkthrough once they're in formation.

Make sure you have everyone's attention as you begin the walkthrough. As mentioned below under "Teaching Tips," the most effective way to do this is to call for some action on the dancers' part. Even "Hands four" will get them listening to some extent, but the first movement of the dance must follow without delay.

During the Walkthrough

The timing of your instructions is just as important during the walkthrough as it is during the dance itself. If the dancers are walking a simple movement that will be followed by another simple one, but the movement is easy for them to extend too far, you'll need to prompt the second movement before they finish the first, just as you would when calling. An example of this is a circle left once around followed by a ladies chain; if the circle goes too far, the dancers will be unsure which way to face for the chain.

On the other hand, if you feel the movements or transitions are difficult, you may want to freeze the action. You could do this with the example above by telling the dancers to circle exactly once around and then stop; once they had done that much, you would tell them that the ladies chain should be across the set to their partner (or whoever). In this particular example, either method will probably work equally well with most groups, but in other cases – such as the transition from the line of four to the hey in *Flirtation Reel* (see Chapter 16) – freezing the action is safer.

Whether you choose to prompt the next call or freeze the action, always make sure the dancers are in the right place, facing the right way, before you go on. Larry Jennings points out in *Zesty Contras* that the failure to do this is a prime source of trouble.

A Sample Walkthrough

Here's an example of a walkthrough, using *Jefferson's Reel* from Chapter 16.

"Take a partner and line up for a contra dance." [Allow time for dancers to line up.]

"Now take hands four from the top." [Give them time to do so.]

"The couple nearest the music in each circle, change places with your partner." [Wait while they cross over; be ready to help sort out any confusion.]

"Notice where you are; this is your starting position. Join hands again in your groups of four, and circle to the left." [Wait until they've taken five or six steps.]

"Now circle right, the other way back." [They'll have gone about two more steps to the left while you spoke, which is why you cut in after six. Now let them take about six steps to the right.]

"The same four people put your right hands into the middle of your group and move the way you face. Rest your hand on the wrist ahead of you – that's a right-hand star." [Again, let them take about six steps before you speak.]

"Change hands, and go the other way back with a left-hand star. Make sure you stop when you get back where you started." [This is a good place to freeze the action, rather than giving the next call as a prompt. If the dancers are new, they'll be fairly overwhelmed with just the circles and stars. It's time for some positive reinforcement.]

"You're doing really well – and you've done half the dance already!

"Now the couples who crossed over, you're number ones, or actives. Would you face up this way, toward me? Good!" [It's all right occasionally to phrase a command in the form of a question, for variety, if you speak it firmly. Beware of sounding too tentative.]

"Now roll out – turn away from your partner, and keep turning till you face down the hall, away from me. Go down the outside of the set, behind the number twos." [Let them take a few steps.]

"Turn around alone and come back – retrace your steps." [Wait while they do this, but not too long. Catch them with your voice before they have a chance to turn the wrong way.]

"When you get back to place, turn in toward your partner and face down. Take hands with your partner, and get in between the twos. Take hands with them in a line of four, all facing down. Good! Everybody go down the hall, four in line." [Wait about four steps – no more – then say firmly:]

"Stop right there! Keep your hands joined. The ones raise your partner's hand and make an arch. Twos, come around and duck through the arch. Everybody hold your partner's hand and let go of the others. We're going to move up this way, but I want the ones to keep facing down and walk backwards. Ready – go!" [This time, make sure everyone moves up to original places. Dancers tend to stop moving too soon after a duck-through.]

"You're facing a new couple. This is the couple you're going to dance the next round with. If there's no one there, just turn around, change places with your partner, and wait a few seconds – we'll have a couple for you real soon."

"Now let's go back to your original facing couple, so the first time through the dance will be with people you've seen before. With the music, get ready to circle left." [And the music begins.]

How Many Walkthroughs?

How many times should you walk people through a dance before calling it to music? At least once!

That's not a joke. Sooner or later you'll be tempted to leave out part of a routine when you're walking your dancers through it. It's easy to say something like "The next move is a circle left followed by a circle right – but you all know how to circle, so let's not walk it." What's wrong with that?

What's wrong is that people have body memory. No matter what the scientific explanation may be, it's true in practice. If you don't let people walk through the whole routine, the part you left out will hit them like a brick wall when it comes up in the dance. If the sequence is "ones swing; circle with the twos; down the outside," and you leave out the circle, the ones will try to go directly from their swing to "down the outside," because that's how their bodies remember walking it.

In the same way, it's best to continue the walkthrough into the beginning of the second round of a contra. In the example above, if the circle is the last movement of a dance and "down the outside" is the first, give the number one couples a chance to separate and go down the outside as soon as they've finished circling with the twos. Otherwise, when the music is playing, their bodies won't know what comes after the circle, even if their ears heard you give the next call.

So the first part of the answer is: Always walk through the whole dance at least once. (See Chapter 17 for an exception that applies to squares.) But should you ever walk it through more than once?

Multiple Walkthroughs

Whether a second walkthrough is necessary depends on your group. If they're all new to country dancing, they'll most likely benefit from it. Repetition is one of the keys to learning, and beginners have a lot of concepts to sort out, especially in a contra. On the other hand, if most of your dancers are experienced, one walkthrough may well be enough. It will almost certainly be enough if the dance is made up of familiar movements, with no unusual transitions.

Some callers make a point of walking through two successive rounds of a duple contra, then starting the music with a new active couple at the head. I prefer to have the dancers return to their original places, whether they've walked through one round or two. Doing this means that everyone will be dancing with familiar people at the outset. If you decide on a second walkthrough, make sure to specify whether you want the dancers to return to their original places or continue from their new ones.

A third walkthrough is nearly always counterproductive. It's usually inspired by the sight of a small number of dancers in serious trouble. If they don't understand the routine after two dry runs, they probably won't after three, and a third walkthrough will try everyone else's patience. It's better either to go down and help the folks in trouble, letting the others relax, or to start the music and hope that the normal mingling of couples will solve the problem.

Classes or Parties?

The question often arises: Should beginners be taught to dance in a class, segregated from experienced dancers, or should they be encouraged to come to the regular dance parties and learn on the fly? There are sound arguments on both sides.

Proponents of separate classes argue that beginners can learn the right way to dance each movement only if a teacher spends time exclusively with them. ("The right way" here means the way that has stood the test of time as being comfortable and enjoyable.) If new dancers are thrown into a mixed group, they may learn bad habits from the more exhibitionistic of the "old hands." And if the caller takes the time at a dance to go over the fine points of styling, the experienced dancers will lose patience and eventually desert the series.

Those in favor of teaching beginners at the regular dances maintain that it's the easiest way for new folks to learn the posture and pace of the basic walking step. Then, too, beginners can find their way through the maze of the squares and contras faster with seasoned dancers to guide them than if they had only each other to lean on. And finally, a dance party with a mixed crowd fosters an atmosphere of excitement that will inspire beginners and induce them to come back. This spark is not easy to create at an all-beginner session.

Combinations and compromises are possible. Some groups provide half an hour of instruction before each dance party, and encourage experienced dancers to come early and help out (especially by creating sets of a workable size if only a few beginners show up). If there is no established dance series in your area, you'll have to deal with a group made up entirely of beginners; but a good teacher can overcome some of the drawbacks of such a class. (See "Teaching Beginners" in Chapter 10 and "How to Move" in Chapter 11 for ideas.)

A beginners' class can be treated like any other dance session, as a series of dances with walkthroughs. Instead of inventing drills, choose one or more dances that include the movement being taught, preferably routines in which the movement is danced from different formations or positions in the set. For instance, in teaching the ladies chain, you could start with a progressive circle formation, in which the dancers begin and end the chain with their partners, and then use a contra dance such as *Newbury Reel* (see Chapter 16), in which they begin and end the chain with their neighbors.

Demonstrations

Many square and contra dance movements are easier to show than they are to describe in words. Demonstrations are an effective teaching tool that many callers fail to use to the best advantage.

There are two kinds of demonstrations. In one, the caller remains on stage as two or four dancers perform the figure. In the other, the caller comes down to the floor and actually does the figure, taking the place of one of the dancers. Both kinds have their advantages: it can be easier to maintain continuity and crowd control from the stage, but joining the dancers on the floor makes the caller seem more human, building rapport with the group. (A wireless microphone, particularly of the headworn type, makes it much easier for the caller to demonstrate from the floor.)

In either case, everyone must be able to see the demonstration group. This often means that some people must either squat on the floor or leave their position in the set. The larger the crowd or the fuller the room, the more time and effort this will take. With a hundred or more people in a crowded hall, it's best to limit demonstrations to once or twice a night.

Whether to demonstrate a particular sequence is a matter of judgment. At a typical dance series, you wouldn't show "circle left" and "circle right"; you'd expect people to be able to walk through those movements from the calls alone. But if you were instructing a group of beginners, you might well get down and demonstrate a circle left, to give them an idea of the difference between walking and dancing.

A hey for four, on the other hand, is a prime candidate for demonstration at any time. A helpful technique in showing a hey is to suggest that each person in the crowd watch only one demonstrator, the one doing the part that the watcher is about to try. Even after this, the hey normally takes a while to smooth out; but at least the dancers will have some idea of what's expected of them.

Teaching Tips

Following are some of the things that should be in your mind when you plan your teaching time beforehand and when you stand up in front of your dancers.

Keep Them Winning

People will learn more and retain it longer (and certainly feel better about returning) if they're allowed to succeed most of the time. This is true regardless of age or experience level, but it's especially important to remember when working with beginners. The way to keep people "winning" is to present new concepts in a logical order, relating new material to things already learned, and to give the group only as much new information at one time as they're likely to absorb. Not only will they be more confident when given "bite-sized" pieces, but they're less likely to make mistakes. And each mistake requires many correct repetitions to erase the mistake from their mental and bodily memory.

As an example of this "bite-sized" approach, notice that in the walkthrough of *Jefferson's Reel* above, no mention is made of couple numbers or progression in the set until the group has actually walked through half the routine. The circles and stars are easy for almost everyone, and walking through them will give people the confidence to respond more favorably to the second half of the dance, which introduces more difficult concepts.

Get Them Moving

Studies have shown that people learn faster if they participate actively than if they just sit and listen. Fortunately, dancing lends itself well to a teaching style that involves the whole group. This may seem obvious, but it's not. Too many dance leaders waste precious time on lengthy explanations while their dancers stand around and do nothing. Much of the time, the dancers aren't even listening.

The most effective way to teach dancing is to let people dance as much of the time as possible. This means telling them only what they need to know in order to start moving, as mentioned above under "Keep Them Winning." With this one technique, you can hold their attention and build their confidence at the same time.

Once the dancers have gone through a few moves, they are more likely to be listening when you go into the fine points of style. It's wise to watch carefully for signs of wandering attention – a sure indicator that any further preoccupation with detail will be lost on the group. When people are about to tune out, it's time to get them moving again!

Teach Basics, Then Name Them

There are thousands of contra dances, ranging from the very easy to the almost impossibly complex. But nearly all of them use the same few basic movements, each with its distinctive call. These movements and calls – circle, star, do-si-do, ladies chain, and the like – are the building blocks that enable dancers to learn a little at a time, yet make possible an infinite number of combinations. But their very names form an arcane language that can intimidate dancers.

The secret of using these special names is to walk the dancers through a movement, making sure they understand it, and only then to tell them its name. Teaching the movement and its call in this order will build the group's confidence. Particularly in the case of calls like "do-si-do" and "allemande left," which most people have heard in films or on television, beginners will get a sense of accomplishment from being able to dance them. Teaching the movement first also avoids the common problem of dancers thinking they know what the names mean. If you use the term "do-si-do" before defining it, nine times out of ten at least some couples in the group will link arms and do an elbow swing. As usual, incorrect actions require several correct repetitions to undo the damage; it's better to avoid the mistake in the first place.

Tell Dancers Where They'll Be

Beginning dancers are easily disoriented, and most of them are afraid of getting lost or looking foolish. An effective teaching technique is to tell the group where each person should be after executing a movement. The first few calls presented in this book, when used in their elementary form, return all dancers to their starting positions. This will not be obvious, though many people will instinctively return "home" after each call. It's well to emphasize that each movement ends where it starts unless other directions are given.

Some calls leave one or more dancers in new positions. When teaching these calls, you should alert the group to this, and begin by explaining clearly where each person will be when the move is completed. For instance, in teaching the right and left through, you might say, "You're about to change places with the opposite couple. When you're done, you'll still be facing them, but you'll be where they are now. The lady will still be on the right in each couple." Then the movement itself can be taught and practiced. This will build confidence. In addition, if any dancers don't yet understand how to execute the move, they can easily go to the correct ending position. You won't have to spend time adjusting the sets; they'll all be in the same formation, ready to go on from there or to return to an earlier point as you wish.

Tell Them How to Recover

That last point – that dancers who are lost can and should go to the ending position of the current movement – applies not only during the walkthrough, but during the actual dance as well. Everyone forgets a figure now and then, and it's good to emphasize this to beginning dancers, who will otherwise blame themselves and their inexperience when they blank out. Tell them that nobody's perfect, that a good dancer is not one who always goes the right way, but one who can quickly recover from going the wrong way. The best thing for a dancer or a subset of dancers to do if they get tangled is to stop, take a deep breath, figure out where they should be at the end of the movement that's currently being danced, and go there as quickly as they can without panicking. Many a dance has been saved this way. In the dance, as in life, it's the recoveries that count!

Be Positive

This comes last because it's so important: Tell people what they're doing right!

There are at least two good reasons for taking a positive approach. The more obvious one is that people don't like to have their mistakes pointed out, especially in front of a group who may well be their friends or classmates. It's saddening to watch a teacher with a negative attitude try to present a square or contra dance, commenting on people's mistakes but not rewarding correct actions.

The second reason is that it's less confusing to be positive. If you see one or two people skipping instead of walking as they circle left, and you say "Don't skip," you'll put the idea of skipping into the heads of many dancers who may not have thought of it. It's better to say things like "Just walk it" or "Nice and easy."

The same technique works with more complex movements. When new dancers are first exposed to the right and left through, many of them will incorrectly turn to their own right, individually, after the initial pass through. If you say "Don't turn to your right," it's likely to be counterproductive: what sticks in a lot of people's minds will be "Turn to your right," even though you prefaced it with a "don't." Instead, say "Stop" or "Freeze" as soon as you see them passing through correctly, then have them take promenade position immediately, which will keep them from turning alone.

Once the dancers are doing something correctly, praise them. Some of them won't be sure they're doing the right thing unless you tell them so, and everyone responds to a pat on the back. You won't want to sound insincere, of course, but an occasional "That's it!" or "You're looking good!" will go a long way toward brightening the atmosphere at your sessions.

If you do this consistently, telling people what to do instead of what not to do, and praising them for doing things right, you'll reap huge rewards. Not only will your dancers like you better, they'll learn much faster!

6

Choosing Your Material

There's a story about a television repairman who turns a single screw inside a customer's set and writes out a bill for $50. When the customer demands an itemized account, the repairman writes, "$1 for turning screw; $49 for knowing which screw to turn."

Knowledge is important in any field, and country dancing is no exception. It's not enough to be able to call a dance, or even dozens of dances. You need to know which dance to call at any given time. Whether you're doing a guest set at someone else's dance or at a festival, or calling an entire party or even a whole series, programming is an essential part of your expertise.

The Guest Set

Calling a single dance isn't strictly "program planning," but it's important to choose the right dance for the occasion nonetheless. Many if not most callers got their start doing guest sets, and it's good practice for programming skills as well as calling skills.

Your primary aim whenever you call should be to give the dancers a good time. When you're appearing as a guest caller, that can be hard to remember. It's tempting to choose a flashy or tricky dance because you think it will make you look good to the crowd or the sponsors. You'll look a lot better if you call a well-constructed, well-timed, smooth-flowing dance that everyone can do.

The routine doesn't have to be the simplest one you know. It can have what songwriters call a "hook" – something that makes it different enough to be interesting. But the whole figure, including the "hook," should be straightforward enough that the group is unlikely to have any trouble with it. You should have danced it yourself, preferably several times, and be able to call it almost in your sleep.

As to the level of difficulty, you may not know what the crowd can and can't do until shortly before you go on. It's good to have more than one dance picked out, and to watch the floor carefully as the session progresses. Notice which moves and transitions, if any, are causing trouble. Watch the other callers; note the dances they use, so you won't repeat one or use a theme that's been overworked. When it's your turn to call, you'll be able to make an informed decision.

For a guest set, it's better to underestimate the dancers' ability slightly than to overestimate it. Although dancers like to be challenged, they also enjoy dances that let them relax. Remember that this is your one chance to succeed at this event. If you pick too hard a dance and the crowd has trouble with it, you won't be able to recover by doing an easier one.

The Evening Dance

The most common type of event you'll need to plan for is the single evening (or afternoon) dance. Whether it's billed as a workshop or a party, whether it's a special event or part of a series, the evening dance has certain definite requirements.

Level

You'll need to stay in closer touch with the experience level and proficiency of your dancers than you would for a guest set. Fortunately, you'll have more time to establish rapport with the crowd and size up their ability.

Most dance events attract both beginners and frequent dancers. You should be prepared to please both groups in the same program. It's a challenge, but not impossible, and meeting the challenge can be rewarding. How much you cater to one extreme or the other will depend on who's in the majority. But in general, you can aim at the broad middle ground, presenting a range of material from the fairly easy to the fairly demanding.

Two keys to successful programming are variety and flexibility.

Variety

Country dances can differ from one another in many ways. Almost everyone would agree that it's more fun to do a variety of dances during an evening than to know that the next number will be just like the last one. An important part of your job as a programmer is to pick dances of different types and put them in an order that will achieve maximum contrast.

You should, of course, choose dances that you know and like; your dancers will accept them more readily if you're sold on them yourself. But learn to like as many different dances and styles as you can, to help balance your program.

Variety can itself be achieved in a variety of ways. One obvious way is to use dances done in different formations. Contras, squares, big circles, progressive circles, scatter promenades, whole-set longways, couple dances, and folk dances from other ethnic traditions can all contribute to an enjoyable evening. Note that you don't need to know how to call squares in order to vary the shape of your sets: most of the formations in this list can be called exactly as if they were contras.

Dances can vary even within their basic setup. If you want to use two contras whose dominant figure is a hey, and two that feature "down four in line" but no hey, it's better to intersperse the types than to put the two heys together. Even if you're using two or more dances to teach a movement – contra corners, for example – you'd do well to put something different in between them. Your dancers will appreciate the mental rest, and they'll probably do better at contra corners after the diversion.

Other ways to gain variety include:

- Music – it can be fast or slow, smooth or bouncy, sedate or rowdy. Jigs, with their rocking 6/8 rhythm, can break the monotony of "oompah, oompah" all night.
- Degree of difficulty – everyone likes to be challenged now and then, even if it's only a little, but people need to rest their brains, too.
- Social interaction – some dances let you spend a good deal of time with your partner; others keep you with your neighbor or corner so much that they amount to mixers even if you keep a nominal partner throughout.
- Level of physical energy – many swings or none, everyone moving or inactives standing still. Even dancers who like to be in motion most of the time will appreciate a breather now and then.

Flexibility

Often you'll find that a group isn't quite what you expected it to be in one or more respects. Some of the dances you chose beforehand may not be ideal for the people who actually came. The evening will be more fun for everyone if you're able to change your program on the fly.

It will help, therefore, if you sit down at home and make a list of the dances you know, then divide them into categories to suit your needs. Use as many factors as you think will be helpful: easy/hard, strenuous/relaxing, fast/slow, interaction with partner/neighbor. This set of lists won't take the place of your program for a specific evening, but it will enable you to substitute a better dance for an upcoming one that's beginning to look inappropriate.

Factors that should influence your choice of material include:

- Age – very young or old people may have trouble with "normal" material for various reasons (see Chapter 9).
- Dancers' experience level – quite often, even a series dance you've called at before will attract a different crowd the next time you're there. If you plan for seasoned dancers, you may get mostly beginners, and vice versa.
- Dancers' attitude – people at a party where the liquor is flowing freely will be less willing to learn new figures than students at an adult education class.
- Balance of the sexes – if the men vastly outnumber the women, or vice versa, you may need to be creative (see Chapter 9) or switch to international folk dancing for the occasion. There are many good folk dances for trios, and innumerable ones that require no partners at all.
- Couple status – if everyone came in couples and it looks as if they want to stick together, use mixers sparingly. People will learn faster if you separate them for the first number or two, but give them time with their spouses or sweethearts later. Groups of singles, on the other hand, will appreciate plenty of mixers (and contras that have the effect of mixers).
- Hall size and shape – A long, narrow hall would seem to be ideal for contra dances, but if the sets are longer than about ten couples, routines that don't keep everyone moving present a problem (see "How Long Should a Contra Run?", Chapter 4). Circle dances work best in a squarish hall.
- Other hall factors – A slippery floor demands a slower tempo to avoid accidents; a hard surface will make forceful balances a painful experience. If the dancing space has posts supporting the roof or an upper story, take care not to let exuberant dancers get out of control.
- Degree of crowding – If the hall is jammed with people, stick to dances with compact figures. If there's extra space, take advantage of it by doing things like "sashay" or "promenade outside the set."
- Number of people – Some dances are practical only with a large group. Progressive circles in particular require a minimum of about thirty people. If your group is small, you can have fun trying all the older contras that would be deadly in long lines.

Chapter 6: Choosing Your Material

- Weather – If the night is hot and humid, do at least a few leisurely dances and make the rest periods a bit longer. If it's cold, the first dance or two should keep everyone moving; after that, the hall will warm up from body heat.

Keep a record of what you actually use, including any changes from your original plan. It helps you remember what worked and what didn't, and it can help you avoid repetition if you call often to the same group.

Pacing

There are two mental and psychological factors you'll need to be aware of at a country dance: the difficulty level and the energy or excitement level. Both of these levels should change as the evening progresses, but not in unison.

The difficulty level should reach its peak around the middle of the dance. By then, people are sufficiently warmed up to be able to deal with tricky material, and they haven't started tuning out yet. Mental fatigue sets in toward the end of the evening; the last few numbers can be physically strenuous, but they shouldn't be too intellectually demanding.

The excitement level, on the other hand, should increase from the beginning to the midpoint of the dance, and then increase again from the midpoint to the end. (Normally it will have dropped a bit during the intermission.) This means that during the first half of the evening, the difficulty of the dances and the excitement level will rise together; but during the second half, the difficulty level should go down even as the excitement continues to increase.

The Only Graph in This Book

——— Difficulty level
‒ ‒ ‒ Excitement level

When you plan a program, then, try to put the trickiest material, or the dances least familiar to your group, near the middle of the evening. If such a dance is also exciting because it goes well to fast music or affords plenty of physical contact, especially between partners, it should go just before the intermission. Dances that are slower in tempo or "cooler" in their social atmosphere can go after the break, when a "hotter" number might feel forced.

The beginning of the evening calls for dances that are easy, to build the confidence of newcomers, and that feature frequent partner changes to mix the crowd. A circle mixer, in which the dancers never return to their original partners, is almost essential. Not only will it give people a look at potential partners for the rest of the evening, it will provide a change from the contra or square formation. If beginners make up the majority of the group, the circle can well be the first number. (This is particularly true if the party follows another event such as a dinner, so that everyone is present when the dance begins.) With a mixed crowd that drifts in a few at a time, it may be better to start with a contra, letting couples join in at the foot during the dance, and postpone the circle until most people have arrived. (Note that many newcomers arrive late; if everyone present at the starting time is experienced, you may call one or two more advanced dances, then drop the level if and when the new folks show up.)

The last few dances of the evening, as mentioned above, may or may not be physically strenuous, but should never be mentally taxing. They should allow the dancers to spend plenty of time with their partners; presumably they know by now whose company they prefer. Some groups enjoy a real rouser at the end of the night, while others prefer to be let down gently, perhaps with an elegant number. But the movements and transitions should be familiar enough to your dancers that you don't anticipate any trouble.

In general, pace yourself. Remember that the energy level should rise through each half of the evening. If you start out at a fever pitch, you'll have no room to go higher, and you're likely to burn out before you finish.

The Dance Series

If you're the primary caller at a monthly or weekly series, you have a double challenge: each event needs to be planned as carefully as if it stood alone, but also needs to be different from the other events in the series. This presupposes that you know enough material to call several nights without repeating yourself. An experienced caller with a weekly series will try not to use a particular dance more often than once every four to six weeks. With a monthly series, the crowd will have more time to forget the last program and to anticipate their favorite numbers, and repetition between events can well be more frequent, say every two or three months.

If you're presenting a dance to your group for the first time, you may want to repeat it deliberately, especially if it's quite different from your usual material in some way or appears to need extra teaching for some other reason. After you've used it two or three times in a row, you can add it to your active list (assuming the dancers like it!) and put it in the regular rotation.

It's essential to keep a log of your programs if you call at a series. It will enable you to look back over the year and avoid too much repetition, and it will give you a place to make notes on what worked well with the group and what didn't. Even if you're not the only caller for the series, a log is helpful: it will let you compare notes with the other callers.

Don't be in a hurry to raise the level of a series. One of the things that many people find attractive about traditional square and contra dancing is its accessibility. The fact that a newcomer can walk in and participate immediately has encouraged thousands of people to join our activity through the years. True, a group of people that dances together for any length of time will improve their dancing skills, such as reaction time, ability to see what's happening in a set choreographically, and ability to recover from a lapse of mind. Such a group will undoubtedly ask for harder material sooner or later. As a leader, you owe it to the dancers to keep the level down to where beginners can still be assimilated – not just for the beginners' sake, but for the sake of the experienced dancers who will otherwise see their numbers start to dwindle for lack of new blood.

Some callers ask, "How can I avoid becoming bored if I don't use challenging dances?" The answer is to identify with your dancers. Put yourself in their shoes. Many experienced callers agree that easy dances can be exciting when viewed through the starry eyes of a beginner. After nearly half a century of teaching and calling, I still find that there's nothing more inspiring than seeing beginners' eyes light up and hearing them say "Wow! I can dance!"

The best way to deal with requests for something more demanding is by taking advantage of our old friend, variety. Choosing dances that are "easy but different" will go a long way toward holding the interest of the old hands, while giving beginners just enough of a challenge to let them know you won't baby them. If the requests continue for a higher level of difficulty, it may be time to run an occasional evening for experienced dancers only.

Choosing the Right Stuff

Thousands of contra dances (and even more thousands of squares) have been written over the last century and a half. Obviously, some are better than others. With so much material to choose from, there's no point in using less than the best.

Judgment, here as everywhere, has to be developed over time. It's hard at first to tell a good dance from a lesser one. It's especially hard to do it by reading their descriptions in a book or on a website. This is one of the many reasons why frequent dancing is essential to your development as a caller: the only sure way to tell whether a routine is comfortable to dance is to try it!

Most dancers don't worry about technicalities. If they like a particular dance, they'll simply say "It's fun." If they don't like it, they may get a little more specific, saying "It's boring" or "It's awkward." As you look at dance routines with a critical eye, you'll become aware of some of the criteria for a good one.

Smooth Flow

Smooth flow is important. In general, dancers should not be called on to use the same hand twice in quick succession. Clockwise movements (such as swings, do-si-dos, and right hand turns) should be preceded and followed by counterclockwise ones (such as left hand turns and courtesy turns). The routine should not require anyone to stop short from a running start. For instance, a pass through to a new couple followed by a ladies chain would be fine for the ladies, but awkward for the gents, who must stop in their tracks. A better sequence would be "pass through, right and left through, ladies chain."

Smooth flow has become more of an issue since the 1970s. Until then, nobody objected to two consecutive "balance and swing" combinations, or to a "cast off" followed by "turn contra corners" that forced the active lady to wrest her right arm from behind someone's back in order to do a right hand turn. Many older dances with awkward spots are still done and enjoyed as a part of our heritage, but in spite of those flaws, not because of them. Like anything, smooth flow can be overdone, but in general it's a reliable indicator of whether dancers will like a given routine.

Easy Memorization

Good routines are memorable. They hang together well enough that both caller and dancers can remember them easily. A good test of this for a dance you're just learning is to put the written routine where you can see it during the walkthrough, but to avoid looking at it once you've started to call it. If you can't remember a dance for two or three minutes after reading it aloud (assuming you've also studied it at home), your dancers are likely to have trouble with it too. And if you quit calling midway through the dance, to let people enjoy the music, the trouble will compound.

If the dancers can't remember a routine, there's almost certainly something confusing about it. The most common problem is a move that occurs twice from the same position and at a similar point in the music, but is followed by a different move each time. An example is my own dance, *California Contra,* in which a neighbor swing occurs during the second half of the A.1 music and a partner swing during the second half of the B.1 music. The gents, who normally lead from a swing into whatever follows it, are on the same side of the set both times. The neighbor swing is followed by a forward and back, the partner swing by a circle. Dancers consistently have trouble remembering what comes after the swings. The dance is enjoyable in other ways, but it's not my best work.

Story Line

The concept of "story line" has been introduced to explain what makes a dance memorable. The best routines are those that "tell a story"; they start somewhere, end somewhere, and hold the dancers' interest in between. Too many dances feel as if they begin with "Happily ever after" and end with "Once upon a time."

What makes a good story line? It usually begins with one of two elements: a figure that brings the whole set together (such as forward and back) or a sequence that defines the minor set (such as "circle four"). Many modern contras begin with a bit of flirtation between neighbors (do-si-do and/or swing), but even this serves to define the minor set. From there, an ideal story line progresses from interaction with one's neighbor and the other dancers toward interaction primarily with one's partner. Many good routines either end with a partner swing or add a figure that solidifies the feeling of being in a group (such as a right and left or a ladies chain).

Bad story lines come in many forms. They may contain a long series of movements that appear strung together in no particular order. Or they may have a sequence that actually gives the feel of a backward progression. The least satisfying of the newer contras place a partner swing early in the routine and a neighbor swing toward the end, undoing the feel of zeroing in on one's partner. (There are a few good dances, such as Ted Sannella's *Fiddleheads,* that put the swings in this order; but they typically have redeeming factors like an unusual and interesting main figure.)

Note that a good story line will not only make a routine more satisfying to dance; it will also make the sequence easier for the dancers to remember, enabling you to reduce or eliminate your calls and let the dancers enjoy the music!

Judging Difficulty

For several reasons, you'll need to have some idea of the difficulty level of each dance you use. First, you need to know whether a given dance is even appropriate for the group you're working with, or whether they'll find it boring or childish on the one hand or hopelessly frustrating on the other. Then, once you have your dances graded by difficulty, you can put together a well-paced program, with the hardest material in the middle. And finally, if you know a dance is likely to give trouble, you'll be able to prepare a careful explanation of the tricky spots.

It will pay to determine the probable level – easy, intermediate, or advanced – of each dance you know, and to make a list of all your material sorted by level. "Easy" dances are those you would choose for a group made up entirely of complete beginners. "Intermediate" material is what dancers at your local series could handle after a single brief, though careful, walkthrough. "Advanced" dances would require enough teaching to break the flow of a party-style evening, and are best reserved for separate workshops. Occasionally a dance will seem to be on the borderline between two categories; you can put it on both lists, with a note or symbol reminding you that it's easier or harder than the others on each list.

Following are some of the things to look for when you're judging the difficulty of a dance:

- Basic movements – New England style dancing, both square and contra, uses only about two dozen basic movements with special names; but even this is too large a number for some groups. Certain basics – right and left through, contra corners, hey for four – require more time than others to teach the average group, and dances using those basics should be disqualified from the "easy" list.
- Transitions – Some dances are more advanced than others, not because of the basics used but because of the way they're put together. You may think a routine is suitable for your dancers because they know all the movements in it, when there are one or

more transitions that could prove disorienting. Examples are a right-hand turn with one person followed by a swing with another, a series of several fractional hand turns in succession, or a circle four followed by a ladies chain (the circle must end with the dancers precisely where the author intended, or the ladies may be confused about which gent to chain to).

- Timing – Even if all the movements in a dance are known to your group and the transitions are straightforward, the dance may be harder than it appears at first if the timing is tight. Much as we would like them to, basic movements don't always take exactly eight or sixteen beats of music to do comfortably; often the dancers must speed up or slow down a little to stay with the musical phrase. If a movement that takes effort to complete on time is followed by one that must be started on time, such as a balance or a forward and back, the timing is said to be *demanding*, and the dance is more difficult than the written calls would indicate. Conversely, a dance whose movements can all be done quite comfortably in less time than the music allows would be *undemanding*. Such a dance is likely to prove easier than it looks on paper (though groups accustomed to dancing energetically might consider it boring).

- Forgiveness – Similar but not identical to the concept of demand is that of *forgiveness*. (Both concepts arose from discussions between Larry Jennings, Al Olson, and Ted Sannella in the early 1980s.) Whereas demand has to do with timing, forgiveness is determined by the nature of a movement or sequence with little reference to timing. The cooperation required of the dancers, rather than their speed, is the crucial factor. An example of an unforgiving sequence is a star three-quarters around in eight beats, followed by a hand turn with a dancer from another star. Even though the timing of the star is not demanding, the sequence is unforgiving because the star must move exactly three-quarters around – no more, no less – or the dancers will have trouble finding the correct person for the hand turn. Everyone must be alert in order for the sequence to work. By contrast, imagine a hand turn for two ladies or two gents in the center, twice around in eight beats, followed by a partner balance and swing on the side of the set. Although the timing of the hand turn is demanding, the sequence is fairly forgiving: presumably the center people will have no trouble identifying their partners, and the dance can go on even if a few couples are late for the balance.

- Piece count – This concept was introduced by Al Olson as a further measure of likely difficulty. The term "piece count" refers to the number of movements that the dancers will perceive as separate elements. For example, a "circle four" followed by a "neighbor swing" would count as two pieces, but a "circle left" followed by a "circle right" would count as only one. Naturally, the higher the piece count, the more difficult the dance is likely to be, other things being equal. Piece count is probably most useful in planning for groups that do a lot of contras and are used to dancing without calls, as it becomes more of a factor when the dancers must work from memory. Of course, a dance with a high piece count will be a greater test of the caller's memory, too!

A few other factors more or less related to difficulty are worth mentioning here:

- Certain dances "quote" other routines, usually distinctive ones like *Rory O'More*. If the dancers don't know the original, some of the point is lost. It's like reading a book that quotes Shakespeare or the Bible, or the author's earlier work; it's more enjoyable if you know what the author is referring to. (Quoting has become much more common since this book was first written, but I still feel this way to some extent.)
- Beware of the "dance camp romance." Often at an advanced workshop or a dance week or weekend, where almost everyone is an accomplished dancer, you'll find yourself falling in love with a routine because it's being done under ideal conditions. The band is hot, the crowd is hot, you have a wonderful partner, and if the dance is at all challenging, you get a feeling of satisfaction at having mastered it. This is all well and good. But if you bring it home and try to teach it at a regular series, you may find that hardly anyone has the background or experience to appreciate it. Do collect material at camps, by all means, but analyze it carefully before you use it with an average group.
- Make sure you have several dances that are as close to foolproof as is humanly possible. You'll need them for guest sets, non-workshop slots at festivals, and beginners' workshops if you do them. And it pays to be able to pull one out if your group shows signs of frustration after a harder dance.
- Don't feel you have to use everything you find. Thousands of dances have been written over the years; probably less than half of them are truly satisfying to do. If you know only a hundred dances, you can call eight full evenings without repeating yourself. Learn to be selective in adding new material to your repertoire.

Organizing Your Material

You'll need a way to keep your material organized, so that you can find a given dance or type of dance when you want it. Probably a majority of working callers use index cards, either 3 by 5 inches or 4 by 6 inches, and keep them in a small box. An increasing number of callers keep a master file of dances in their computer and print their working cards from that file; this ensures that if they lose a card, they haven't lost that dance.

On the front of each card is a dance description, in whatever form the caller finds easiest to read. Normally a caller doesn't expect to borrow another caller's card and work directly from it, so the descriptions can be as cryptic as you like. If you find a kind of homemade shorthand is best for you, by all means use it. If you plan to read from the card during a teaching session or walkthrough, you may want to use a bigger card and spell out all the words in bold print.

I work both ways, using a form of shorthand to copy dances when I hear them called and writing them out in longhand when I transfer them to my working file. My shorthand is based on a system used by the Hilton company, which used to sell a cue-card system for modern square dance callers in addition to sound equipment. The premise was that every symbol should be available on a standard typewriter keyboard, so for example the "¢" sign stands for "corner" and the "@" sign means "around." By the time I get to my keyboard I'm ready to spell everything out (and the "¢" sign no longer appears on keyboards), but the symbols are easy to use when I'm jotting calls down at a dance.

Rather than cards, I use letter-size sheets of paper with ten or twelve dances on each. This is because a memory for dance routines is one of my strong points, and normally the only dances I need to look at are the ones I'm just learning or don't use very often. I keep the sheets in a notebook that also holds my recent programs, along with a list of titles of the dances I use frequently. Without my title list I'd have trouble putting together a program, but I can remember the sequence of a familiar dance just by looking at the title.

The dances on my title list are sorted into categories: by difficulty; by whether the dancers swing partner, neighbor, both, or no one; and in the case of squares, whether or not there is a partner change. Classic contras or "chestnuts" are on a separate list so that I can make sure to program one or two in an evening, or lead a workshop on them at a camp or festival. If you use cards, you can make up your own categories, putting symbols in the upper right corner of each card or using different colors of paper. An obvious distinction is between circles, squares, and contras; other possible categories are dances that work well with beginners or with children, less strenuous dances that are good for older groups, and contras suited to longer or shorter sets.

On the back of your cards, you can make notes about each dance: teaching techniques that work well, spots that are likely to give the dancers trouble, tunes that fit the character of the dance (especially when played by a certain band), and so on.

Writing Your Own Material

Sooner or later you'll be tempted to put together your own dance routines; every caller is. Some people get the itch to write dances before they take up calling; a few even compose dances with no thought of calling them. The creativity of callers ranges from recombining standard basic movements in fairly predictable ways to dreaming up new concepts that no one else seems to have thought of.

Of the thousands of existing contra dance routines, many are only slight variations on each other. Others are downright awkward to do. Relatively few are both truly original and satisfying to dance. There's certainly nothing wrong with using standard movements to create what's known as a "glossary dance." Many such routines are enjoyable to do, and writing them is good practice. If you get the urge to be more creative, it will help if you learn something about what has been tried in the past and found wanting. (It's been said that many of the so-called new basics that have been written in modern square dancing are movements that the dancing masters discarded long ago.)

It's not necessary, though, to read and memorize all the existing dance material before you try writing your own. Indeed, it might be counterproductive: some would say you're more likely to come up with an innovative new dance if your mind hasn't been trained to run in traditional channels.

The best approach is probably to alternate writing and reading. Try doodling patterns on a clean sheet of paper, with little or no thought to what has gone before or what supposedly can't be done. Then look through a few dance books and websites, as well as any figures you've collected firsthand, and see if you've unconsciously re-created an existing dance. As you do more reading, you'll develop a better sense of what's been done and what's practical. And as you do more composing, you'll strengthen your creativity – as a muscle grows stronger with exercise – to the point where your knowledge of tradition won't keep you from thinking up new concepts.

You should, of course, apply the same criteria to your own creations that you would use in evaluating a dance you got from any other source. Does the routine flow smoothly? Is it easy to memorize? Does the story line make sense? If there are two closely related movements in a row, are they done to the same phrase of music rather than crossing the phrase? In addition, you should ask yourself if the figure is worth adding to the existing body of dance knowledge. Does it have a unique feature, one that will distinguish it from the run of the mill? If not, does it do an ordinary thing extraordinarily well? For instance, does it use the same basics as an existing dance, but in a different order that creates smoother transitions? If it does none of these things, think twice before you introduce it to the world. But don't discard it; leave it on the drawing board, and look at it again in a year or so. At that point you may see a way to improve it, based on your experience in the meantime.

Once you've decided to release a dance to the public, test it several times. First, diagram it on paper, from beginning to end, looking for obvious errors (such as a contra routine that doesn't result in a progression for all four people in the minor set). Next, put on a recording of suitable music and dance it with an imaginary set, preferably from all possible viewpoints (ladies, gents, ones, twos). If it passes all these tests, try it with a few friends and ask for feedback, encouraging them to be honest. Trust your friends rather than the crowd, who will be in a frame of mind to enjoy your dance whether it's good or not.

Specific suggestions about dance composition are hard to make; one person can't be creative for another. But if you have the urge to write your own material, you probably have a few ideas already. One time-honored approach is to take a gimmick you like – an unusual movement or combination of movements – from an existing dance and build a new dance around it. I've done this with some of my own routines: for instance, I decided to use the "horseshoe" figure (down four in line, couples wheel through each other and come up the other side) from my contra *Ocean View Reel* in a simpler dance. *Ocean View* is double progression, with no partner swing, and has two neighbor swings at similar points in the music, which often leads to confusion as to what to do next. I liked the horseshoe pattern, but found that I didn't feel comfortable using *Ocean View* with most groups. So I deliberately set out to write a dance that would incorporate the gimmick but would be easier overall. The result was *Menotomy Reel:*

Ocean View Reel
(Tony Parkes, 1975)
Contra dance, duple improper
Double progression

A.1 Do-si-do neighbor (8)
    Swing neighbor (8)
A.2 Down four in line (4)
    Couples wheel in (4)
    Pass through, wheel up (4)
    Up four in line (4)
B.1 Arch in the middle,
      ends duck through (6–8)
    Swing new neighbor (8–10)
B.2 Half promenade across (8)
    Left-hand star (8)

Menotomy Reel
(Tony Parkes, 1990)
Contra dance, duple improper

A.1 Swing neighbor (8)
    All forward and back (8)
A.2 Ladies do-si-do
      once and a half (8)
    Swing partner (8)
B.1 Down four in line (4)
    Couples wheel in (4)
    Pass through, wheel up (4)
    Up in fours; bend the line (4)
B.2 Right and left through (8)
    Circle 3/4, pass through (8)

One word of caution to composers: Be sure to keep using material other than your own, including the older traditional dances. Almost every writer's routines, no matter how good their quality, bear a certain family resemblance to one another; it's hard to achieve the variety essential to a good series using only your own dances. And most writers tend to think more highly of their own creations than the dancers do. But used sparingly, your original routines can act as the seasoning in your program.

To those of you who feel driven to create new dances, more power to you! Not everything you write will be a gem, but one day you may take the dance world by storm. Every classic routine that we enjoy today was new once; in many cases we know the name of the author. And some of today's creations may be tomorrow's classics. Go ahead and write – you have nothing to lose and everything to gain!

7
Working with Music

Music, as was discussed in Chapter 3, is the basis of all dancing and certainly the foundation of square and contra dancing. It behooves us, then, to spend a good deal of time thinking about our music and the way we use it.

Choosing Tunes

One of the questions that new callers ask most often is "How can I know what tune is best for a given dance?" There are two schools of thought on this. One school believes that almost any tune will serve any dance, the other that you should find one tune for each dance in your repertoire and stick with it. My position is somewhere near the middle of the road: I deal in types of tunes rather than specific tunes, but I do try to match each dance with the tune type that seems to fit it best. This approach not only produces pleasing combinations for the dancers but also simplifies my work with musicians, as will be seen later in this chapter.

The first and broadest distinction I make among tune types is based on meter. Regardless of its name or musical genre, any tune used for contra dancing can be classified as a jig, a reel, or a march. Reels are written and played in 2/4 meter (or "2/4 time"), marches usually in 4/4, and jigs in 6/8.

Remember that every contra dance tune is 64 beats in length, regardless of how those beats are grouped into measures or phrases. This is because contra dance routines are written to require 64 steps from the dancers, and it is an important part of contra dance tradition that once through the dance equals once through the tune.

Remember, too, that the normal contra dance tune is played in four parts: A.1, A.2, B.1, and B.2. Each part contains 16 beats, and corresponds to a part of the dance containing 16 steps. In most tunes, A.1 and A.2 are identical, as are B.1 and B.2, although in some tunes there are slight variations between A or B parts. Occasionally a tune will be used for contra dancing that has no repeats; in this case the parts are often referred to as A, B, C, and D. The parts of the dance, however, usually retain their customary names: A.1, A.2, etc.

Reels

Reels are the most common type of tune used for contra dancing, and are even more common in most square dance traditions. When people think of square dance music, almost any tune that comes to mind is a reel. Examples are Arkansas Traveler, Devil's Dream, Flop Eared Mule, Little Brown Jug, Old Joe Clark, and Turkey in the Straw. Some of these tunes were originally songs, and some have had lyrics added over the years, but they are all reels from a metrical point of view.

Reels often used for contra dancing include Batchelder's Reel, Farewell to Whisky, Gaspé Reel, Miller's Reel, Ross's Reel, and St. Anne's Reel. Most of the classic contra dances that have their own tune are in reel time: Lady of the Lake, Lady Walpole's Reel, Money Musk, Petronella, and even Chorus Jig, in spite of its name.

Reels are normally written in 2/4 time, which means that each measure contains two beats and each beat is represented by a quarter note. (A measure is the length of musical staff between two bar lines, along with the notes and other markings it contains; it is commonly, if loosely, called a bar.) For contra dance purposes, each beat is further divided into the downbeat and the upbeat, each represented by an eighth note. The actual melody may contain four sixteenth notes to one downbeat.

In some books, to avoid a cluttered appearance, reels are written in 2/2 or "cut" time (represented by a C with a line through it, somewhat like a cent sign). This doubles all the note values of the 2/4 notation: a half note gets one beat, the downbeats and upbeats become quarter notes, and the fast passages become eighth notes. Occasionally a reel is written in 4/4 time; this is downright wrong, and taking such a notation literally will result in playing the tune at half speed.

Most people find that reels sound "even," "steady," or "smooth," especially when compared to jigs. This is because the downbeat and the upbeat of a reel are exactly the same length, producing an effect that may be thought of as

                One   and   two   and

or

                Oom   pah   oom   pah

The "oom" or numbered beat is the downbeat. This is the beat on which the dancers' feet should hit the floor. The "pah" or "and" is the upbeat. The upbeat is not just a space-filler between downbeats; it gives "lift" or energy to the music and therefore to the dancers. Good contra dance musicians emphasize the downbeat and the upbeat almost equally.

The "ooms" should come at the rate of about two per second, or 120 per minute. This is the tempo adopted by the army for comfortable long-term marching, and it has been standard in contra dancing for several generations. The tempo can be varied during an evening, to provide contrasts in energy or excitement level, but should probably not be altered by more than about eight beats per minute either way (down to 112 or up to 128). Including traditional Western squares or Southern big circles in a program can allow for more variety in tempo, up to about 136; but the dancers' physical condition, the floor, and the weather should always be taken into account.

Hornpipes

Hornpipes were originally in slow, dotted 4/4 time, like schottisches, and in English and Irish dance music they still are. But in the Scottish and American traditions, hornpipes have been speeded up and evened out so that they sound almost identical to reels. The chief difference is that hornpipes often appear to have longer phrases than reels (see the discussion of phrase length under "Marches," below). They are usually written in 2/4 or 2/2 time.

Hornpipes used for contra dancing include Cincinnati, Durang's, Fisher's, Forester's, Garfield's, Lamplighter's, Quindaro, Rickett's, Staten Island, and Vinton's. The classic contra tune Hull's Victory is usually considered a hornpipe. The stereotyped "sailor's hornpipe" that makes many people think of the cartoon character Popeye is an old tune called College Hornpipe.

Marches

Marches have a lot in common with reels. They share the smooth, even feeling that is caused by a downbeat and upbeat of the same length. In a march, however, the measure and the musical phrase are both twice as long as in a reel. Most marches are written in 4/4 time (though some, notably in the Scottish tradition, are in 2/4 or 6/8 time). When a 4/4 tune is written or printed, each measure contains four beats, represented by quarter notes. This doesn't change the way a contra dance routine is written out; it just means that each eight-beat movement will occupy two measures of music rather than four.

The phrases of a march are generally sixteen beats long, rather than eight as in a reel. The phrases feel longer because there is no sharp break after the first eight beats, and often because the harmony is unresolved at that point – in other words, the chord is not the "home" chord (a G chord if the tune is in G) that is played at the end to give the tune a "finished" sound.

Marches, with their long phrases, are ideal for dances with long flowing movements. The hey for four is perhaps the prime example of such a movement; others would be a promenade along the line or a trip down the hall four in line. In a routine danced to a march, eight-count movements should be followed immediately by their counterpart or mirror image. Examples are a circle to the left followed by one to the right, or a ladies chain across the set and back. If a dance contains several short movements that don't fit comfortably into long phrases, such as a succession of hand turns, or a single star followed by a single ladies chain, it will probably feel better if it's danced to a reel or a jig.

Some familiar 4/4 marches are Caissons, Marines' Hymn, and Stars and Stripes Forever. Marches in 4/4 commonly used for contra dancing include McQuillen's Squeezebox, Meeting of the Waters, Mount Cashel's Brigade, Rollstone Mountain, Scotland the Brave, and Snowy Breasted Pearl (also known as Boys of Wexford).

Note that many popular songs used for square dancing have phrases of the same length as marches and can be used for the same type of contra. Examples are Just Because, My Little Girl, Swanee, When You Wore a Tulip, and You're a Grand Old Flag. Songs that everybody knows can give an extra lift to an evening, but like strong seasonings, they should be used sparingly.

Jigs

Jigs give an altogether different feeling to the dance than reels or marches. Jigs are "bouncy" tunes, due to their uneven pattern of downbeat and upbeat. They are written in 6/8 time, which strictly speaking ought to mean that each measure has six beats represented by eighth notes. In the real world, however, those six notes are grouped into two sets of three, with each set worth one beat. So jigs, like reels, have two beats to the measure. The difference is that in a reel each beat is again divided into two (downbeat and upbeat), but in a jig each beat contains not two but three parts:

                One and ah two and ah

or

                Sat ur day Sat ur day

Where, then, is the upbeat?

In dance work, the second note in each group of three (the "and") is ignored by the rhythm section of the band, leaving the first note ("one" or "two") as the downbeat and the third (the "ah") as the upbeat. This makes the upbeat much shorter than the downbeat, as follows:

One — ah two — ah

You can get a feel for this effect by galloping as children do when they play horse, shifting quickly from your left foot to your right. This is similar to the footwork used in the buzz-step swing, and indeed one of the many uses of jigs is in teaching a buzz step. Unfortunately, 6/8 rhythm also encourages many new dancers to skip when they should walk, and so I prefer to use reels for the first dance of the evening when I'm working with beginners. The swing can be avoided entirely until the group has learned a smooth dance-walk, and taught later using 6/8 music.

Jigs are ideal for any dance containing side-steps ("chassez" or "sashay" steps) or extended periods of buzz-stepping (a basket or several long swings). They also seem to work well with dances containing a large number of balances, possibly because of the extended downbeat. Finally, jigs can be used for variety's sake with almost any dance that would normally be done to a reel. If the program includes three dances in succession that appear to call for reels, the second one can be danced to a jig without any problems.

Calling to jigs is much like calling to reels or marches, with one exception. Occasionally most callers find themselves using wording that groups four syllables on one downbeat, as in

<u>Part</u> - ner <u>swing</u> in the <u>mid</u>-dle of the <u>ring</u>

where "mid-dle of the" all comes during one beat (the third of the four beats on the line). This poses no problem if the music is a reel, as each downbeat or upbeat can be further divided into two parts, each part represented by a sixteenth note. Indeed, most 2/4 tunes contain many sixteenth notes. But if the tune is a jig, the caller must speak those four syllables while the band is playing three notes. It can't be done – at least not comfortably. It's better to change the wording to conform to the rhythm of the tune:

<u>Swing</u> 'em a - <u>round</u> in the <u>mid</u>-dle of <u>town</u>

Three syllables against three notes is a much easier mouthful.

Jigs that can be heard at contra dances include Brisk Young Lads, Coleraine, Dusty Bob's, Fair Jenny's, Haste to the Wedding, Irish

Washerwoman, Maggie Brown's Favorite, Rakes of Kildare, and Tobin's Favorite. Of the traditional dances that are associated with tunes of the same name, Jefferson and Liberty, Pop Goes the Weasel, Portland Fancy, and Rory O'More are the only ones in jig time, although *Sackett's Harbor* is often danced to the 6/8 tune Steamboat Quickstep. Familiar marches in 6/8 include Semper Fidelis and Seventy-Six Trombones.

Live Music

Live music has always been the norm for traditional square and contra dancing – indeed, until the 1940s it was the only possibility. Since then, many recreational dance groups have adopted records, tapes, or CDs, and the branch of square dancing that became the modern "Western" movement has shifted almost completely to recorded music. There are several likely reasons for the latter phenomenon. The dominance of the caller over the music in the Western square dance tradition may have made playing for dances unrewarding; the many small clubs that evolved during the 1950s felt they couldn't afford live music; and a typical string band specializing in fiddle tunes found it hard to keep up with the expanding repertoire of singing calls and round dances.

In the New England tradition, however, live music is highly valued as an integral part of the dance. This is largely because of the strong connection that has been maintained between the dance movements and the musical phrase. Very few New England dances have a particular tune associated with them; this enables a band to get by with a limited repertoire if necessary.

A live band has some clear advantages over recorded music:

- The sense of immediacy that live music produces is impossible to duplicate with recordings. There is no substitute for the feeling that the people making the music are right there in the hall, interacting with the caller and the dancers.
- Live music is spontaneous. Often the tunes are chosen on the spot, based on the band's and caller's mood of the moment. Even if the music has been planned in advance, the level of excitement on the floor may inspire the players to new heights. Or the band may commemorate a chance happening with impromptu vocals or sound effects. Even the occasional mistake can add to the sense of community, as it reminds everyone that the musicians are human.
- Live music is flexible. If the caller has planned to run a dance seven times through the tune, but the band is hot and the dancers

are eager for more, it's a simple matter to ask the band for "one more time." Medleys, key changes, special singing call arrangements – all are easy with live music, difficult with recordings.

True, it takes a little forethought and some hard work to form and use a live band. But the same can be said of learning to call – or indeed any worthwhile human endeavor. You get out what you put in.

Musicians Are People

From a caller's point of view, the first thing to remember about dance musicians is that they're people. You'll be sharing the stage with them, egos and all. Don't expect them to crank out music all night like a machine, with no help from you except "Let's go." They're proud practitioners of a valuable and time-honored craft, just as you are.

Happily, the band's goal is identical to yours: to give the dancers a good time (and, if at all possible, to have fun themselves). If you can all remember that you have a common purpose, and look for ways to cooperate to achieve that purpose, you'll make each other sound better than you ever thought you could. The dancers, of course, will benefit beyond measure from this kind of shared energy on stage.

The very way you stand can make a difference. If you stand in front of the band, you'll be blocking their view of the dancers and the dancers' view of them. They'll be looking at your back all night; if you need to communicate with them, you'll have to turn completely around, losing touch with the dancers. And you'll be saying to the band (and everyone in the hall) that you're the big cheese and they're the hired hands.

The best place to stand is at one side of the stage. From here you can attain eye contact with the band, or at any rate the lead musician, by turning only slightly in their direction. This motion soon becomes second nature, like the eye shift between the road and the rear-view mirror when you drive a car. Standing at the side tells everyone that you and the band are in this together, equal partners in a joint venture.

The key to any successful relationship is communication: the more the better. It will help your dances greatly if you can meet with the band away from the hall occasionally, to discuss any ideas you may have or problems that arise. At the least, if you're due to work with an unfamiliar band, plan to arrive at the hall early – at least half an hour sooner than other responsibilities would dictate – and ask the band to do likewise. This will allow time to go over the program line by line, and the band won't be taken by surprise later when you ask for a particular tune or type of tune. Better still, get in touch with the band before the night of the dance to discuss strategy.

Two things that most bands and callers find helpful to communication are a tune list and the appointment of a lead musician. The tune list indicates to the caller the breadth and depth of the band's repertoire: Do they know Hull's Victory? Should I avoid asking for a high proportion of jigs? And having one musician to deal with simplifies the caller's job and eliminates a good deal of anxiety on the band's part.

The Tune List

A band and caller who work together regularly can develop a joint tune list that takes some of the caller's preferences into account. Yankee Ingenuity, the band that played with me in Concord, Massachusetts for many years, had a tune list on which the tunes were grouped by "flavor": bouncy reels, flowing reels, laid-back tunes, cut-loose tunes, and so forth. (A tune could be in more than one group.) If I wanted a bouncy reel for a particular dance, I wrote a "B" next to the dance title on the band's copy of my program, alerting them to look at the "Bouncy" list for possible tunes. This method made everyone happy: I got the type of tune I wanted, and the band got to choose the specific tunes rather than have me dictate to them. (Once or twice a night, I used dances for which I preferred to choose the tune myself. The band didn't mind because they picked the vast majority of the tunes.)

Tune flavors, of course, are subjective. No two bands will agree completely on which category a tune belongs in, and the categories themselves will vary from one band to another. It's important to create a list that works for the people who will use it. Some bands like to put tunes in medleys on the spot; others prefer to work them out ahead of time and develop a medley list.

Starting the Music

To start the music, if you know and like the band's usual tempo, you can simply turn to the band and say "OK" or "Ready." If you want a particular tempo that you're not sure the band will play on their own initiative, you'll need to get their attention first and then tap your foot at the proper speed. If they're on the ball, they may start playing after four of your taps, but be prepared for them to come in at any point. Note that it's your job as the dance expert to set the tempo, but the band's job to maintain it.

Most bands prefer to begin each number with a four-beat introduction: either a shuffle on the fiddle ("*dah*-didi-*dah*-didi-*dah*-didi-*dah*") or a vamp on the piano (four "oom-pahs"). This is long enough to establish the tempo in everyone's mind: yours, the band's, the dancers'. Unfortunately, it's not always long enough to let you give the first call of the dance comfortably. If you can convince the band to play eight beats before starting the first tune, you can wait four beats and give your initial call on the next four. If not, as mentioned in Chapter 4, you can tell the dancers beforehand what the first move of the dance will be, and then as the band plays the introduction, say "[One, two,] Ready, go!"

Changing Tunes

Until about 1970, most bands played only one tune for each dance number. Ralph Page, the most influential caller in New England for fifty years, used to say, "If a tune is good enough to play at all, it's good enough to play for the whole dance." Dance tunes in those days tended to be fairly simple and put relatively little strain on the musicians. As bands became more sophisticated and learned more intricate tunes, they began to prefer playing two or three tunes per dance. This was probably both to lessen the strain of playing difficult tunes over and over and to make things more interesting for themselves and the dancers.

Normally the band will take care of tune changes with no effort required on your part. Most bands, however, will appreciate knowing roughly how long you plan to let a dance run, so that they can pace themselves and play each tune about the same number of times. This is especially important if some of your numbers are to be longer than others – for example, if you plan to run an old-style contra "all the way down and all the way back" for the original head couple, but are willing to cut off an all-active contra or a circle dance after a shorter time. Contra medleys, which are becoming increasingly popular, require close coordination with the band so that a new tune and a new dance routine start together.

If you're calling New England squares (see Chapter 17), which last a definite number of times through the tune, tell the band how long each square will be. Ask them whether they plan to play medleys for the squares. If they do, they'll need to change tunes at a specific point, halfway through the dance. If a square has a middle break, the tune change can come either just before or just after the break. If you often prolong your ending breaks, you should encourage the band to delay any tune change until after the middle break, or they may find themselves playing the second tune longer than they would have liked.

An inexperienced band may need help in putting together workable medleys. The most likely problem is that they will choose two tunes with markedly different flavors, such as a march and a Southern reel. This will change the feel of the dance drastically at the halfway point; you may want to do that deliberately on occasion, but normally the flavor of a dance should be consistent.

Signals during the Dance

Occasionally you may need to signal the band while a dance is in progress. This will usually be to ask them to play either faster or slower. There are no universally accepted signals for speed changes; I've found after years of trial and error that a loud "Faster!" or "Slower!" is the most effective signal.

Don't worry about offending your musicians by sounding too imperative. They're concentrating on their playing, and a politer request will distract them as they try to figure out what you said. A single sharp word will penetrate their consciousness without breaking their concentration.

It's best, too, to avoid telling them what not to do (as in "Too fast" or "Too slow"). On a noisy stage, they may hear only the "fast" or "slow" and think that's what you wanted. Keep your directions consistent, and tell them what you do want. Once they've fixed the tempo, thank them with a smile and nod or an "OK" sign.

Some callers like the band to play louder or softer at certain points in the dance, for dramatic effect. In my experience, any band good enough to play at different volume levels is likely to be sensitive enough to develop their own drama. But a little direction from the caller is probably all right. Although volume signals can be given in the same manner as tempo signals, an open hand raised palm up for "louder" or lowered palm down for "softer" is commonly used and easily understood.

Ending the Music

The most critical aspect of caller-band communication is the procedure at the end of each dance number. Presumably the caller is the only person on stage who knows how long the dance should run. How can a caller most effectively signal the end of a dance to the band?

The key here is timing. Whether you use hand signals or spoken signals is less important than when you give them. Most bands prefer to be warned in plenty of time that you want one more round of the dance, so that they can build to a musical climax as they play the last time through the tune. You can do this by holding up one finger or by saying "One more!" In either case, look for signs that everyone has seen or heard you. The time to signal is during the "B" part of the tune preceding the last round. If you call for "one more time" during the "A" part, it won't be clear whether you mean this round or the next round.

A band that has played together for a while, and is good at varying dynamics for dramatic effect, may prefer to be warned *two* rounds before the end. Many bands like that much warning if the dance is a "chestnut" and they've changed tunes in midstream; if you tell them "Two more" they'll have a chance to switch back to the original tune. Be sure to signal for one more, even if you just did for two more.

It's wise to signal the band again just before the end of the last round, even though they might not need it. People do draw mental blanks on things they've just heard, and musicians are no exception. Again, you can either hold up a hand, traffic-policeman style, or say "Out!" The spoken signal is more common; try to give it just off the beat so it will be easier to hear. Musicians often signal the end of a tune to each other by raising one foot. If you're sure your band will understand it, this can be a useful alternative to the other signals, especially if you're calling a complicated square or improvising an ending for a contra.

Recorded Music

Someone once said "Good recordings are better than a bad band." This is a half-truth at best. The finest recordings available, chosen with care to fit each dance and played through a top-quality sound system, are better in some ways than an unsteady or indifferent band. Some, but not all. With even the worst live band there is still that sense of immediacy that no recording can match.

Even so, recorded music can be a lifesaver in certain situations. A dance group newly formed, in an area where no one seems to know any dance musicians, will rejoice in the availability of good recorded square and contra dance music. Some groups, such as small churches and parent-teacher organizations, that would love to try dancing but whose budgets genuinely will not allow for live music, may have to hire a caller with recordings or forgo the activity altogether. Often such groups enjoy their initial taste of dancing so much that they hire the same caller again, this time with a live band!

The key to using recordings successfully is to capitalize on their strong points. I hesitate to term them "advantages," but recorded music does have certain strengths:

- Variety is the chief asset of recorded music. Since it's possible to dance to a dozen bands in one night through the miracles of modern science, why not do it? Not only can you use different bands for the squares and contras, you can add ballroom, novelty, or international folk dances that a live band might not know. Variety will go a long way toward compensating for the loss of the excitement that a live band would provide.
- Predictability isn't always an advantage, but you can turn it into one. Knowing how many times each tune will be played, or how a recording is going to end, will enable you to reach a climax as the music does. With live music, only a band and caller that have worked together for years can achieve this kind of effect.
- Recorded music has definite advantages if you're running an out-and-out class. The income from most classes won't do more than cover the expense of renting a hall, and recordings will save a bit of money. They'll also save wear and tear on musicians, who might otherwise have to sit around a lot while you worked on fine points of style (though it's not a good idea to go too long without letting people dance to music). You can always plan a live-music party for the last session of class, to add excitement and give your students the feel of the dance events you hope they'll be attending.

Recording Formats

In the first edition of this book, published in 1992, I wrote "The recording industry is currently in a state of flux." This is, if anything, truer than ever. Following is a brief rundown of the media used by folk, square, and contra dance leaders in 2010.

Compact discs (CDs) have, of course, become the standard for music in the home. Many fine albums of contra dance music have been produced on CD in the last several years, and some older recordings have been reissued on CD. The advent of recordable CDs, which can be loaded with music using a home computer, has made this format popular with callers and instructors. CDs are small and light; many selections (over an hour's worth) can be put on one disc; and, unlike cassette tapes, CD equipment allows instant access to each selection. Many CD players allow the user to vary the music's pitch, tempo, or both in small increments across a wide range.

Cassette tapes, which were a favorite of folk dance groups in the 1990s, have almost completely disappeared from the dance hall. Their chief advantage, the ease of recording them at home, is now shared by CDs. Access to individual tunes was always a problem with tapes; it could be addressed by putting each tune on its own short cassette or by using a player that searched for the brief silences between tunes, but the results were never wholly satisfactory. In addition, tapes wear out with repeated use, although they can easily be re-created if a master has been kept on file.

Vinyl records have many drawbacks when used for playback at a dance: every use wears them down; they attract dust, which causes more wear; and the playing arm is sensitive to vibration from the dance floor and to the wind at outdoor events. But they have made a comeback in the new role of source material for CDs and computer files: they're the most stable of media, and any scratch or hiss on a record can be reduced or eliminated in the computer. Many wonderful tunes, recorded only on vinyl, can once again be enjoyed by dancers, with better sound than ever.

Minidiscs (MDs) enjoyed a spurt of popularity in the 1990s, before recordable CDs became available. They look like smaller versions of floppy computer discs (which are now themselves nearly obsolete) and have most of the advantages of CDs. Their chief drawbacks are that very few MD recording and playback devices are on the market, and that the sound is not as good as that of CDs (some information is removed in order to fit the music on the MD).

Computer files are extremely popular and will probably remain so for a long time. One can now easily convert music from any format – tapes, CDs, vinyl records, or files purchased from a website – to files on a home computer. One can then create one's own CDs, transfer the files to a portable digital player, or use the computer itself as a playback device. The two most frequently used formats are MP3 and WAV (pronounced, and sometimes spelled, "wave"). WAV files have better sound quality than MP3 files but take up more computer storage space; they are used primarily for master files kept in the computer. MP3 files are compressed like minidisc files, though not as drastically; they're probably the most-used format for playback. They can be downloaded into a portable player such as the Apple iPod or kept in a laptop computer; player or laptop can be taken to dances and connected to the PA system. Several software programs have been written that allow music to be played through a computer, including such features as tempo and pitch control and electronic "cue cards" (see the Resources section). At present the iPod does not have variable speed, but most of the fancy CD players made for disc jockeys can now play MP3s with variable pitch and tempo.

A big advantage of both CDs and computer files for dance work is that you can start the music instantly with the press of a key. This lets you give the first call of a contra and then start the music in rhythm, even if the recording has a short introduction or none at all. With tapes and vinyl records there was a period of silence, whose length was hard to judge, before the music began.

Note that there is some question as to the long-term stability of CDs, particularly CDs recorded at home. If recordable CDs are your format of choice, it's wise to keep copies of the source files on your computer or in a removable drive.

Using Recorded Music

It's important not to let the mechanics get in the way of the dancers' fun. Organize your music so that you can find the selection you want instantly. The most common system is to set up categories – jigs, reels, marches, Southern tunes, waltzes, other couple dances – and arrange titles alphabetically within each category. MP3 players and computer programs allow you to create "playlists"; you can make up a playlist of the selections you plan to use at an event, then switch easily from one tune to the next (unless you change your program on the spot). If you're using tapes or discs, you can pull selections from your case as you need them, or stack the ones you think you'll be using if you have trouble picking them on the fly. Either way, get in the habit of switching to your next tape, disc, or file as soon as each dance ends, so you won't have to hesitate once you've started the next walkthrough and dance.

Along with the tune title, it's helpful to mark each selection with the number of times the tune is played. If a selection goes seven times through a 32-bar (64-beat) tune, you know that it can be used for any square dance figure of that length, with breaks at the beginning, middle, and end. If you use a tune that's played only six times, you'll have to omit the middle break.

For contras, you'll need to decide what to do about recording length. Until recently, most recordings of contra music ran only seven or eight times through the tune. Most traditional callers prefer to run their contra dances at least twice that long. You can play a selection twice, use one of the longer tracks that have become available, or splice your computer files to repeat some of the rounds of a tune or to join parts of two tracks. (Many digital players have a "looping" feature that lets you repeat part of a track as many times as you like, but I have yet to encounter one that's precise enough to keep the beat steady as it passes from one part to another.)

You should know, however, that when you're calling without the excitement of a live band, 18 or 20 times through may make for too long a dance. Thirteen times through is an excellent length for recorded contra music. It seems to be long enough to satisfy most dancers, and it ends with a couple dancing at the head of the set whether you're calling a duple or triple dance.

Caring for Your Media

If you're still using records or tapes, it's important to keep them clean. For tapes, this means keeping them in their boxes except when you're playing them, and rewinding them when you're done so the actual tape isn't exposed to dust (and possible tangling). Records seem to pick up dust no matter what you do to them or where you keep them. There are cleaning systems on the market, but few callers have the patience to use them. If you can find a lint-free cloth, you can try moistening it slightly and wiping the record gently just before you play it. CDs are somewhat less trouble-prone, in that a minor scratch won't affect the sound; but it is possible to destroy or seriously damage a CD by careless handling.

Records and tapes are both susceptible to heat. Everyone knows by now what happens if you leave one in the sun – under the rear window of your car, for instance. Use common sense when you're transporting and storing your music; avoid any place that's likely to get that hot. Outdoor dances can be a problem if you're using recorded music. Often there will be little or no shade for your equipment. Keep your discs or tapes out of direct sunlight if you can, even if you have to put them under the table. (If there's little or no shade, keep all your cases shut except when you're changing selections. This is one time when a delay between numbers is justified.)

Make sure, too, that your equipment is being kind to your media. If you're using tapes, demagnetize your tape deck's heads regularly. A demagnetizer costs only a few dollars and is easy to use. If you're using records, even just to enter the music into your computer, check your stylus (the "needle") at least twice a year. Audio repair shops have microscopes for doing this. If you can't find someone to check it, replace the stylus once or twice a year, depending on how often you use your turntable. The cost is easy to justify: your record collection may be worth more than your sound system, and would probably be a lot harder to replace.

8
Sound Equipment

If you plan to call dances anywhere bigger than your living room, you'll need to learn how to deal with sound equipment. Like any skill, it may seem like a lot of trouble at first, but once you have the hang of it you'll be much more versatile as a caller.

In the old days, callers worked crowds of a hundred or more with nothing but lung power (and occasionally a megaphone). Bands likewise played to huge assemblies with no help from tubes or transistors. But people couldn't hear amplified music anywhere else, either, and so they weren't used to it. No one expected to catch every note of the band's performance, and as for the caller, he had either to develop industrial-strength lungs or trim his commands to mere prompts.

Nowadays people have come to expect good sound. Everywhere they go – at home, at work, in stores and restaurants, and in the theater – they're exposed to music played in ultra-high fidelity. When they come to a dance, they assume they'll be able to hear the band and caller even through normal crowd noise. A sound system, carefully chosen and correctly operated, can make your job much easier.

Sound System Theory

A sound system consists of three parts: one or more microphones ("mikes" or "mics"), an amplifier ("amp"), and one or more loudspeakers. The microphones convert sound waves from the band and caller into tiny electrical impulses; the amplifier turns the tiny impulses into bigger impulses; and the speakers convert the big impulses back into sound waves. If recorded music is used, the band's microphones are replaced by a turntable, a tape deck, or a CD or MP3 player. These components "read" sound waves that have been captured and stored on a tape, disc, or computer file and convert them into the kind of electrical impulses that a microphone would deliver. The amplifier includes circuits and controls that enable the signals from the microphones and playback devices to be "mixed"; that is, the volume of sound from each source can be adjusted separately until every voice or instrument can be heard clearly.

The quality and versatility of sound systems have improved vastly over the years. For practical purposes, amplifiers have been perfected: they produce superb sound, have controls and connection ports to suit almost any need, and are more trouble-free than most consumer products. Mikes and speakers, which are partly mechanical devices, have traditionally been the weak links, but even they have improved quite a bit.

Choosing Equipment

If you work exclusively with live music, it should be easy to find an appropriate sound system. Almost any music store will have what you're looking for. It's generally referred to as a "PA system" (short for "public address"), but it bears little resemblance to the "squawk boxes" that have been common for years in schools, factories, airports, and hospitals. The kind of PA system to get is made specifically for bands: rock, country, gospel, and the like. The PA handles the vocals of such a band, as well as any non-electric instruments. (Some bands also run the sound of their electric instruments through the PA, for better balance.)

A typical PA system is sold as a package including a mixer-amplifier (often called a "powered mixer" in stores and catalogs and a "board" or "amp" on the job) and a pair of speakers. (Having two speakers doesn't mean the system is stereophonic; it simply makes it easier to aim the sound where you want it.) Cables to connect the amp and the speakers are usually included. Microphones are included in some systems, but mike stands and speaker stands are almost always extra. Note that amps and speakers can usually be purchased separately; many people prefer to do so, perhaps to get components of different makes that appeal to them.

Amplifiers

The amplifier is the brain or control center of your system. It has two parts: a mixer-preamplifier, with volume and tone controls for each mike or other sound source, and a power amplifier, which does most of the work of magnifying the sound.

How big an amp do you need? Amps are measured in two ways: by the number of separate microphone channels and by the amplifier power. Many small systems have four mike channels, and are adequate for a caller and a three-piece band. If you think you may need more channels in a year or so, it's better to get a six- or eight-channel system now. Each channel should have its own tone controls in addition to a volume control (more about tone controls later in this chapter, under "Equalization"). Look closely at any model you're considering: a board advertised as eight-channel may have only four channels suitable for microphones.

As for power, 100 watts of continuous power is about the least you should settle for. If you have grand plans for the future, 150 or 200 is better. More and more powered mixers are being made with two power amplifiers (see "Monitors" below for their uses); again, higher wattage is better if you can afford the unit and it's not too heavy for your taste.

Ideally, the catalog or the product tag will state the continuous power rating; this is usually referred to as "RMS" (root-mean-square) power. Other rating methods, such as "peak power" or "music power," result in exaggerated and often meaningless numbers; if the wattage is not clearly labeled "RMS," you can assume that the true continuous power is one-half or even one-quarter of the stated figure. With contra dance music, it's safe to feed each speaker about twice its RMS rating; any peaks in the music will be short, and speakers are built to deal with such peaks.

You'll be spending a lot of time at the control board, so it's important to get one you can live with. Does the layout of the knobs and sliders make sense to you? Can you find a crucial control fast? Do the controls operate smoothly, and are they comfortable to the touch? Is the control panel easy to see? Look for a good viewing angle and legible labels. These are not minor issues: think of the different cars you've driven.

The ideal sound system, in a word, is simple. You may not be able to find a system with adequate power and enough channels that's also as simple as you'd like. Buyers who want a powerful system usually want it to be flexible, so manufacturers put more bells and whistles on their larger models: more ways to shape the sound and more places to send it. If you can't find a board that has only the controls you want, see whether the extra controls can be turned off or set to neutral positions and whether it's easy to tell this at a glance.

Popular mixer-amplifier brands include Behringer, Crate, Mackie, Peavey, Soundcraft, Yamaha, and Yorkville. The contra dance standard for years was the Electro-Voice Entertainer, one of the first amps to offer a lot of power and features in a relatively small, lightweight package. It's no longer made, and secondhand examples are likely to be near the end of their useful life, but many other companies now make similar units.

Impedance

One more pesky little detail that can't be ignored is the matter of impedance matching. Impedance is such a technical term that dictionaries have trouble with it, but basically it refers to the opposition that your sound system puts up to the flow of electricity. This affects you in two ways: the impedance of the mikes must match the input impedance of the amp, and the output impedance of the amp must match the impedance of the speakers.

The mike-to-amp impedance match won't be a problem if you buy only "low impedance" mikes and an amp that will accept them. "High impedance" equipment is slightly cheaper to build but less versatile. (For instance, you can't use more than about 18 feet of mike cable with a high impedance mike.) At one time, low impedance systems were priced out of reach of most callers and bands, but now all but the very cheapest PA systems include low impedance mike inputs.

The amp-to-speaker impedance problem used to be critical – the wrong number of speakers plugged into an amp could destroy the amp – but modern amps are built to withstand a wider range of impedances. As long as you use only the two speakers that came with your system, the problem will never arise. If you're piecing together a system from separate components, remember that in most cases impedance goes down as the number of speakers goes up. For example, two 8-ohm speakers equal a 4-ohm load; four of them equal a 2-ohm load. Most amps won't work with less than two ohms, and some (especially smaller ones) need at least four.

Microphones

With microphones, more than any other component, there is a wide range of price and quality levels. Get the best mikes you can afford; good ones will make an audible difference to your dancers.

Mikes built for PA use are either "dynamic" or "condenser." These terms refer to the way sound is converted to electricity. Condenser mikes are cheaper to make for any given level of quality; in other words, if two mikes cost the same, the condenser mike is likely to sound better. Condenser mikes are more sensitive than dynamics (and are therefore much used in recording studios) but are more prone to damage from wet or humid weather. They also need a source of electrical power: either a battery (which typically lasts about a year) or a special setting on your mixer called "phantom power." Dynamic mikes are more rugged and need no power source. They used to be fairly heavy, but there are some good lighter ones on the market now.

Look for models with a "unidirectional" or "cardioid" (heart-shaped) pickup pattern, which will hear only the sound that's fed directly into them. "Omnidirectional" mikes are cheaper but will hear sound in all directions, including the sound from nearby loudspeakers. When a mike hears sound from a speaker, which has already been amplified, the system will try to amplify it over and over again, and the result is the howl or squeal (known as "feedback") that is all too familiar to audiences and dancers. (Note that unidirectional mikes have a quality known as "proximity effect"; that is, they emphasize the low frequencies if you hold them close to your mouth. See the section on mike technique in Chapter 4.)

Wireless mikes have become popular with callers, especially callers who do a lot of teaching from the floor. There are three styles: lapel, handheld, and headworn. Lapel mikes, by their nature, are omnidirectional and not suitable for dance work. Handheld mikes give slightly better sound than the other types. They can hamper you when you're trying to demonstrate a figure, but they're easy to move away from your mouth when you're talking to the band. Some callers think a headworn mike is the best of both worlds: it sounds almost as good as a handheld but leaves both hands free, so you can teach or even join in the dancing. One caller who prefers this type says that he quickly learned to swivel the mike out of voice range when necessary. Some models don't swivel readily, but they're likely to have an easy-to-use mute control. (The power switch on a wireless mike should stay on throughout the evening; the mike's mute switch and the amplifier should be used to control the sound level. If the mike is turned off while the amp is on, the mike's receiver may pick up nearby radio signals and broadcast them through the speakers.)

Note that any wireless mike will need at least one battery; it's concealed in the body of a handheld mike and in a small transmitter on your belt for other styles. (The wireless receiver generally runs on wall power; it's connected to the caller's mike channel on the amp just as a wired mike would be.) Unlike an ordinary condenser mike, a wireless mike has a ravenous appetite for batteries: expect a set to last two or three evenings at most. Rechargeable battery systems are available for $20 or so; if you use disposables, look for a battery recycling program in your area.

There are many well-regarded brands of mike, including Astatic, Audio-Technica, Audix, Beyer, Electro-Voice, Sennheiser, and Shure. The Shure SM58, which sells for about $100, has been the industry standard for decades – a phenomenal run for a piece of electronic equipment. Its ice-cream-cone shape and its vocal characteristics have been copied by just about every other company. I currently use a Shure Beta 58, which looks just like the SM58 but is completely different inside; it has what I would call a more open, natural sound. (It also has a tighter cardioid pattern, allowing more gain before feedback sets in.) The Electro-Voice N/D series is also good and includes several lightweight handheld models. Wireless mikes are made by Audio-Technica, Electro-Voice, Nady, Sennheiser, Samson, Shure, and Telex. They seem to get cheaper and better every year; still, it's wise to listen to a friend's mike before you buy, especially in the case of a wireless. Equally good mikes can have vastly different "personalities" or sound contours, although they can be modified using the amplifier's tone controls.

Mikes to avoid include those sold for around $20 as upgrades for portable recording devices, and indeed almost anything that sells for less than about $100 new. If you're on a tight budget, it's better to get used mikes of standard grade. (See below for more information about buying used equipment.)

Mike stands and cables are less standardized than mikes: most stores will have only one or two brands, often under private labels, making it hard to compare models. Stands should be examined in the store. Try adjusting all the movable parts: Are the knobs comfortable? Do the parts stay put once you've adjusted them? Any stand meant for musicians should have a boom mounted on top, so the player can maintain a comfortable distance from the upright part. As for cables, it's hard to judge quality by looks alone. Don't get the cheapest available if they look and feel flimsy, but there's no need to buy "super-premium" cables at two or three times the price of standard grade. Most stores will have adequate cables at medium price. Be sure to buy at least 20-foot cables; 25 feet will give you more versatility. This assumes that you've decided on low impedance equipment (see above), which is all but standard these days. Make sure the cables have the right connectors for your mikes and amp.

Speakers

Loudspeakers are nothing but paper or plastic cones mounted in sturdy boxes; the cones vibrate to produce sound. Because they're simpler to build than other components, a lot of people have gotten into the speaker business. Anyone can slap together a speaker, but good speakers are as tricky to design as any other part of a sound system. Stick with recognized brand names that have been around for a while. These include Electro-Voice, JBL, and the brands mentioned above under "Amplifiers." If you're considering a brand you don't know, get a recommendation from someone you trust.

Some contra dance groups use speakers built for home use, but I don't recommend this. Home stereo speakers, especially the smaller and lighter ones, are not likely to be made to take the high sound levels you'll need at a dance (or the banging around they're likely to get in transporting and setting up). It's better to get good PA speakers, which are designed for the kind of work you'll be demanding of them. If money is a problem, look for used speakers (see below).

The main problem with PA speakers, and one of the reasons some groups don't use them, is that most of the good ones are quite heavy. This is fine if you have a roadie to carry your equipment, but it can be discouraging to bands that do their own sound work. Fortunately, many manufacturers now produce a line of lightweight speakers, with cabinets made of space-age plastics; some of them weigh in at less than 20 pounds. It should be noted, however, that the lighter the speaker, the less substantial it's likely to sound, particularly in the lower or bass frequencies. If possible, listen to speakers before you buy to make sure the sound quality is adequate. Better yet, attend all the dances and folk concerts you can; see what other performers are using, and listen to the sound.

Speakers, like amplifiers, are rated in watts, but speaker ratings indicate how much power the speaker can accept from the amplifier. A typical speaker rating is "100 watts RMS (or continuous), 200 watts program, 400 watts peak." It's generally considered safe to feed a speaker its program rating, or twice its continuous rating; in other words, you can connect a power amp rated at 200 watts RMS to a speaker rated at 100 watts RMS. The amp will be putting out less than its full rated power most of the time. And because PA equipment is built to withstand the high sound levels of rock bands, a contra dance group will have plenty of safety margin or "headroom."

Powered speakers are a relatively recent development, and some contra dance groups are using them successfully. Each powered speaker has a built-in power amplifier whose impedance and wattage are perfectly matched to the speaker. This means that the mixer can be unpowered; in fact, many powered speakers have a basic mixer built into the back of the cabinet (though you'll probably want more flexibility). The chief drawback of powered speakers is their weight, but as with unpowered speakers some lighter ones are being made.

One unusual type of speaker worth considering is the line array. Research has shown that if a number of speakers are put in a vertical line, they throw sound a great distance to the right and left with hardly any throw to the ceiling or floor. This, of course, makes line arrays ideal for halls with problematic reverberation caused by ceiling reflections. In addition, as you move away from a line array, the sound drops off only half as quickly as sound from a conventional speaker. This enables the music and calls to be clearly audible at the back of the dance area without blasting the people near the speaker. The taller the array, the more pronounced these effects are. Modern square dance callers have been using arrays (under the name of "sound columns") since the 1950s; a typical enclosure has four to eight small speakers. Bose has recently taken the line array concept to a new extreme: the Bose L1 has 24 tiny speakers in a seven-foot tower. The L1's designer intended it to sit behind the band (ideally a separate tower for each musician) and function as a monitor as well as a main speaker. Contra dance musicians, however, won't like having the caller's voice in a speaker facing them. If you have two towers, you can put the calls through one (in front of the band) and the music through the other (behind the band), but this still takes some getting used to on the musicians' part. I've had better luck using one or two towers as house speakers in front of the band, with the musicians getting their own mix – minus the caller's voice – through conventional monitors.

Speaker stands are often thought of as optional, but in many situations they can literally save a dance from being a disaster (see "Speaker Placement," below). Most brands are built pretty solidly, and are more than adequate to support the weight of the kind of speakers we use. Examine various types in the store or at dances, and buy the one with the features you want: light weight, ease of folding, extra height, compactness when folded, etc. A recent innovation is a friction height adjuster that locks with a twist, so the speaker doesn't come crashing down when you're trying to raise or lower it.

Speaker cables, like microphone cables, are an unglamorous but important part of a sound system. As with mike cables, the medium-priced ones will probably be the best suited to your purposes. The 25-foot length is more or less standard; for more versatility, get one or two 50-footers or extra 25-footers with adapters that let you connect them end to end.

Monitors

A monitor system is a distinct advantage in all but the smallest halls. It's simply a second system – amplifier and speakers – that sits on the stage and lets the musicians hear themselves. (The main or "house" speakers are usually in front of the band and don't help them much.) A separate set of volume controls lets you give the band a mix that suits them, typically without the caller's voice. If you want to hear yourself over the PA system (which will help you avoid straining your voice), stand next to a house speaker and very slightly forward of it so you can hear the actual mix of music and calls that's going out to the dancers. If you start to get feedback, move away from the speaker.

Most PA amplifiers have these monitor controls built in, but the smaller and cheaper models require an external power amp as well as speakers to complete a monitor system. Many mid- and higher-priced boards contain two power amps that can be used for the main and monitor channels, eliminating the need for a separate monitor amp. In large halls or outdoors, you can flip a switch and use the built-in amps to drive the left and right house speakers, doubling your useable power. (In this case you'll again need a separate monitor amp; your main board will have a clearly marked place to plug it in.)

Most of the companies that make PA systems for bands also sell monitor systems; often these are identical to the company's smallest PA, without the mike mixer controls. Powered speakers are popular for monitor work, including the mini-monitor, a small box that can be mounted on a mike stand. The mini is lighter and cheaper than a conventional monitor system; the ideal is to have one for each band member, but current models put out enough sound that one or two may be enough for a whole band.

Sound for Recorded Music

What kind of sound system should you buy for recorded music? That depends on which recording/playback format you plan to use, and on whether you'll be working with live music too.

If live music figures in your plans at all, your best bet is to buy a system designed for live bands and plug your playback device (tape deck, CD player, MP3 player, or laptop computer) into it. This is true even if you don't anticipate working with live music very often. There are portable sound systems built specifically for dance leaders who use recorded music, but because of the limited market, those systems tend to be expensive compared to the PA systems made for bands. Ideally your playback device should have variable speed; that is, the speed of the music must be continuously variable to about 10 percent above and below the standard speed, to compensate for recordings that are faster or slower than you'd like and to facilitate working with dancers of different abilities. Many players have an additional feature, called "pitch lock" or "master tempo," that keeps the music in the same key while you vary its speed. The market for playback devices is changing so rapidly that it's impossible to make recommendations of models, brands, or even formats that will still be valid by the time you read this; the Internet and word of mouth will be your best sources of information. (See "Recorded Music" in Chapter 7 for a discussion of currently available formats.)

If you think you won't be working with live music in the foreseeable future, you may still be better off with the kind of setup described above. But if portability and ease of use are more important to you than cost, you can buy one of the systems designed for use by schoolteachers and professional dance instructors; typically they combine a small amplifier with one or more playback devices (CD or MP3 player, tape deck, or turntable). Note that the turntables built into portable units are typically not kind to records; if you have a vinyl collection you'd like to use for dancing, your best bet is to buy a good turntable, play the records into your computer at home, and create CDs or MP3 files to use at dances. Karaoke machines, sold for sing-along use at home parties, are cheap copies of the type of equipment used in bars and nightclubs. They may be less expensive than units built for dance work, but their construction may be flimsy and their sound quality is often disappointing.

Any of the above systems will need an external speaker for best results. (If a speaker is included in the unit, it is usually small and often not mounted in a way that will give good sound in a large hall.) And you will, of course, need a microphone for calling even if your music is recorded. The advice above on buying mikes and speakers applies equally to live and recorded music.

Cutting Sound System Costs

Many fledgling callers, bands, and dance organizers reach the point at which they need a good sound system long before they feel they can afford one. There are several ways to lessen the financial bite.

One time-honored method is to buy used equipment. Live-music systems are especially easy to come by; watch for "Band Breaking Up" notices in your local classified-advertising media. It helps to have a knowledgeable person examine the goods. In general, if equipment produces a good clean sound and nothing appears to be loose, you're fairly safe in buying it. Don't forget to lift each amp and speaker before you agree to the transaction: rock equipment is heavy! (You can also search online auction sites such as eBay, but the cost of shipping and the risks of buying delicate equipment sight unseen make auction sites less attractive for sound gear than for books and recordings.) Pawn shops are another possibility, but based on my experience, you're more likely to find lookalike systems of inferior make there than any of the recommended brands.

Some cost-cutting measures should be avoided. These include buying low-grade microphones (as outlined previously) and buying your PA system at the electronics store in your shopping mall (the kind of store that carries cellphones, radio parts, and cheap home audio and video). The systems you see there will look much like those at your music store, but their sound quality is abysmal. Stick with the music store, or buy secondhand.

If even a few hundred dollars is too much, you can get one of several mini-systems that have come on the market in the $100 to $200 range. A typical one consists of a small powered speaker with volume controls for one or two microphones. Such systems can come in handy for calling at small parties where the band doesn't need to be amplified. Their sound quality varies from good to very bad; as always, it's advisable to listen before you buy.

No matter how much or little you choose to spend on a sound system, the process will be less painful if you set aside funds regularly toward the purchase: a certain amount from each private party you call at, or everything over expenses if you're running a dance series.

Using Your Sound System

The technical term for what a PA system does is "sound reinforcement." Keep in mind that reinforcing is all you should be doing. When you use a sound system for square and contra dancing, you're not trying to blast people out of the hall. You're simply trying to help the music and calls get to the far corners of the hall, where they would otherwise be drowned out by the dancers' feet or the normal conversations on the sidelines. It's all too easy to set the sound level too high if the crowd is noisy. Encourage them to quiet down, especially during the walkthroughs, and you won't need as much volume.

Two factors are especially important in achieving good dance sound: speaker placement and volume settings. (A third factor, microphone technique, is covered in Chapter 4.)

Speaker Placement

In placing the speakers, it helps to think of them as spotlights. If they are placed on the stage or on a table, they will only "shine" on the front row of dancers. If you turn the volume up in an attempt to reach the back of the hall, the front row will get blasted and the dancers in the back will probably still not be able to hear well – bodies absorb sound. For best results, the speakers should be raised above the dancers' heads. Speaker stands are the easiest way to do this; if stands aren't available, the speakers may be placed on chairs on top of tables on the stage. Whatever the mounting method, make absolutely sure the setup is stable.

The sound will be even better if the speakers are not only raised but also angled down so that they're aimed at the dancers' heads. Note, however, that some methods of doing this make the speakers unstable on their stands. Hilton Audio, which specializes in sound for modern square dance callers, used to make a gadget called the "Hilton Tilter" that offset the speaker behind the top of the stand, so that the center of gravity only shifted a few inches. The angle of tilt was adjustable. If you're handy, you can build tilters out of wood; you probably shouldn't try to make them adjustable.

In general, the sound should all appear to come from one source. Unless the hall is very long and narrow, it's best to have the music and caller at one end, and to put all the speakers at that end. The best sound will be obtained if the speakers can be placed in the middle of the stage area and angled slightly away from each other; this is usually practical for recorded music, but gets in the way of a live band. The next best solution is to put the speakers one-quarter to one-third of the way in from the side walls and to point them straight toward the back of the hall (that is, pointed neither to the left nor to the right; they can still be angled down). Avoid putting them in the corners and angling them in toward each other; dead spots may occur where their sound crosses in the center of the hall.

In a long narrow hall, it's often better if the caller and music can be set up in the middle of one of the long sides, with speakers aimed straight across the room flanking the stage area. If the dancers at the extreme ends of the hall can't hear the calls, it may be necessary to use four speakers, spaced evenly along one wall. The two speakers farthest from the stage can be angled outward. If your system allows you to assign the power amps to the left and right speakers, you may want to plug the two inboard speakers into (say) the right channel and the two outboard ones into the left channel. This will let you control the level of the outboard or "corner fill" speakers independently, assuming your mixer has separate level controls for the left and right channels.

Speaker setups that should be avoided if possible include putting speakers opposite each other (this takes a lot of experience and some painstaking experimentation) and using a pair of speakers at one end and a second pair halfway down the hall (this requires a special device to cancel the time lag between the two pairs and, again, should be left to a professional).

Remember in all cases that (1) if some people are not within the throw of any speaker, raising the volume will not reach them; it will simply blast everyone else. On the other hand, (2) increasing the number of speakers will not in itself give you more sound; it will only disperse it more evenly. Some speakers are more efficient than others, but the only way to get more sound from a given speaker is to use more amplifier power, either by raising the volume or by getting a larger amplifier.

Once your speakers are set up, check the sound by putting on a recording or having the band play a tune while you walk around the floor. Listen from every part of the hall: the center, the front, the back, both sides, and all four corners. The sound probably won't be ideal in every possible spot, but it should be acceptable. Allow enough setup time before the dance to let you play with speaker placement and amplifier settings (see "The Sound Check," below).

Note that monitor speakers must be placed carefully on the stage to avoid interacting with the microphones and causing feedback. The usual place for monitors is at the front of the stage, facing the musicians and angled up at them. Using unidirectional mikes will greatly reduce the chance of feedback.

Volume Settings

In theory, adjusting the sound level is simple: set it so that everyone can hear the music and the calls, but no one is annoyed by the volume. This is easier said than done.

In the first place, your dancers are not holding still and listening the way they would listen to a concert or a lecture. They are walking around, rather heavily perhaps, and they may even be shouting exuberantly. Even if they're not, the folks on the sidelines are talking. This is right and good – a dance is a social event, and if no one felt like talking, it would be time to worry. But it complicates the task of setting the sound level.

In the second place, the optimum level of sound changes during an evening. Bodies absorb sound, and the more people there are in the hall, the higher the volume controls must be set in order to produce the same perceived sound. The level you carefully set before the dance will need to be increased as people come in. Toward the end of the night, when people start to leave, the sound may become too loud even though no one has touched the controls.

Fortunately, most of the settings on your amplifier don't need to be changed once they're set for the evening. These include tone control settings, now generally known as equalization, and the volume levels of the caller's voice and the various instruments relative to each other. Once these are set, all you need to do in most cases is to turn the "master volume" control up or down as the evening progresses and you need more or less sound overall.

Balancing the levels of the calls and music is similar in principle to setting an overall sound level: make sure everyone can hear the caller and each instrument, but nothing is loud enough to be irritating. This may take several trips to the middle of the floor combined with signals from a trusted assistant, but the job becomes easier with experience. The caller's level should be set a little higher than the music; otherwise the calls may be heard but not understood. But the music is an essential part of New England style dancing, and the band needs to be showcased.

Equalization

Equalization, or "EQ," refers to adjusting the high- and low-pitched tones of each instrument or voice to compensate for faults in the hall's acoustics or in the way the mikes are picking up the sound. Guitars, for instance, tend to sound boomy when played close to a mike, and often benefit from having the "bass" or "low" control cut back. Fiddles occasionally sound too shrill and can even interfere with the intelligibility of a caller's voice, especially a female caller's. The solution is to cut back the upper end of the fiddle's sound with the "treble" or "high" control.

The caller's voice presents a unique problem: it must be heard over the music and every call must be crystal-clear, yet the voice must be pleasant to listen to. Clarity is most easily achieved by boosting the high tones and cutting the lows, whereas a pleasant voice is one that contains all the audio frequencies in a more or less even balance. The answer to this dilemma is to begin with the "flat" tone settings (neither cut nor boosted) and to alter them only as much as you need to for clarity's sake.

A female caller, unless her voice is unusually low, poses even more of a challenge to the sound operator. Most women's voices, when projected as they need to be for dance calling, fall in the same range of tones as the fiddle or other lead instrument. The competition from the music can make the calls hard to understand. The normal solution is to cut the bass on the caller's mike channel and to cut the treble on the fiddler's, but this can lead to complaints that the caller's voice is too harsh or the fiddle sounds muffled. Again, any changes to the tone controls should be made sparingly.

Some higher-priced sound systems include a third tone control on each channel to control the middle frequencies. A mid-range boost can make a voice "stand out" from the rest of the sound, but this effect can be overdone. Carried to extremes, it can make you sound as if you're calling over the telephone!

Feedback

Equalization has one more, very important purpose: to eliminate feedback. Feedback is the howl or squeal that is caused when amplified sound from a speaker is picked up by a mike and amplified again in an ever more vicious circle. Speaker placement is the biggest single factor in avoiding feedback, but there are times when that alone won't do the trick and the offending frequencies must be cut back.

Most modern sound systems have a "graphic equalizer" mounted on the amplifier case. This is a set of handles mounted side by side, each of which can be slid up or down a track to control a particular part of the audio spectrum from very low to very high notes. The position of the handles gives you an instant picture of how they're set, somewhat like a bar graph. Unlike the tone controls on the mike channels, the graphic equalizer affects the overall sound. When you hear a high-pitched squeal, for example, you can slide the handles downward one by one, starting at the upper end of the row, until the squeal goes away. Some newer systems have tiny lights that flash to tell you which frequency (pitch) or even which mike is causing feedback. A few models include circuitry that automatically cuts the offending frequency; I haven't heard any of these in action, but I've read reports that they're far from perfect. Fortunately, most of them can be switched off.

Remember that you are actually changing the tone of the overall sound when you use an equalizer, and move the controls only as much as you must to get out of trouble. If sliding a control down doesn't help, slide it back to the "flat" or normal position right away.

Older sound systems, and some smaller ones, lack this feature. If you have persistent problems with feedback, you can buy a separate graphic equalizer that plugs into your amp. It may cost nearly as much as a new amp, but it will probably have more sliders and therefore better pinpoint control. If you work regularly in a hall that has an annoying "ring" at one particular frequency, an equalizer may be a worthwhile investment.

Speaking of "ringing": If your amp has a "reverb" or "echo" feature, make sure it's switched off or turned all the way down. Leaving it on is one of the surest ways to cause feedback. In an outdoor setting, a very small amount of reverb can make the calls and music sound more natural, but if you use any, stay alert for signs of trouble.

The Sound Check

It's good practice for the band and caller to arrive at the hall at least half an hour before the dance is scheduled to begin. Whoever is in charge of the sound equipment should plan to have it set up by then. This will give everyone time to unwind from the daily routine, and will facilitate a proper sound check.

The primary purpose of a sound check is normally to make sure the volume and tone of the caller and each instrument are satisfactory. If a group is using a hall for the first time, the sound check will also include a check of speaker placement (see above).

The main power switch on the amplifier should not be turned on until all cables are connected and all other components are switched on; the master and monitor volume controls should be all the way down. If the operator is not familiar with the system, the level controls for each performer should also be low or off at first. Few things are more annoying than a sudden blast from the sound system. Tone controls and equalizers should be in their "flat" or neutral positions to start, unless you're in your regular hall and you know what your preferred settings are (bits of colored tape can be used to indicate these).

An easy way to check the band's sound is to have the pianist (or rhythm guitarist, if there is no piano) play a "vamp" (oompah, oompah) while you bring up the level on that mike. Add the bass, if there is one. Then ask the other musicians to play along with the rhythm, one at a time, while you adjust each one's level. Finally, have everyone play together, and check the overall sound to make sure it's not too loud but everyone can be heard.

This will require you to shuttle from the board to the middle of the dance floor and back, unless you have someone you trust to set levels while you signal from the stage (or vice versa). At a concert, the mixing board is usually in the center or back of the hall, with a full-time sound operator who can hear what the audience hears and make adjustments as needed. Dance bands don't normally have the luxury of a sound specialist, and as the board needs to be handy, it usually ends up on the stage, complicating the sound check.

A musician who plays two or more instruments should check them all before the dance. If one is especially loud – a banjo, for instance – the player may have to hold it farther from the mike than, say, a mandolin. (At a concert the sound operator would compensate for the difference by "riding" the level of that mike.) If your mixer has enough channels, you can use a separate one for each instrument.

Don't blow into a mike to see if it's working – if you can't wait for the band to play, just say "Check" or "Test." Blowing too hard can damage some mikes, and any blowing will introduce moisture, which can be harmful. (The caller's mike will get a certain amount of spray during the dance, but a foam windscreen can reduce the effect; it will also cut down on "pops" when the caller hits a consonant too hard.)

Care of Your Sound System

Many problems that might arise due to wear and tear on the sound system can be avoided with a little common sense. Mike and speaker cables are the most likely components to fail. Disconnect all cables as soon as the last waltz has ended and you've said goodnight; someone may be about to pull on one. Coil your cables in a way that doesn't bend them too sharply or put kinks in them. Inspect all cables frequently for wear, and repair or replace any damaged ones. And be sure to carry spare cables, spare fuses (if your system uses them), a heavy-duty extension cord or two, and a roll of duct tape!

A Final Word about Sound

It's possible to get so involved with the sound system that you forget why it's there. It's a tool, a means to an end. If it furthers people's enjoyment of the dance by making you and the music easier to hear, it's doing its job well. But if running it takes your time and energy away from *your* primary job, it's time to lighten up. You may have to settle for adequate sound, rather than perfect sound. That can be frustrating, especially if you have a sensitive ear for sound. But given time, you can probably put the sound system in perspective, as an adjunct to the smooth running of the dance, and not the whole show.

9
Calling for Special Groups

As long as square and contra dances have been done, the normal dance group (using "normal" in its strict sense of "most usual") has been made up of adult mixed couples. Anyone looking for chances to call, however, is likely to encounter many groups that depart from the norm in one way or another. This chapter discusses some of the more frequent exceptions to the rule.

Children

Squares and contras are often thought of as ideal for children. This is undoubtedly because these dances are a splendid form of exercise and encourage a group spirit. What people often overlook is that country dancing also has a strong element of flirtation, making it more suitable for older adolescents and adults than for school-age children.

This element can be more or less ignored if the children are below about twelve years old, and the dances done as recreation pure and simple. But it's better to make sure that at least some of the adults in your community know and enjoy the dances before you present them to the primary grades. Otherwise, the children may have fun dancing for a while, but by the time they reach junior high school they'll feel they've outgrown the dances and look on them as "kid stuff." A sad fate for a sophisticated adult pastime!

In designing a country dance program for the primary school, whether as part of the music or the physical education curriculum, it's essential to stress the enjoyable aspects of squares and contras and avoid treating them as a kind of drill. In the most successful programs, the students eagerly look forward to the dance sessions and regard taking part in them as a privilege. If grade-school children have to be coerced into square dancing, something is terribly wrong.

Summer camp is perhaps the ideal setting for a child's first exposure to square dancing. The atmosphere is informal, the country air invigorating, and the activities (one hopes) presented as exciting new worlds to explore rather than busy-work to keep the kids out of trouble. Again, dancing should be viewed as a privilege rather than a duty. At one camp, a single mid-season dance was planned for the nine- and ten-year-olds, preceded by a boys-only "bull session"

113

where etiquette was discussed and the boys were encouraged to voice their anxieties about the event. The dance was such a hit that another one was quickly scheduled for two weeks later.

Of course, in teaching squares and contras to children you should be thoroughly familiar with the material to be used, and ideally with country dance history and style as well. You must also wholeheartedly believe this kind of dancing is fun. Any uncertainty or negative attitude will transfer to the group in short order.

The actual dances best suited to school-age children are whole-set longways, in which one couple at a time is active, and squares, in which everyone has a home position to retreat to in case of confusion. True contras, with their constant shuttling back and forth and frequent change of roles, are best saved for groups aged about sixteen and older. But a group that has danced and enjoyed many of the simpler formations and figures for several years may be introduced to contras sooner.

A small number of children can be integrated into an adult dance without any special treatment from the caller. Such an event will be more successful if the children are physically big enough to "give weight" to the adults during swings and hand turns. In a group that includes a wide variety of ages, smaller children should be paired with adults or adolescents, not with one another.

The father-daughter dance is a well-loved tradition for many groups, especially Brownies and Girl Scouts. As half the dancers at such an event are children, and the other half are almost certain to be complete novices, the program should be similar to that of a school or camp affair: easy squares, circles, and whole-set longways.

Other events billed as "family dances" may attract a more random assortment of ages and sexes than a father-daughter dance will. Every attempt should be made to encourage "talls" and "smalls" to take one another for partners; it will make things easier for the younger children, and it may cause some adults to dance who would otherwise sit out. Some family groups have imposed minimum ages for dancing without an adult, or for joining in the dance at all.

In recent years a great deal of excellent material has been published for leaders who work with children and families. This material includes books with sheet music and printed directions, as well as audio recordings with and without calls. There are also booklets of essays and at least one video on teaching dance to children. Because this area is so crucial to the future of dancing, I have listed all the materials I know of in the Resources section.

Adolescents

For our purposes, the teen years can be divided into junior high or middle school (ages twelve to fourteen) and senior high school (ages fifteen to seventeen). Although individuals may vary, in general there is a sharp break between the two age groups in their attitude toward square and contra dancing.

Junior High

Junior-high students, whether or not they have been exposed to country dancing in grade school, typically want nothing to do with it. This is due to many factors: their unease with their changing bodies and resulting shyness with the opposite sex; their rebellion against anything endorsed by their parents' generation; and their desire to be like their peers in everything, including their taste in music. Unfortunately, the popular music industry has realized that this age group is vulnerable to the hard sell, and bombards them with music of questionable merit, day in and day out. Every caller who has worked with junior-high groups has heard the complaint: "Haven't you got any regular music?"

It takes a leader with far more than average charisma to teach and call square dances successfully with younger adolescents. My advice to most callers and curriculum developers is to give square dancing a rest for the junior-high years. In the few cases I've seen where students of this age accepted the dances, their parents or camp counselors had exposed them to folk music for years, treating it as something everyone could enjoy, not a style suitable only for children.

If you decide to try a junior-high dance program, I suggest starting slowly, with one or two events rather than a semester-long unit. One middle school hired a caller for a special afternoon party for the seventh grade, which had just completed a social studies unit on the westward expansion of the United States. The teachers were enthusiastic about the event and "talked it up" for days beforehand, which helped immeasurably.

Dance material for junior-high students should be more challenging than that for the lower grades, but contras should still be avoided unless the group is well above average in ability and in their enjoyment of the squares.

Senior High

Senior-high-school students, while still vulnerable to peer pressure and the mass media, are more likely to enjoy an occasional square dance party than junior highs. By older adolescence most people develop a desire to be like adults in many ways, and one of these ways seems to be the ability to deal with a variety of unfamiliar situations. Young people observe adults having fun at "theme parties" of different kinds and conclude that it's the height of sophistication to be able to laugh at oneself in circumstances that are anything but sophisticated.

Square dancing also gives this age group a chance to hone their new-found social skills. Senior highs are often nearly as shy as junior highs, but are more willing to work toward overcoming their shyness. Left to their own devices, with popular dance music but no adult direction, at least half of the typical group will drift to the sidelines. While many adolescents will groan at the initial mention of square dancing, not a few of them are secretly grateful for the structure of the dance, which relieves them of the obligation to "make the first move."

Senior-high students can appreciate squares and contras in many different settings: during school hours, as an extracurricular activity akin to a camera club or theater group, or at evening parties at school or summer camp. If the exposure to these dances is to be brief, the material should of course be kept simple. But in an ongoing dance program, senior highs can handle anything adults can. Contras have proved successful with many students who saw them as something new and different but would have rejected squares as childish due to unfortunate past experience.

In several cities, people as young as high-school age have started to attend regular contra and square dance series in large numbers; young people in some areas are organizing their own dance events. Long-time dancers are rejoicing at these signs of vitality; some of the youngsters' exuberance needs to be tempered with courtesy and consideration, but the young folks are increasingly dealing with such issues themselves. If you are a caller or organizer trying to attract young people to your dances, the best way is to be young yourself; the next best is to have an already existing positive relationship with your desired audience.

Older Adults

By "older adults" I mean those who would have trouble keeping up with a typical group of mixed ages. Individuals who have danced for years, of course, often look and act far younger than their age.

Many, perhaps most, older adults who are potential country dancers have slowed down only physically. Mentally they are as alert as they ever were, and they will appreciate dance material that is intellectually challenging – indeed, it may prolong their lives by giving them mental as well as physical exercise. The caller should avoid talking down to older adults; not only are they anyone's equal, they often have a fierce self-respect that it is dangerous – and certainly counterproductive – to cross.

Few modifications need be made to the dance material for older groups. The tempo can be slowed slightly, and dances that include long swings (more than eight beats of music) can be altered or avoided. Rest periods may need to be longer than average.

Some older adults may have trouble executing solo movements (such as the do-si-do and the hey) in the number of steps normally allotted. To avoid losing their balance, the dancers must make their steps shorter than the country-dance norm, and so will not be in the correct ending spot when the music for the movement is finished. Dances for such groups should be chosen with an eye to timing; a solo movement or other demanding portion should be followed by a looser-timed segment.

The short steps just referred to are considered normal in modern square dancing (which is discussed later in this chapter). Among the resources listed at the end of this book, those aimed at modern square dance callers may be helpful in choosing material for older adults.

Note that many groups of post-retirement age consist primarily or entirely of women. The additional challenges of calling to such groups are dealt with below under "Same-Sex Couples."

Special Education

People with various physical, mental, and emotional disabilities can learn and enjoy many folk dances, including squares and whole-set longways. I once saw an exhibition team of mentally retarded children and adolescents perform a simple contra, but the dancers appeared to be stretched to the limit of their frustration tolerance, and I would not recommend contras for most "special ed" groups.

Existing dance routines often require a good deal of modification before they are suitable for people with physical, mental, or emotional disabilities. This puts the subject beyond the scope of this book, except to say that it can be done. Anyone working in this field is strongly advised to contact the Eastern Cooperative Recreation School or the Lloyd Shaw Foundation for help (see the Resources section).

English as a Second Language

You may be asked to call for a group of people for whom English is not the primary language. It may be a church with a large immigrant population or a group of foreign exchange students at a high school. If you are fortunate, there will be an equally large number of native English speakers present, as is likely at the high school. Occasionally, however, you will find that those who don't speak or understand English well are in the majority.

There are several things you can do to increase your chances of success at such an event:

- Use demonstrations for most or all of the dances, before the walkthrough.

- Avoid ordinal numbers ("first couple," "second couple," etc.); instead, use cardinal numbers ("couple one," "couple two," etc.), which are among the first things people learn in a new language.

- Use primarily moves (like circle and star) in which people are physically connected and can help keep one another going in the right direction.

- When teaching, keep your language plain; avoid figures of speech, slang, and similar idioms that the group may not understand quickly.

- Make your calls short and to the point; avoid patter and extraneous language.

Same-Sex Couples and Gender-Free Dancing

There are three broad categories of group in which male-female couples are not the norm. They are dealt with together here because they present similar challenges to the caller.

Chapter 9: Calling for Special Groups

The first type of group consists primarily or entirely of members of one sex. Because men in our culture are not socialized to dance together, such a group will usually be female. Girl Scout events (other than father-daughter dances) are one example. Dance classes in retirement centers and other groups of older adults are predominantly female, partly because women tend to live longer than men and partly because the men are more reluctant to dance.

The second type of group consists of children or teenagers who are not comfortable taking partners of the opposite sex. Parents and teachers are increasingly reluctant to insist on boy-girl couples, and left to their own devices, many young people will adopt same-sex pairings.

The third type of group is organized to do what is commonly referred to as "gender-free" dancing (short for "gender-role-free"). Most such groups are founded and run by members of the LGBT (lesbian/gay/bisexual/transgender) community, though "straight" people are usually welcome to attend. In contrast to the single-sex group, at a gender-free dance one may see same-sex couples, mixed couples dancing the traditional roles, and mixed couples dancing the opposite roles. This can be disorienting to a caller who is used to getting visual cues from the sex of the dancers as to whether they are in the right place; with practice, a caller can learn to get along without these cues.

There are three ways to approach calling to a group in which same-sex couples are the norm:

1. Use only dances in which both sexes do exactly the same thing (or a mirror image of the same thing).
2. Refer to the dancers as "ladies" and "gents" (or similar names denoting sex roles).
3. Devise new names for the two roles.

The first approach, using only gender-free dances, is the easiest once you have determined your repertoire, but it requires some forethought in choosing material. Many relatively simple dances are gender-free; examples are *Sanita Hill Circle* (Chapter 14) and *Jefferson's Reel* (Chapter 16). No mention need be made of "ladies" or "gents" in teaching or calling such dances, as the only difference between the two members of a couple is that one will find his or her partner on the right, the other on the left. You don't even need to point this out; simply calling "Face your partner" will produce the desired effect.

In addition to true gender-free dances, there are numerous routines in which only one or two movements are "gendered." These moves can usually be replaced without too much difficulty. A sequence of "ladies do-si-do" followed by "gents do-si-do" can be changed to "do-si-do your neighbor" and "do-si-do your partner." A ladies chain over and back, if it is in the routine merely to fill out the music without regard to body flow (as is the case in many older dances), can be changed to right-hand and left-hand stars, or to some other 16-beat movement.

The second approach, using "ladies" and "gents" or similar words, has been widely used for many years, with varying degrees of success. In the past, all-female groups have generally accepted this terminology, while predominantly male groups have not. There has apparently been a greater social stigma attached to boys acting as girls (except for blatantly comic effect) than to girls acting as boys. In any case, there is more resistance to the use of such terms than there used to be.

This leads to the third approach, inventing new names for the sex roles. In the past twenty years or so, this has become the prevailing method of dealing with the issue. Many different names have been tried: A few leaders have used "ones" and "twos" (in squares and contras, of course, those terms have other meanings). More common are names like "reds" and "blues," "lions" and "tigers," and "moons" and "stars." With such neutral names, it can be a challenge to remember which name refers to which role. To the dancers, it doesn't matter, but the caller must keep track of who is on the right side in each couple, and of who must do what in an adapted traditional routine. My wife Beth often uses "birdie" for "lady" and "crow" for "gent," from the traditional square dance *Birdie in the Cage*. This has two advantages: it's easy for the caller to remember which role is which, and the new names have the same number of syllables as the old ones and can be readily substituted when calling in rhythm.

In addition to new names, dancers can be distinguished by articles of clothing such as armbands, vests, or loose cloth yokes. Typically only one member of each couple is so equipped; in a single-sex group it will be the one playing the "opposite" role, and in a gender-free group it is likely to be the one playing the "lead" or "gent." Chris Ricciotti, a pioneer in the LGBT contra dance field, refers to the roles as "armbands" and "bare-arms," or "bands" and "bares" for short – although his dancers now wear short clip-on ribbons rather than full armbands. Hats are less practical than armbands or yokes; they come off easily, they can muss the hair, and they are sometimes suspected as a carrier of head lice.

Modifying Dances

As noted above, a simple dance routine that includes one or two sex-role-defined moves can often be modified to eliminate them. This is often done when working with children and families. Some callers, for either ideological or practical reasons, may want to go further toward eliminating movements in which the sexes do quite different things. Usually this involves movements in which the gent leads the lady, such as the swing and the movements involving promenade position (promenade, ladies chain, right and left through). There are ways to modify such moves to make the two parts similar and enable partners to dance together without leading or following.

- The swing can be modified to a "unisex" handhold (see Chapter 12), or a simple two-hand swing can be used.
- The promenade position can be changed to a "front skaters" hold, with right hands joined in front of the right-hand person, left hands joined in front of the left-hand person. (This hold is customary in modern square dancing and in traditional dancing as practiced in some localities.)
- The right and left through can be danced as it is in some parts of northern New England: after the pass through, adjacent dancers put their near arms behind each other's back for the couple turn (or simply keep their near shoulders adjacent as if they were glued together).
- The ladies chain is the most difficult to modify. A few people have objected to it altogether, resenting the implication that the woman has to be handed in and out of any movement she makes on her own. Some dances can be modified for such a group by replacing the ladies chain with another movement; other dances will have to be left out of the repertoire. But most groups will accept the ladies chain as part of the folklore of country dancing – particularly if a "gents chain" is used occasionally.

Modern Square Dancers

From the viewpoint of the traditional caller, modern square dancers (see "History" in Chapter 2) constitute a "special" group; that is, a group of people who must be dealt with slightly differently than the average adult. Callers unfamiliar with the modern square dance network are likely to be surprised by many of the responses of its devotees.

Traditional callers may encounter modern square dancers in several settings. Often a small number will show up at a traditional dance, either by mistake or for a change of pace. Occasionally a traditional caller will be asked to lead a workshop at a modern festival or convention. And any caller who accepts private bookings will occasionally find that a high percentage of the crowd are modern square dancers who have come to help the beginners.

When you as a traditional caller deal with modern square dancers, the main source of confusion is this: Most people in your experience either do or don't know how to dance. In either case, you know how they're likely to respond to various calls and instructions. Modern square dancers have a different body of knowledge. They know some of what an experienced traditional dancer knows, but not all. In addition, they have learned many things that a traditional dancer hasn't. And they will respond to the calls and music in quite different ways than a traditional dancer would.

A New England style dancer will listen to the call, which is given at the end of a 16-beat musical phrase, and step out boldly on the first beat of the following phrase. An experienced dancer will do this even if the caller is unseasoned or careless and gives the call at the wrong place in the music. But a modern square dancer has been taught to follow the caller, not the music.

Most modern square dancers will rush through a ladies chain, for example, in five or six steps. If they haven't heard the next call by the time they finish, they will come to a dead stop. You'll probably need to encourage them to "use up the music," to time their movements so that they begin and end with the changes in the music. There's no need to burden the dancers with a long explanation of phrasing; a simple reminder that this isn't a race will usually suffice. ("There are no prizes for finishing first – one of the nicest things about country dancing is that everybody wins!")

The swing is also problematic. Modern callers hardly ever use it except as a means of changing partners in singing squares, and allow very little time for it even then. As a result, modern square dancers have evolved a move that consists of a swing about once around, followed by a twirl for the lady under the gent's arm as the couple begins to move in promenade direction. A mere reminder to use up the music probably won't be enough in this case. It may help to say "Swing twice around."

Another hidden danger in the swing is that many present-day New England style dances use it as a method of progression. Often a couple will be told to end a swing facing in a given direction, *with the lady on the right.* Modern square dancers have trouble doing this, even though the practice was first developed on a large scale in their style. Frequently they will end an initial neighbor swing in a contra by putting their neighbors back where they found them, even though the caller has clearly instructed them otherwise. A little demonstration may be the best way to deal with this problem.

Balances were used in modern square dancing at one time, but have not been taught for several years. Some dancers know what the term means, but few can do it at the right place in the music. If most or all of those present are modern square dancers, any "balance and swing" combinations should be changed to "do-si-do and swing," both to avoid the balance and to shorten the swing to eight beats (about twice around).

The walking step itself is another point of difference. Whereas traditional dancers take long steps, with the feet leaving the floor, modern square dancers are taught to take short shuffling steps. The body is held more erect than in traditional styles, which usually favor a slight forward lean. The short steps make it hard for modern dancers to get through a hey or a "turn contra corners" in the music normally allotted. Several modern callers have written contra dances with timing adapted to the needs of their dancers.

A final point to be aware of is that modern square dancers are conditioned to respond only to code words, not to plain English. That is, if you call "ladies chain" they will do it immediately, but if you call "two ladies turn by the right hand round" they will need an extra beat or two of music to figure out what the words mean. (This conditioning is done so that the dancers can enjoy an entire evening without any walkthroughs.) If you are dealing with a high percentage of modern dancers, be aware that plain English will confuse them more than calls with accepted names. If you want them to do something that can't be described using standard calls, try to use the same wording each time you come to it.

One contra dance formation was actually developed for modern square dancers: the one in which each couple stands together on one side of the set, facing another couple in the other line. This setup is usually known as "Becket formation," after *Becket Reel,* the first dance to use it. (The dance was written by Herbie Gaudreau, the pioneer of all-active contra choreography, and named for the YMCA camp in Becket, Massachusetts, the site of many dance gatherings in the 1950s. The camp has been rediscovered by present-day contra dancers and is once again being used for dance events.) The advantage of Becket formation for modern square dancers is that many enjoyable dances can be called in it using only movements and concepts that the dancers have already learned in conjunction with squares. Many Becket dances are double progression with no neutral couples, making them even easier for people unfamiliar with traditional contra dancing.

10
Reaching Your Community

Throughout the first half of this book we've hinted at various ways of introducing contra dancing to a community. Now it's time to consider them all together and look at them in greater detail.

The Schools

School children are not the most appropriate group to begin with if you're trying to get your community interested in contra dancing. This is especially true if your long-range plans call for a solidly established adult group. Once an activity is perceived locally as "kid stuff," few adults will be drawn to it. Dancing in the schools can be made to work, though, particularly if other avenues of dance promotion are pursued at the same time, or if there are no plans to start an adult series in town.

In general, the older the children, the easier it will be to get them dancing, with the notable exception of the junior-high-school ages (see Chapter 9). Circle and square dances, and whole-set longways, can be introduced at almost any time. True contras are best saved for senior-high students and adults.

Dancing in a school setting can take place in several situations:

- It can be a semester- or year-long unit. This is usually done as part of the physical education curriculum, though it could also be handled by the music department. Care should be taken to avoid the appearance of a drill or exercise class. The social aspects of the dance should not be forgotten, and casual clothes rather than uniforms or leotards should be worn. It is crucial to involve the boys as well as the girls.
- It can be an extracurricular activity, along the lines of a camera club or theater group. As this is likely to be promoted on a voluntary basis, it works best if the students already see country dancing as an attractive form of recreation. This is most likely in areas where many adults enjoy it regularly.
- It can be saved for special occasions, either to celebrate the successful completion of an academic unit or as a feature of one or more school dances during the year. This may meet some student

resistance at first, but often develops into a tradition that students remember favorably and look forward to each year.

A leader using traditional dance with children or teenagers should have all the qualities a caller normally needs, plus an extra measure of patience and good humor. Often young people will test a leader with good-natured heckling and horseplay. In most cases, simply waiting out the storm and quietly but firmly holding to the planned program will be enough to move things along. Occasionally the resistance will be stronger and not so friendly, especially from junior-high groups. If the usual firmness doesn't work, it may be productive to sit down with the students and ask what the problem is. They may have been forced to dance in grade school by a leader who took a precious or patronizing tone. If you can convince them that dancing doesn't have to be like that, they may give it another chance.

Adult Education

If there is no country dancing in a community, one place to start is in the adult education program. Typically, this is organized into courses that meet weekly for one semester, or about twelve weeks; some courses last as few as six weeks, while some continue for two semesters, depending on the depth of material covered. Six to twelve weeks is probably the best length of time for a country dance class.

The advantage of a class, as opposed to an open community dance, is that the same people attend every week. This gives the leader a chance to build each week on what has gone before, and lets the students develop confidence as they meet in a relatively private setting.

The greatest challenge of teaching a class is that the students don't have any experienced dancers to use as role models. At a community series, new people are swept into the flow of the dance and usually develop a sense of the local style (posture, length of stride, amount of weight given) fairly quickly. A group made up entirely of beginners has no one but the leader to look to for guidance.

This means you must be careful to cover the fine points of style that you might not mention at an open dance. When you call for a circle, for instance, you'll need to tell the students to bend their elbows and put some spring into their forearms. If you ask for a star, you'll not only have to specify the kind of star (wrist-hold or hands across); you'll also be obliged to tell or show people exactly how to form it.

Chapter 10: Reaching Your Community

This kind of careful teaching will dictate a relatively slow pace, compared to that of a community dance evening. Whereas at an open dance you might use fifteen or twenty basic movements in one night, at a class you'd probably introduce no more than two or three basics each time you met. The first night is normally an exception; half a dozen movements or more are commonly presented, to enable you to call complete dances. But many of those movements, like the circle and the forward and back, require relatively little explanation.

It's not necessary to use a wide variety of dances during a class. In fact, most groups will build more confidence if they're given the chance to repeat some routines from week to week. If you use *Chorus Jig* to teach "turn contra corners," for example, you should repeat it at least once and preferably twice or more during the course. It follows that anything you plan to repeat several times should be introduced early enough to let you do so.

Beginning at the third or fourth week, your students should be encouraged to attend local community dances, if any exist. Such dances normally make some kind of provision for absolute beginners, and your group will have a head start. It doesn't matter if some of the movements used are unfamiliar to them; by attending your class, they will have developed the ability to move well, to listen well, and to recover when necessary. Those qualities are more essential to a casual dancer than knowing all the movements; anything unusual is likely to be explained during the walkthrough anyway.

Similarly, it shouldn't be a cause for concern if you haven't covered everything in your lesson plan by the time the course ends. Teaching beginners how to move well is more important than exposing them to all the movements they're ever likely to see. The more classes you teach, the better idea you'll develop of what people can handle in a given time – though some groups are bound to surprise you.

The One-Night Stand

One type of country dance gathering stands apart from the others in many of its demands on the leader. This is the so-called one-night stand, an evening designed for people who have never done this kind of dancing before and may never try it again. At most, such a dance will become an annual event. (Some people object to the name "one-night stand," which originated in show business, because of the sexual connotations it later acquired. But dance callers have long used the term among themselves with no negative implications, and so far no substitute has gained widespread acceptance.)

A one-night stand differs from a class session or a community series in many ways: it requires different material, different pacing, and even a different attitude toward the whole evening. This is because the people who attend it are there for a slightly different reason: they came to have fun. Not to have fun while learning a folk art or a worthwhile recreation; to have fun, period. Comments on the fine points of the game are likely to be lost on them. They don't want a teacher; they want an entertainer.

One-nighters, by definition, are sponsored by an affinity group of some kind: a school, a church, a fraternal order. The one thing these groups have in common is that they're not organized around country dancing. Your big night is just another monthly meeting to them. Last month it was a Las Vegas night; next month it may be a scavenger hunt. Your job is to sell them on dancing – not as a lifelong hobby, just for that night.

Material needs to be of the utmost simplicity. Any dance you use needs to be teachable in less time than it takes to perform. This is a good rule of thumb in most situations, but it's crucial at a one-nighter. Every dance has to be a showpiece – just as if you were a pop singer – and you only get one chance to put it over. (Around the middle of the evening, after you've won the group's confidence, you can bend the rule a little and spend a few extra minutes on one tricky dance. But only one.)

Contras are usually problematic at one-night stands. Remember that it takes a while for people to understand the contra formation and progression. Even though hundreds of different contras can be done from the same setup, this fact will be lost on the crowd, who aren't planning to dance again till next year – if ever! At many one-nighters, the liquor flows like water, making contras even less advisable. It's safer to stick with whole-set longways, with one couple active at a time, plus any circles and squares you know.

In fact, you may need to change your attitude toward all-moving dances when you call a one-nighter. Country dance enthusiasts usually prefer material that keeps everyone moving most of the time; they often look down their noses at some of the older dances that have inactive couples. One-night-stand crowds will not only tolerate those older dances, they'll actually appreciate them. Casual dancers tire faster than seasoned ones, and they'll welcome the chance to stand still part of the time.

By the same token, people at a one-nighter are likely to take their time forming sets and even finding partners. If your background is in the contra dance community, you may think this reflects on you. Be patient: the people are there to socialize, and dancing is only a means to that end. In addition, they don't have the understanding of the size, shape, and placement of sets that comes automatically to you. Their slow pace doesn't mean you've failed in your job; keep encouraging them without seeming to nag, and they'll get set when they're ready.

Phrasing is another important element of contra dancing that is less crucial at a one-nighter. True contras, where each couple performs the same routine many times in succession, need exact phrasing to keep the set together, particularly if the caller drops out after a few rounds. But the kinds of dances you're likely to use at one-nighters are less dependent on phrasing. In a whole-set longways, with only one couple active at a time, people experience the dance differently in each round. And you'll probably be calling each dance all the way through, so the dancers won't be relying on the musical phrase to find their place. If your dancers take longer than the prescribed number of beats to do all or part of such a dance, my advice is to let them – and not to call their attention to it.

The pacing of the evening is critical. While you're on the mike, you need to convey excitement. But people are going to need longer and more frequent breaks from dancing than a crowd at a typical series. This is partly because they're not used to this particular form of exercise, and partly because they would rather hop and skip than do everything "just so." Let them burn themselves out if they want – it's their party. Have some music (live or recorded) ready to play during the breaks, to keep the party atmosphere going between sets. If you're working with a live band, you may want to bring some recorded background music so the band can rest occasionally.

Organizations sponsoring once-a-year square dances often feel a need to decorate with a "Wild West" or "farmer" motif. The urge to decorate is understandable; the dance is a special event for the group. It's too bad, though, that country dancing is seen by so many as a quaint or corny activity rather than a normal pastime for normal people. The decorations themselves are generally harmless, with one exception: Never call a dance with hay on the floor. People will almost certainly slip on it. Insist that any hay or straw be swept well away from the dancing area before you begin.

If you approach it properly, a one-night stand can be an enjoyable time in itself (and will probably be more lucrative than other calling jobs). And once in a while, a group will be more serious than usual about dancing and will want to turn a one-nighter into a series!

The Community Dance

The ongoing community dance series is the backbone of the activity. Held weekly or once or twice a month, it provides a meeting place for people of many different ages, backgrounds, and degrees of experience. At its best, the community dance combines the fun of a one-night stand with the educational aspects of a class.

To start a series, it's essential to have a core of people. This can be an existing affinity group, such as a church or synagogue or a singles' or couples' club within one, an outing club, a food co-op, or the parents and teachers of a small school. Or it can be a group of friends who have shown an interest in country dancing. In either case, the core must commit themselves to support the series, both by working behind the scenes and by showing up at the dances.

The series can be sponsored by the caller, the band, the hosting school or church, or a committee of dancers. The less formal organization you can get away with, the better. Most people have enough demands on their time without having to attend lengthy meetings. But it is important to make sure each of the necessary jobs is assigned to someone.

The jobs that need to be done include:

- Hiring a hall and maintaining good relations with the hall management
- Lining up one or more bands and callers (if they're not the ones running the series)
- Scheduling the dances
- Creating publicity
- Arranging for refreshments
- Setting up and cleaning up before and after dances
- Collecting money at the door or during intermission
- Decorating the hall (optional)
- Teaching beginners before the dance (optional)

Following is a look at these jobs from a caller's point of view, in case you decide to run your own series or find yourself to be the most knowledgeable member of a dance committee.

Hall Rental

Finding a hall suitable for dancing is the first job on the time line; if you don't have a hall, you can't have a dance. The task may seem overwhelming at first: it's no small feat to call every organization in town that might offer dancing space. But it needs to be done.

The ideal country dance hall has a smooth wood floor, plenty of ventilation, a stage or platform for the band, enough room for several sets to dance while people sit around the edges, and no pillars or posts to bump into. A kitchen or lounge is an added attraction; both are even better. The hall should have adequate parking space, either on the street or in a lot, and be close to public transportation if any exists in the area. Obviously, no hall is likely to have all these assets, but it's a challenge to see how close you can come to the ideal.

Possibilities for dancing space include:

- Houses of worship
- Public schools
- Private schools
- Colleges
- YMCAs, YWCAs, YMHAs, and similar groups
- Fraternal organizations – Masons, Elks, Pythians, etc.
- Nationality groups – Irish-American, Sons of Norway, etc.
- Veterans' organizations – Legion, VFW, etc.
- Trade unions
- Granges
- Town or city recreation centers
- Restaurants, lounges, function halls

Many hall managements will be more welcoming than you might expect. Some will specify clean shoes (or no street shoes) on the dance floor – a small price to pay for a high-quality surface. You may be required to hire a police officer or a custodian, but this is often negotiable, especially after you've rented the hall a few times with no problems.

One person should be given the responsibility of dealing with the hall management, to avoid misunderstandings. The dates, time of day, rental fee, any paid personnel required, and cancellation policy on both sides need to be firm before you put out any publicity.

Check the condition of the dance floor and all the facilities you'll be using. Note any problems, and make sure everyone agrees who is responsible for correcting them. Find out whether the dance must end promptly at the stated time (perhaps due to complaints about noise, or for religious reasons), or whether the ending time is flexible.

Hiring the Band

Finding a band may be a challenge, especially if there's little or no dancing in your area. It may appear hard to track down musicians who are competent and interested. If you have no word-of-mouth leads, check at the nearest music store that caters to the folk trade (do a Web search and check the wording of various stores' advertisements). They may be able to refer you to bands or musicians who play traditional music; often the store has a bulletin board where you can look for offers or make your own wants known.

The talent of the musicians you find will range from outstanding to minimal. If everyone you find seems to be at one extreme or the other, don't panic. Expert instrumentalists may welcome a steady local job. If you hold your series on a weeknight, you may be able to hire top-drawer talent for less money than they'd ask for a Saturday concert. Beginning or casual musicians, on the other hand, may be happy to play for the experience and exposure (and a little gas money). Even total beginners may be an asset to your dance: they can play for one or two numbers in an evening while you use recorded music for the rest, and work their way up to a full evening.

Fiddle and piano are the traditional backbone of a New England dance band. Other instruments can be substituted if necessary, as long as you keep certain requirements in mind. Country dance melodies are often technically difficult, and must always be played for long periods of time without a rest; it usually takes two wind players to do the work of one fiddler. (A single wind player, or a beginner on any melody instrument, can choose tunes with longer and fewer notes.) An accordion or a guitar substituting for a piano must be played with plenty of "punch" and be loud enough for the crowd and the hall.

If your budget allows for more than two musicians, you may have to decide between an extra lead player and an extra rhythm player. There are advantages to both. An extra lead can take the burden of carrying the whole evening off the first lead player. A bigger rhythm section can provide more of an upbeat, avoiding the feeling of tent-peg hammering that a lone pianist, especially a new one, may produce. My advice on choosing extra players is to go with whoever is available and good.

Some dance series encourage sit-in musicians – people who play along with the hired band but are unamplified and unpaid. Many fine musicians got their start in the dance world this way. A few series feature a large band, in which learning new tunes and learning to play together are important parts of the experience. Such a setup requires one or two strong players (and possibly a conductor) to set and hold the tempo.

It's important that everyone be happy with the financial arrangements. Whether the band works for a flat fee, a guarantee plus a percentage, or a share of the receipts, no one should feel exploited. Many musicians don't mind low pay if they believe they're being treated fairly and no one else is making a fortune either.

Make sure you agree on the details. The band needs to know location, dates, starting and ending times, and pay scale (amount of money or formula for determining shares). Directions to the hall will be appreciated. And do establish who is expected to bring the sound system. It's no joke when two systems arrive at the dance, each owner expecting a rental fee. The only thing worse is no system at all!

Scheduling the Series

Scheduling is closely related to hiring because the schedule must be worked out in consultation with the band.

In scheduling a dance series, the most important thing is to avoid conflicts with other events. These include:

- Dances of the same kind (contra, traditional square)
- Other kinds of dances (swing, international folk, English, Scottish, modern square)
- Folk concerts and storytelling events
- Major holidays
- Major sporting events (local or national)
- Other things your group enjoys (or is likely to enjoy)

Conflicts should be noted on a single calendar, to avoid problems due to lack of communication. If one special event, say a regional folk festival, poses a conflict, you may want to cancel or reschedule the one conflicting dance rather than move your entire series to another night of the week.

Publicity

Creating publicity for a dance series can be fun, but waiting for it to work can be frustrating. There's no quick way to build interest in country dancing. Over the long haul, you'll get more people from word of mouth than any other way – one person telling or, better yet, bringing another. But some effort on your part will be needed even then, and it's even more crucial at first.

Historically, the two most effective methods of publicizing dances have been flyers and press releases. Paid advertising has been tried from time to time, but the results seldom justify the expense. Look on the bright side: the best methods are also the cheapest!

Flyers can be simple or elaborate, depending on the talent you have available. They are easy and inexpensive to produce. Make sure all the information anyone will need is not only on the flyer but easy to read: dates, time, names of band and caller, admission fee, location, and the phone number of someone who's willing to answer questions. Emphasize the fact that no partners or experience are necessary. Provide a map and/or directions if you think a street address won't be enough. And be sure to include the year – some people save flyers a long time, and yours may confuse them a year or two from now.

At first you'll probably want to post flyers in store windows, on community bulletin boards, and anywhere else that won't get you into trouble with property owners or the local government. And of course you'll have stacks of them handy at your own events and at any other dances or concerts in the area. Be sure to let other groups know that their flyers are welcome at your dance too.

A mailing list can be effective if it's made up of people you know are interested. Experts on direct-mail selling will tell you that you'll be lucky to get a one percent response from a mailing, but that's if you use a list that someone else has compiled. If you ask for names at the dance, you'll have a list of people who have proved their interest by attending.

E-mail is now the norm for group mailing lists: it's free or very cheap compared to postal mail, and people are used to dealing with it. It's important, though, to make sure everyone "opts in" and to immediately honor anyone's wish to "opt out." There are strict laws regarding the sending of unwanted e-mail.

Press releases and their radio equivalent, public service announcements (PSAs), are a second tool in your publicity kit. They should be kept brief and simple; many papers will send a style guide on request. PSAs, in addition, need to fit a specific amount of time, usually thirty seconds. If you're given a time limit, read your PSA aloud until you're sure it fits. As with flyers, be sure to include the essentials: who, what, where, and when. Admission fees are better left out, as they smack of advertising.

If there are any local or regional dance newsletters in your area, be sure to put them on your mailing list. Whether you send them flyers, press releases, or both, they will help spread the word of your series to people who are already interested in dancing.

Social networking websites such as Facebook are a recent development that many groups have used successfully. The mechanics of such sites are beyond the scope of this book, not least because they change frequently. It may help to put one of your younger members in charge of managing your Web-based publicity.

In the end, word of mouth will make or break your dance. The best publicity of all is a dance where people feel welcome, enjoy the music and calling, and get a sense of accomplishment from dancing.

Refreshments

The most important refreshment at a dance – indeed, it's an absolute necessity – is water. More elaborate fixings are not strictly necessary, but are traditional in some areas and can make a dance feel more like a party. Drink is more important than food; cider, iced tea, lemonade, and punch are all popular. Some groups buy a few boxes of cookies for each meeting; others encourage baking on a potluck basis, or ask people to take turns bringing something. A potluck supper before the dance takes a little work and extra publicity, but it can further the party mood and give people a chance to talk more than they normally do at a dance.

A word about alcohol: In some places drinking and country dancing have been mixed for many years, but this normally happens only where the dance serves a purely social function and a very limited number of figures are done. If, like most present-day dance groups, you want the variety of figures to be one of the attractions of the series, you are advised to discourage the use of alcohol. If the hall owners insist on having their bar open, you can suggest that they lay in an extra stock of juices, mineral waters, and other soft drinks. Dancers won't mind paying slightly inflated prices for these items if they know the bar is enabling the group to use the hall at a lower cost.

Setup and Cleanup

Preparing the hall for the dance, and leaving it clean for the next user, must be the most thankless job in the country dance world. But it needs to be done, just like any other job. Some people will do it out of sheer community spirit; if you can't find anyone like that, try offering free admission.

Before the dance, chairs and tables may need to be moved. Electricity and plumbing should be checked. Signs should be put up if things like toilets or drinking water are hard to find. Spare fuses, light bulbs, toilet paper, and towels should be on hand, as well as drinking cups if there is no fountain.

The floor surface should be clean. Sweeping before and after the dance is the single most important way to prevent damage to the floor. Special sweeping compounds are not normally needed; a push broom or damp mop should be enough. Occasionally a floor will be too sticky, or too slippery, for comfortable dancing. Any measures to correct this should be taken in consultation with the hall owners.

During the dance, the crew can relax for the most part, but one person should watch for spills of food and drink. During intermission, trash cans should be handy.

After the dance, the floor should be swept again, and furniture replaced where you found it if the management so requests.

Collecting Money

Another job that usually proves necessary is that of collecting admission fees at the door. This is not as thankless a duty as setup and cleanup, as the door-sitter will enjoy greeting people and chatting with them. But it is a responsible job, and needs a responsible person.

Some smaller dances get by with the honor system, leaving a basket at the door or passing it around during the break. If you decide to do this, check the receipts against the size of the crowd once in a while. If more than three or four people appear to be "forgetting" to pay, you'll be better off financially if you use door-sitters and reward them with passes to future dances.

Decorations

Some jobs are entirely optional; one such job is decorating the hall. Whether or not you do it depends on several factors:

- Whether anyone in your group has the imagination and commitment to do the decorating
- How attractive and festive the hall is to begin with
- How special this particular event is

Many groups dispense with decorations entirely, particularly if they meet every week or two in pleasant surroundings. But if your hall is stark and uninviting, a minimum of effort can work wonders. Crepe paper streamers ten or twelve feet off the floor will make a room with a high ceiling appear less cavernous (though it probably won't improve the sound). Cardboard cutouts with a seasonal or regional flavor can be mounted on the walls. Fresh flowers on stage are a nice touch, as are pumpkins and ornamental corn in the fall. But as mentioned above under "The One-Night Stand," hay should be kept off the dance floor.

Teaching Beginners

Holding a separate teaching session for new dancers is another optional part of running a dance series. It's optional, not because beginners don't need instruction, but because people disagree on the best way to provide that instruction. The pros and cons of various teaching formats are discussed in Chapter 5.

If you elect to hold a session before the dance, two things are critical: publicity and the selection of a teacher.

Publicity. For a teaching session to do its job, it's essential that people hearing about your dance for the first time are aware that the session exists. To that end, every bit of publicity for the dance – flyers, posters, articles, press releases, calendar listings, radio announcements – needs to include a line about teaching. It can be as simple as "Beginners welcome – arrive at 7:30 for special instruction."

Choosing a Teacher. Whoever is to lead the teaching session must be thoroughly familiar with the basic movements used in the area and their most common combinations and transitions. The teacher must be a good dancer, aware of the others in the set and quick to recover from the inevitable lapse of mind. And he or she must be able to present in a nutshell the basic movements and something of the philosophy of country dancing.

This is a tall order, and not many dancers will feel equal to the task. (Some who do may not actually be equal to it!) An obvious candidate is you, the caller. Many callers would rather do the preliminary teaching themselves, in order to maintain continuity and control over what gets taught. But you may welcome a chance to relax before the dance and let someone else teach. And you're likely to be preoccupied with other things at that point, such as comparing notes with the band and checking the sound.

If you decide not to teach, work closely with whoever leads the session to make sure you're both using the same definitions of terms, and that things you feel are important are being taught. You may or may not want to have the turn-under ending to a ladies chain taught in addition to (or instead of) the courtesy turn, but you certainly don't want to have the instructor twirl his partner and announce "This is called a courtesy turn" (I have actually seen this done).

In general, it's better if you don't try to teach all the basic movements in half an hour. Some things, like "turn contra corners" or "hey for four," must be taught and walked through carefully during a dance anyway. Accordingly, you may as well omit them if you're pressed for time. (You might do one each time you meet, especially one that's the key figure of your hardest dance that night.)

But some things need to be taught every time. The balance and the swing require more footwork than other movements, and they're both tricky for people who are just learning how to hold their body weight. This makes them physically hard to master, and suggests that they be given plenty of practice. The right and left through should also be included, but for a different reason: it may be the most difficult call to learn intellectually. It's a compound movement: you go straight and then you turn, and you turn in a way you couldn't possibly have guessed. And it appears in a good many dances.

A facet of country dancing that often gets short shrift is the basic step, or dance-walk. Many people have learned all the basic movements and can get from one place to another in the set, but know nothing of how to hold their bodies and what kind of steps to take for the most enjoyable dancing. It's worth taking a few moments at the outset to practice circling to the left and right, emphasizing the difference between dancing and ordinary walking. The concepts of strong connection and giving weight are vital to New England style dancing; work on them can begin with a circle as well.

If possible, the teaching session should start on time. People who arrive late can be brought into the group if this is comfortable for you; otherwise they can be encouraged to come early next time.

One effective way to end a teaching session is to present the first dance on the program, walking it through extra carefully. When the newcomers get into sets with the rest of the group, they'll have the confidence of knowing what's coming. Make sure that they do disperse and dance with the others, rather than clinging to each other; explain that they'll actually learn faster if they mingle with the old hands. (Of course, you'll also encourage the old hands to mingle with the new folks!)

The Family Dance

In some ways, the best of all possible country dance worlds is the family dance. Many traditional dances over the years have been family affairs, with three or even four generations dancing together. Even where the crowd comprised mostly adults, small children would often form their own set in a corner, safely out from underfoot.

Chapter 10: Reaching Your Community

If you're fortunate enough to be involved with a group of mixed ages that wants to dance together, a family dance can be rewarding in the extreme. But you'll need a good deal of patience, as people will learn at different rates and be interested in different aspects of the dance.

If the bulk of your group is made up of adults and adolescents, you can probably plan much the same kind of program that you would for any dance. You may want to start with easy dances and encourage younger children to participate. These first few dances should be circles, easy squares, or whole-set longways – not true contras, which can be disorienting and frustrating for small children. For the rest of the evening, the younger dancers can form their own set, or dance with adults who don't mind the disparity in size and weight.

A larger percentage of children dictates a larger period devoted to their needs. One proven format divides the evening into an hour of dances exclusively for the young folks and a two-hour session for adults and teenagers. A variety of folk and square dances are presented during the first hour, including several that don't require partners. The children end with a "grand march" – a snake dance that winds its way in and out of the hall or even the building – before being taken home to bed.

This presupposes that you, the caller, are comfortable with many different types of material. Folk dances from around the world are often more popular than squares and contras with young children, largely because less time is spent forming sets and remembering one's place. Middle-school and junior-high students who are reluctant to choose a partner of the opposite sex are often willing to do big circle dances that need no partners. A few games interspersed with the dances are often well received. (See the Resources section for books on these subjects.)

Another way to run a dance for all ages is to bill the entire event as a "family dance." In this case, it should be made clear that all the material will be within the capabilities of young children, and that parents are expected to dance, not just watch. A minimum age is sometimes specified, below which children will probably not appreciate the dances. A family series run along these lines in the Boston area became so popular that it had to be changed from once to twice a month.

If you have the privilege of calling at or helping run a family dance, you're in an enviable position. Not only will you have the time of your life; you'll be able to watch the next generation of country dancers in the making!

PART TWO
Basic Moves and Dance Routines

11
Before the Basics

Country dancing is more than the sum of its parts. It's possible to learn all the basic movements, even to master the transitions between them, and still not be a good dancer. The two areas in which the majority of problems occur are etiquette and posture. It may sound picky and old-fashioned to dwell on such topics, but attention to them can make the difference between an enjoyable evening and a wrestling match.

Most of this chapter is written as if it were addressed to a group of dancers. As a teacher and caller, you won't be able to make all these points at once; trying to do so would be counterproductive. But you can keep them in mind and mention them one by one as the need arises. Some callers and dance organizers prepare a handout, primarily for newcomers, explaining country dance customs and touching on the matters outlined here.

Etiquette and Dress

Someone has defined country dancing as "an exercise in controlled abandon." The phrase is an apt description of the age-old tension between the dancing masters and the common people. Both the control and the abandon are important; to overstress one at the expense of the other will spoil the fun. The ordinary dancer, if unchecked, will move in the direction of abandon. You, the teacher and caller, have the job of introducing the element of control in a way that won't alienate the dancers.

While the specifics of etiquette vary from one time or place to another, the guiding principle remains the same: to give other people the same consideration you would like from them. This, of course, is nothing but the Golden Rule, espoused by all the great religious leaders and given at least lip service by most of humankind. That we so often ignore it when our own comfort or convenience is involved takes nothing away from its eternal wisdom.

In country dancing, the Golden Rule dictates courtesy in at least four directions:

- Toward your partner
- Toward the other dancers in the set
- Toward the other sets on the floor
- Toward the caller and band

Courtesy to your partner means using common politeness when asking for a dance and expressing thanks afterward. It also means not abandoning one partner suddenly in the rush to find the next. "Booking ahead," or securing partners for the next several dances, leads to hard feelings and frustration on the part of those who don't practice it. It can also backfire when an inveterate booker forgets to redeem a pledge!

Another form of courtesy to partners is physical. People come in different sizes, weights, and degrees of strength. Not everyone likes to be handled firmly; on the other hand, many dancers are irritated by too tentative a hold. It's important to read your partner's signals and adjust your pressure to his or hers.

The others in the set are important, too. Country dancing differs from most forms of social dancing in that each person moves in harmony with several other people, not just one. A common fault of country dancers is to ignore the set almost entirely, refusing to give weight on a move as simple as "circle left" and twirling one's partner into bystanders after every swing or ladies chain. Courtesy toward the set means not just the absence of such antics but a positive awareness of everyone else in the circle or line. Each dancer should, at least subconsciously, be thinking, "What is this person's relation to me? What can I do to make him or her more comfortable? What can we do together to make this set feel more like a team, and not just a bunch of people who happen to be in close quarters?"

To some extent this applies not just to the other people in the set, but to everyone on the floor. Each set needs to be aware of the sets around it. This is obvious in the case of a movement like "forward and back," but it's also true for other calls. In a ladies chain, for instance, whether a couple chooses to twirl or do a courtesy turn, the gent often rotates in place and so forces the lady to travel in a wide arc around him. If the sets are closely spaced, or if a couple in the next set is doing the same thing, a collision is likely.

Last but not least, the caller and band deserve some courtesy. True, people normally come to a dance to socialize, not to learn; but if the socializing continues into the walkthrough, the caller's directions will fall on many deaf ears, forcing a second walkthrough. A wise caller will give the dancers a minute or two to greet old friends and

Chapter 11: Before the Basics

introduce themselves to new ones, each time they form sets. But once the walkthrough has started, the dancers owe it to the caller – and to themselves – to listen quietly. And both caller and band will appreciate a crowd that dances with enthusiasm and applauds freely!

Here are a few specific points of etiquette that have stood the test of time:

- Always accept graciously an invitation to dance. If you must refuse, don't accept any subsequent offers.
- In a contra dance, join the shortest line. In a square, join the nearest set that needs you; don't pass by an incomplete set.
- Always join a contra line at the foot – the end farthest from the music.
- Let the caller do the teaching. Don't assume you know what's coming.
- During a dance, if you see someone floundering, it's all right to direct them (pointing and gently steering work better than talking). But make sure you really do know what you're doing before you try to help others.
- Stay in your set until the caller tells you the dance is over.
- Change partners frequently – it helps the group spirit, and if you're new, you'll learn faster. Experienced dancers, if you ask the beginners to dance, you'll benefit from an improvement in the group's ability.
- Look the other dancers in the eye in a friendly way (but don't stare or, worse, leer).
- Learn the standard way to execute each movement before trying variations.
- Avoid clapping in time with the music. It makes the calls harder to hear, and it can throw the band and caller off the beat because it's delayed in getting back to them.
- When you travel to other dances, do things their way.
- Don't drink alcohol before or during a dance – it slows your reaction time.
- Avoid wearing sharp-edged jewelry, especially rings.
- Don't use highly scented soaps or cologne before a dance (but do make sure your breath is fresh).
- Feel free to applaud at the end of each number. It makes the band and caller feel good, and you're really applauding your own accomplishment as much as theirs.
- It's nice to thank the caller, band, and hosts at the end of an evening. And it's always good manners to thank your partner. If your partner is new to the group, you might introduce him or her

to some of your friends, or otherwise see that he or she is comfortable.

A note on clothing: Country dancing has no dress code as such, but clothes should be neat and clean. Most women prefer skirts to slacks, finding them cooler to dance in (and more fun to twirl in). Many men bring extra shirts to change into as the evening warms up. On cold nights, it's smart to dress in layers which can be peeled off. Women especially should beware of wearing a sweater with no blouse!

Shoes should fit and be well broken in. Most dancers prefer a low but definite heel; flat shoes can be tiring, and high heels are downright dangerous. Soles should be hard and smooth, unless the hall management requires soft soles. In that case, there are several makes of dancing shoes with soft felt-like leather on the soles and heels. Dancing in bare feet is popular in some areas, but splinters and other people's boots present hazards.

How to Move

How good a dancer you are isn't measured by how many calls you know. It's not even a function of how long you've been at it, though experience usually helps. The biggest single factor, aside from a willingness to nurture the group spirit, is how you hold your body when you move.

It's often said that country dancing is simply walking in time to music, and that if you can walk, you can dance. This is true from a purely mechanical standpoint: by walking, you can get from point A to point B and thereby make it through any given routine. That fact has enabled thousands of people who had trouble with other kinds of dance to take up country dancing and enjoy it. But for best results, the normal walking step needs to be modified when it's used in the dance.

A great many people lead with their feet when they walk. The right foot reaches out in front; the heel comes down, followed by the rest of the foot. By the time body weight is transferred to the right foot, the walker is already swinging the left foot forward. Walking like this, it's almost impossible to exercise the control over one's movements that dancing requires.

A seasoned dancer, by contrast, is more aware of the backswing of the foot. Body weight is kept well forward, over the balls of the feet. Each foot, rather than reaching forward, touches the floor directly below the body and immediately starts to push back, propelling the dancer forward more rapidly than the length of stride would suggest.

This dance-walk is most effective when combined with relatively small steps. A country dancer must be ready to change direction at a moment's notice. A long reaching step in one direction will unbalance the body. Instead, the dancer needs to maintain the feeling of poise over both feet, like a baseball fielder who is prepared to chase the ball either way even before it's hit. Knees should be kept unlocked to delay the onset of fatigue.

The balance and the swing, of course, are exceptions to the rule that country dancing is done at a walk. But the principles are the same: keep your feet under you, knees unlocked, and take small steps.

Two other important concepts are giving weight and anticipation. Both of these are treated in Chapter 5; giving weight is also discussed in the following two chapters under the movements that require it.

12

The Basic Moves for Two People

Contra dancing, like most forms of square dancing, is made up of a small number of basic movements – not much more than a dozen. Like the letters of the alphabet or the notes of the musical scale, these few moves can be combined in nearly infinite ways. Literally thousands of contra dances have been written using only these terms.

This chapter and Chapter 13 discuss the basic movements of contra dancing in depth. The movements in this chapter, being danceable by two people, can all be taught and called while the dancers are in a big circle. This will give the group a solid foundation of dance knowledge before they need to deal with the various formations and couple numbering systems.

The order of presentation is somewhat arbitrary, based partly on the difficulty of the movements and partly on the frequency with which they occur in present-day contra dancing. These terms and many others appear in alphabetical order in the Glossary at the end of the book. Note that many calls, such as "down the center" and "turn alone," are self-explanatory or nearly so, and are defined briefly in the Glossary but not treated in detail here.

Do-si-do

Done by

Any two adjacent dancers.

Description

The dancers face each other, if they were not already doing so. They both move forward, keeping to the left so that their right shoulders are adjacent, until they have passed each other. Without turning, they move to their right to pass back to back (whence the name, a fractured version of the French "dos-à-dos"). They now move backward, keeping to the right so that their left shoulders are adjacent, until they are in their starting positions. In the standard version of the do-si-do, each dancer continues to face in his or her original direction throughout the maneuver. A left-shoulder do-si-do may be called, with all directions reversed.

Result

Both dancers are in their starting positions. They are facing each other unless the next call sends them to another person or location in the set.

Teaching Technique

Many people have trouble telling their right side from their left. It often helps to have the dancers shake hands with the person they're facing, and then to say "*On that side,* go around each other, back to back – now come back on the other side." In the rare cases when the group can't execute a do-si-do from brief spoken instructions, a demonstration will make it clear.

Variations

Enthusiastic dancers at all levels of experience enjoy spinning as they go around each other. This is one of the more innocuous variations on contra dance movements, as the dancers must stay fairly controlled in order to keep their own balance. Those who opt to spin should remember to end the move facing in the correct direction.

A do-si-do preceding a balance in a wave is actually once and a quarter around. For a do-si-do once and a half, see below under "Timing."

Transitions

Since the do-si-do is a "no hands" movement, most transitions into and out of it are relatively smooth. For example, a do-si-do can be followed by either a right-hand turn (with the dancers continuing in the same direction) or a left-hand turn (reversing the dancers' direction). Certain sequences pose a challenge to dancers who spin: if the do-si-do is followed by a balance in a wave, requiring everyone to face original directions at a precise moment, or if the dance calls for a do-si-do once and a half in 8 beats (see below). Such a case demands a careful walkthrough.

Timing

Traditionally 8 beats. In many modern sequences, the timing is speeded up in one of two ways:

1. The do-si-do shares a 16-beat phrase with two other moves, usually hand turns, giving it an allotment of 5 to 6 beats. The moves typically flow well, and the dancers don't feel rushed.
2. The do-si-do is done "once and a half." In 8 beats, the dancers are expected to circle each other and then pass by the right shoulder a second time. They end back to back, almost in each other's starting place.

Gypsy

Done by

Any two adjacent dancers.

Description

The dancers face each other, if they were not already doing so. They both keep to the left and take one or two steps forward until the other dancer is on a right diagonal, no more than two or three feet away. Holding eye contact, they move clockwise on a circular track, almost all the way around each other. They finish as directed by the call, either swinging each other, moving toward someone else, or backing away to face each other. A left-shoulder gypsy or "left gypsy" may be called, with all directions reversed.

Result

Both dancers are in their starting positions. They are facing each other unless the next call sends them to another person or location in the set.

Teaching Technique

If the dancers know the do-si-do, you can say something like this: "Face your partner. Now do a do-si-do, but keep looking at each other as you go around." A demonstration will help the dancers to appreciate the subtleties of the gypsy, especially if the demonstrators have a bit of the ham in them.

Variations

The gypsy is the occasion for much flirtatious byplay, especially in close-knit groups of experienced dancers. But the nature of the move precludes any real variation. To spin, for example, would be to lose the gypsy's most distinctive feature, its unbroken eye contact.

Transitions

Since the gypsy, like the do-si-do, is a "hands off" movement, most transitions are relatively easy. But if the next move is with someone else, the dancers must remember to break eye contact in time to reorient themselves. For example, if a gypsy with partner in the center (for the "ones") is followed by a left-shoulder gypsy with the opposite, dancers who hold their gaze too long will find themselves in the right place for the next move, but facing the wrong way.

Timing

Typically 8 beats. Occasionally the timing is shortened in one of the ways described under "Do-si-do."

Hand Turn (Allemande)

Done by

Any two adjacent dancers.

Description

The dancers face each other, if they were not already doing so. They move toward each other until they are about three feet apart. (The distance will vary depending on the timing of the move; see below.) They join either right or left hands as directed by the call, as if they were arm-wrestling with their elbows resting on a table: hands are joined chest- to shoulder-high, wrists straight, elbows bent and pointing downward. Fingers are cupped around the other person's hand; thumbs are usually grasping each other. (A dancer who is concerned about thumb injuries can hold his or her thumb and index finger together, relying on the cupped fingers to maintain the hold.) Both dancers "give weight," pulling toward themselves just enough to provide a degree of resistance without leaning backward or turning the move into a tug-of-war. Using a normal dance-walk, they move forward around each other as far as the call dictates, usually between halfway around and twice around. Feet should be pointed in the direction the dancer is moving, not toward the other dancer. Heads are often turned to look the other dancer in the eye. The dancers finish as directed by the call, either moving toward someone else or backing away to face each other.

Result

The hand turn is quite satisfying to dance, and choreographers use it in many ways. Dancers may find themselves returning to their original places or moving toward someone new, often for another hand turn.

Teaching Technique

The hand turn is fundamental to contra dancing, and is one of the few moves that beginners can't comprehend from simply watching someone else. Therefore, it's wise to spend extra time teaching it. A demonstration always helps, but it will also be necessary to describe the feeling of "giving weight." In a small group, the leader can dance with each person, encouraging them to gauge the amount of force required.

Variations

The speed of the hand turn varies from dance to dance (see below under Timing), but dancer-inspired variations are few – a good index of the satisfaction inherent in this move. Occasionally, if experienced dancers perceive the timing of a series of hand turns to be too loose, they will add solo spins after one or more of the turns. (In other styles of country dancing, hand turns are done with a handshake hold or a forearm grasp, requiring slightly different techniques of weight-sharing; but in New England style, the "hands up" hold is standard.)

Some dancers habitually dance hand turns with a sharply bent wrist, forcing the other dancer to do likewise. Or worse, they make contact not with the hand but with the inside of the wrist, an area of delicate bones and blood vessels. The best defense against the bent wrist is to keep one's own wrist straight; the only sure defense against the wrist-to-wrist hold is a limp arm.

Transitions

Most dances that include hand turns pose no problems of physical awkwardness; the turns flow smoothly from one to the next (right hand to left hand, for example). The primary challenge for most dancers will be orienting themselves after each turn: noting which way they must face and what dancer to interact with next. A few dances call for a balance followed by a hand turn with the same person; if the dancers have joined hands in a one-hand hold for the balance, they can shift to a hands-up hold just after they have pulled toward each other following the balance.

Timing

Varies from dance to dance, depending on both the number of revolutions and the speed desired by the choreographer. Dances of the Colonial era often allow 8 beats for a turn once around or even three-quarters around (though in the latter case the 8 beats usually include time to back into a new position in the set). Newer routines may call for a full turn in 4 beats, or twice around in 8 beats. Some older dances, such as *Hull's Victory,* have been modified to the new timing. A happy medium, favored by many modern choreographers, is once and a half in 8 beats. Good dancers will adapt their style to the routine by adjusting the bend of their arms: sharper for fast turns, less so for leisurely ones.

Swing

Done by

Any two adjacent dancers.

Description

The dancers face each other, if they were not already doing so. They move forward, keeping to the left, until they are almost (but not quite) alongside each other. (The other dancer should be on a right diagonal, less than a foot away.) They are still facing in opposite directions: if one dancer's toes are pointing north, the other's are pointing south. They hold each other in one of several ways (described below) and revolve clockwise as a unit, using the "buzz" step: On each downbeat of the music, both dancers step solidly on the right foot, with the little toe toward the other's little toe and almost touching it. On each upbeat or slightly after it, both dancers step lightly on the left foot, taking body weight for a split second, with the toe of the left foot roughly in line with the heel of the right. The next step on the right foot is well ahead of the left, and so on. The motion has been compared to riding a scooter or playing at being a galloping horse, but the steps are smaller and more controlled than this would imply. The scooter analogy is particularly misleading because in a swing, the right foot must be picked up and set down in a new place, whereas on a scooter it never leaves the footboard. The word "pivot" is also misleading because it too implies that the right foot stays in one place.

The Ballroom Hold. This is similar to a waltz position except that the dancers are on a diagonal rather than face to face. The gent's right arm encircles the lady, with his right hand flat on the middle of her back. The lady rests her left arm on the gent's right arm, with her left hand holding his upper arm or shoulder, depending on the length of her arm. The gent's left hand (palm up) holds the lady's right hand (palm down), their arms forming a half circle. In crowded halls, this handhold is often modified, the dancers reaching halfway up each other's arm and holding on with cupped fingers (not grasping with the thumb!).

The Unisex Hold. There are two variations: (1) Each dancer puts his or her right arm around the other's back or waist and rests his or her left arm on the other's right arm. In other words, each dancer's right arm does the part of the gent's right arm in the ballroom hold, while each dancer's left arm does the part of the lady's left arm. (2) Each dancer's right arm encircles the other dancer, with the right hand flat on the back of the other's waist. Left hands are joined between the dancers, underneath their right arms.

In any of these holds, the strongest connection should be the right hand on the other dancer's back. Each dancer pulls toward himself or herself with the right hand, and at the same time pushes back with the whole upper body against the other dancer's right hand. Knees should be slightly bent, and steps with both feet should be small and close to the floor.

To end a swing, the gent comes to a smooth, controlled stop facing in the required direction and carefully straightens and extends his right arm to the side, letting the lady "unroll" until she is at his right, facing in the same direction. (In a very few cases, such as the dance *Rory O'More,* the dancers must release their hold and back away from each other.)

Result

Normally, the two dancers end side by side, the lady on the gent's right, facing in a direction specified by the call. Occasionally, they return to their starting position, facing each other.

More than any other movement, the swing is done for the joy of the dance rather than to propel dancers from point A to point B. However, many modern choreographers use the swing as a positioning device, often to accomplish a progression.

Teaching Technique

The swing takes more effort to learn than any other movement in contra dancing (note the length of the description above!). It's a good idea to set aside a large portion of teaching time to deal with the swing – as much as one-third or even one-half of a pre-dance beginners' session. The newcomers will adequately learn many of the other moves as they participate in the actual dancing.

One way to teach the swing to beginning dancers is to have them join hands in a large circle and move to the left, crossing the right foot slightly over the left foot. This will give them an idea of the buzz step without making them worry about handholds. Then they can pair off, join both hands with partner, and turn clockwise, pulling away from each other and still using the buzz step. Once they have the feel of "giving weight," they're ready to try one of the conventional handholds.

While it's difficult to learn how to swing by simply watching, a demonstration will help. You'll probably want to conduct it yourself, preferably from the center of the room while the dancers are in a large circle. Points to be emphasized include the push-and-pull exchange of weight between the dancers, the need for bent knees and small steps, and the comfortable way to end a swing (gent stops first).

No one can assimilate all these points the first time they try the swing, and even if they could, it's not enough to know what to do – it takes practice. Encourage the newcomers to keep trying. Remind them that everything comes more easily with time. And provide plenty of opportunities for them to change partners, so they don't get stuck in a rut with the same person.

Variations

Some experienced dancers throw in a few moves borrowed from swing dancing, especially while waiting at the end of a contra line; but most dancers enjoy swinging so much that no variation could compete.

One common handhold is not recommended for contra dancing or New England squares: the straight-arm or "bull-by-the-tail" hold. It's similar to the second unisex hold described above except that instead of encircling the other's waist, each dancer puts the right arm straight out and cups the right hand on the other's right shoulder. It's often taught in elementary schools to enable children to learn to swing without having to touch each other more intimately. And it's admittedly easier to learn the buzz step in this position, since dancers can concentrate on the footwork without worrying about the precise curve of their arms. But many New England style callers discourage it because it takes up more space than other holds, and many of the other movements in New England dancing require compact sets. It's also less secure than other holds, as neither dancer has a hand or arm behind the other.

Transitions

As noted above under "Description" and "Result," most swings end with the dancers side by side, lady on the right. The lady's right hand and the gent's left hand are released first; then, as the lady moves to face the same way as the gent, she removes her left hand from his arm. He catches her left hand either with his right hand (for a circle, forward and back, or ladies chain) or with his left hand (for a promenade). If the call following the swing sends the dancers to someone else – to do an allemande left, for example – the gent releases the lady completely just before she reaches the person she is to turn. She executes either a right-face half turn or a once-and-a-half spin, and ends facing the new person, ready to join left hands.

Transitions from a unisex hold are similar in that the dancer playing the part of the gent stops revolving first. But the second unisex hold described above poses a slight problem for the "lady," who must extricate her right arm from the sandwich formed by the "gent's" left arm and body. Many dancers prefer the first unisex hold for its ease of getting into and out of position.

The average dancer finds it difficult to end a swing in the middle of a 16-beat phrase of music (an "A" or "B" part of a tune). If you use a dance in which an 8-count swing falls on the first half of such a phrase, be prepared to call the movement following the swing for more rounds than you would normally keep calling.

Timing

The swing is a flexible movement, both in the time allotted to it and in the speed at which the dancers choose to execute it. The most common lengths for a swing are 8 beats (when preceded, or occasionally followed, by another 8-beat movement) and 12 beats (when preceded by a 4-beat balance). Swings lasting 16 beats are not unknown. As for speed, different couples in the same set may choose to revolve once around in every 4 beats, every 3 beats, or even every 2 beats. Note that dancers don't consciously think about these numbers; they simply decide to go faster or slower as their experience level dictates and the mood strikes them. As long as a couple can end a swing facing in the correct direction, the speed of the swing doesn't matter.

Promenade

Done by

Two adjacent dancers of opposite sex.

Description

The dancers turn (if necessary) so that they are side by side, with the lady on the gent's right. They take hands in "promenade position": gent's right arm around lady's waist, lady's right hand palm out at her right hip to receive gent's right hand, gent's left hand holding lady's left hand in front of gent's chest. (Note that the left-hand hold is not in handshake style; the gent extends his hand palm up, almost as if asking for money, and the lady puts her hand palm down on his, with her fingers at a 90-degree angle to his.) In this position, they travel across or along a contra set or around a circle or square set, as directed by the call. If they meet another couple, they keep to their own right as they pass. Circular promenades are counterclockwise unless otherwise specified.

In a promenade across a contra set, which is often called by the old name of "half promenade," each couple crosses in about four steps and wheels left (counterclockwise) to face the other couple in the remaining four steps. During the wheel, the lady moves forward and the gent turns in place or moves slightly backward, depending on the amount of fudging the two couples must do to face each other squarely. (A full promenade or "promenade four," now obsolete, was a round trip: two half promenades, ending in original places.)

Result

Varies depending on the dance. Promenades are used in contras as a means of exchanging places with another couple (generally across the set) or as a feature of the routine (up and down one side of the set). In circles and squares, they serve as a filler or chorus figure, often giving new partners a chance to cement their relationship.

Teaching Technique

The promenade is a simple movement and requires little teaching. Be aware, though, that it's much easier to demonstrate the hand position than to get dancers to understand it from a verbal description. If the hall is too crowded to allow people to stand back and watch you in the center, you can assume the handhold with a partner on stage, even if you can't travel.

Variations

Several other handholds are used in different parts of North America, including:

- Left hands joined as in New England, but gent's right arm around lady's shoulders instead of her waist.
- Both hands joined in front, right over left.
- Gent's right arm around lady's waist and her left hand on his right shoulder.

The last position, common in French-speaking parts of Canada, makes for an easy transition from a swing; partners simply release the other hands (lady's right and gent's left) and let them hang freely during the promenade.

In the "half promenade" across a contra set, the wheeling turn at the end of the move is similar to the "courtesy turn" at the end of a ladies chain or right and left. Present-day dancers often substitute a twirl for a courtesy turn wherever it occurs.

The term "promenade" is occasionally used for a solo movement along a contra line or around a circle or square. In such cases, the call is usually expanded to "promenade (in) single file."

Transitions

The most common transition into a promenade is from a swing with the same person. Fortunately, this is fairly easy: both dancers release hands, the gent comes to a stop as the lady lets her momentum carry her another half revolution, and they take hands in promenade position. This has been described as "let go and catch," and it's one of the most satisfying transitions in country dancing.

Timing

For a promenade across a contra set (often called "half promenade"), 8 beats. For a promenade up, then down the line, usually 16 beats. In a square, 8 beats to promenade halfway around, 16 to go all the way around.

Balance

Done by

Any two adjacent dancers.

Description

The dancers face each other. According to local custom or the context of the routine, they either join right hands, join both hands straight across, or support their own weight without taking hands. In four beats of music, they move slightly from their starting position and then return to it. The movement may be either forward and back or sideways, again depending on context or local custom. Following are the two most common forms of balance:

Forward-and-back balance

Beat 1: Step forward on the right foot, keeping body weight over it, and almost immediately bring the left foot up to the right foot.

Beat 2: Touch the left foot to the floor next to the right foot.

Beat 3: Step backward on the left foot, keeping body weight over it, and almost immediately bring the right foot back to the left foot.

Beat 4: Touch the right foot to the floor next to the left foot.

Sideways balance

Beat 1: Step to the right on the right foot, keeping body weight over it, and begin to sweep the left foot across in front of the right foot.

Beat 2: Hop on the right foot, continuing to sweep the left foot across in front.

Beat 3: Step to the left on the left foot, keeping body weight over it, and begin to sweep the right foot across in front of the left foot.

Beat 4: Hop on the left foot, continuing to sweep the right foot across in front.

Either of these balances may be done with as much or little energy as the dancers care to put into it. The hop may amount to a mere raising and lowering of the heel while the toe stays in contact with the floor. If the dancers are holding hands, they may pull together on beat 1 and push apart on beat 3. This is common even in sideways balances, and almost universal in forward-and-back balances.

Result

The dancers are still facing each other. The next call almost always directs them to dance together again. They will naturally use their hands (if joined) to pull each other into a do-si-do or swing.

Teaching Technique

The balance is one of the two movements that use footwork other than the basic walking step (the other, of course, is the swing). Like the swing and the hand turn, it can't be fathomed just by watching and should receive special attention during teaching sessions.

Despite the sometimes showy footwork, a case can be made that the key element of a balance is the hands and arms rather than the feet. This is particularly true of the forward-and-back balance, especially when it precedes a swing: the dancers may be thought of as coming close, then having second thoughts and pushing each other away to arm's length before deciding to initiate closer contact.

Dancers should keep their weight (as always) over the balls of their feet, rather than kicking their feet out in front of their bodies. The best way to get this point across is by demonstration.

Variations

The balance probably has more variations than any other country dance movement. One researcher found 50 without half trying! (Ralph Piper in *Fiddle and Squares* [Wisconsin], Feb. 1952; reprinted in *Northern Junket,* vol. 5, no. 1, March 1955.) The things to remember are: do it in four beats; stay in your own space; and do something resembling what your partner is doing.

In a handful of dance communities across the United States, the balance is done starting with the left foot. A century ago this wouldn't have been a problem, but in our day of easy travel and frequent relocation, it leads to confusion and even embarrassment. If contra dancing as a hobby continues to grow, the left-foot areas will undoubtedly feel pressure to convert. (This is a prediction, not a recommendation; regional differences are the lifeblood of any folk art.)

A very few dances prescribe a leftward balance, usually to complement a rightward one earlier in the routine. *Rory O'More* is probably the best known of these.

Transitions

As noted above, the balance is usually followed by a swing or a do-si-do with the same person. Such a transition is easy: the dancers simply use their joined hands to pull each other into the next move. In the case of the swing, they let go just in time to assume the new handhold.

Transitions *into* the balance are a challenge to the average dancer. The balance is unique among contra dance movements in that it must be danced on the specific beats assigned to it, or it loses its whole point. True, contra dancing in general strictly follows the phrasing of the music, but other moves can be fudged; the dancers can speed up or cut corners to get to the right place if they miss the first couple of beats. Not so with the balance. The rule here is "Better never than late."

This being so, every contra dancer should cultivate the habit of anticipating balances even more than most other moves. If a balance is imminent, the dancers must finish the preceding move in plenty of time to arrive at their next position on the last beat of the musical phrase. This will let them begin the balance comfortably on the first beat of the new phrase.

Timing

4 beats for a single balance, 8 beats for a double balance. (Found in a few dances, a double balance is simply a single balance done twice.)

Twirl to Swap

Done by

Two adjacent dancers of opposite sex.

Description

The dancers join hands (see below for which hands) and raise them above their heads. They exchange places, stepping out of each other's way only as much as necessary, with the lady moving under the raised hands. The handhold needs to be supportive yet flexible; the most effective method is for both dancers to curl their fingers about halfway to a closed fist and bear firmly against each other's hand without grabbing. During most of the twirl, the gent's hand will probably be outside the lady's, with the palm of his hand against the back of hers forming a ball-and-socket joint. Following are the most common types of twirl to swap:

Facing. Both dancers use their right hand, unless a left-handed turn is specified. The gent takes four steps in a clockwise semicircle, keeping to his left, as the lady takes four steps in a tighter counterclockwise semicircle. For both dancers, the first two steps are forward and the last two are backward. (This move is called "box the gnat" in modern square dancing; supposedly the name is an English mangling of an old French dance term, *bauxinet.*)

Side by side. The dancers use their adjacent hands: gent's right and lady's left. They move as in the facing twirl, except that all the steps are forward. (In modern square dancing this move is known as a "California twirl" or formerly a "frontier whirl.")

Hybrid. The dancers face each other and join hands (gent's right and lady's left). The gent crosses to the lady's place and makes a quarter turn to his right; the lady crosses (under the raised hands) to the gent's place and makes a quarter turn to her left. The dancers end side by side, with the lady on the gent's right. (Modern square dance callers refer to this move as a "star through." It is difficult for the dancers because there's no easy way to remember which hand to use; in contra dancing, its use is generally confined to situations in which the dancers already have the requisite hands joined.)

Result

The dancers have exchanged places. In a facing twirl, they are still facing each other. In a side-by-side twirl, they are still side by side, lady on the right, but facing opposite to their starting direction. In a hybrid twirl, if the gent was facing north and the lady south, both are now facing east.

Teaching Technique

The twirl to swap in all its forms has defied many attempts at verbal explanation. You are urged to demonstrate the kind of twirl you have in mind, showing it in the context of the dance you are teaching. Remember to mention the ball-and-socket handhold, especially with beginners.

Variations

A new kind of twirl can be, and often is, improvised by two dancers who sense a need for it. In addition, certain standard figures, such as the ladies chain, are often adapted by dancers to include a twirl.

Present-day contra dancers frequently use a side-by-side twirl to change direction midway through the call "Down the center and back," where dancers a generation or two ago might have done a wheel around (a couple pivot with the lady moving forward and the gent backing up). In this twirl, many dancers choose to both move backward, rather than both moving forward as described in this section.

Transitions

In a sense, a twirl to swap is itself a transition, as it's usually done to change a couple's facing direction and/or relative positions as required by the next movement. The various types of twirl have evolved in order to achieve the smoothest possible transition between certain other moves.

Timing

Usually 4 beats, often "stolen" from the time allotted to other moves.

13

The Basic Moves for More than Two People

This chapter continues the in-depth discussion of the basic movements of contra dancing that began in Chapter 12 with one-couple moves. To reiterate:

- The order of presentation is based on difficulty and on the frequency with which a dancer is likely to encounter the movements.
- Calls that are more or less self-explanatory are defined briefly in the Glossary rather than discussed here.

The first two movements in this chapter, the circle and the forward and back, can be taught in the big circle formation. Most of the others can be done by groups of two facing couples in a progressive circle. In this way, beginning dancers can learn most of the basics of country dancing before they need to deal with the peculiarities of the contra dance – couple numbering, progression, neutral couples, and change of roles.

Circle

Done by

Three or more dancers who are already in a more or less circular group. The most common numbers are four and (in squares and four-face-four dances) eight.

Description

The dancers join adjacent hands to form a circle, all facing the center. They turn their bodies to face diagonally either left or right, and using the basic dance-walk, they move in the direction they are facing, staying on the rim of the circle and keeping its size constant. If no direction is specified, a circle moves to the left (clockwise).

Result

The dancers are in a group similar to their starting formation. They may or may not be in their original places, but they are all in the same positions relative to each other. Note that fractional circles are often used in modern contra dance choreography to bring either partners or neighbors from the opposite side to the same side of the set.

Teaching Technique

The circle is deceptively simple in appearance. It's really a demanding movement, easy to spoil by indifferent dancing, and how you teach it can make or break an evening.

Make sure the circle is as perfectly round as it can get without browbeating the dancers; that is, any obvious corners should be smoothed out, and people should all be roughly the same distance apart. Arms should be bent as for a hand turn, with elbows pointing down and hands about shoulder-high to the shorter dancers. To avoid endless false moves when taking hands, it helps to say "Gents' palms up, ladies' palms down."

Giving weight is as important in a circle as in any other move. The precise amount of resistance needed comes with experience, but you can help beginners make a start by telling them to put some spring in their arms. Some teachers say a dancer should be able to feel the motion of a dancer on the opposite side of the circle.

Variations

Some dancers, especially those with experience in international folk dancing or modern square dancing, will do a "grapevine" step while circling. This involves crossing alternately in front and behind with the trailing foot (the right foot in a circle to the left) while rotating the upper body from side to side. If everyone in a circle does the grapevine at once, it can be fun (as in those Israeli dances where it's the prescribed step), but many people think it spoils the sense of strong connection in a contra dance circle. And if some of the dancers are doing it and some are not, the result is a shambles!

Transitions

When coming into a circle, dancers need to anticipate the movement enough to let them join hands strongly at the beginning of the circle. This means allowing one or two beats at the end of the preceding move to release hands and reorient themselves.

A circle can be followed by almost any other movement. Because each dancer has two strong connections, it's easy to use either hand and arm as a springboard into the next move. For example, the gent's right arm and the lady's left arm together can send the lady into a ladies chain.

Timing

Four people can circle halfway round in 4 beats, three-quarters around in 6 beats, and once around in 8 beats. Eight people will take twice as long.

Note that the dancers must move with determination in order to maintain these ideal timings. In practice, an 8-beat "circle left" followed by an 8-beat "circle right" often degenerates into three-quarters around in each direction. Therefore, a "circle left" followed by a "circle right" is less demanding than a "circle left once around" followed by some other movement.

Forward and Back

Done by

Any number of dancers, facing a similar number. (Forward and back may be done by two solo dancers, but it is done that way so rarely that the move is treated in this chapter rather than Chapter 12.)

Description

Adjacent dancers join hands as described under "Circle." They move toward the facing dancers by taking three steps forward and closing the free foot (that is, stepping on it or touching it next to the other foot). They then return to their place by taking three steps backward and closing the free foot.

Result

All dancers are in their original places. Forward and back is used primarily as a "gathering" movement, to emphasize the unity of the set before smaller groups of people are called on to dance together.

Teaching Technique

As with the circle, there's more here than meets the eye. Forward and back is a powerful figure if it's done well, and completely useless if it's not.

Caution the dancers to keep their lines straight, staying aware of the people on either side of them even if they choose to flirt with the one they're facing. Make sure they allow the full eight beats for the movement.

Variations

Some dancers enjoy swinging the free foot forward on the fourth beat (in the circle dance *La Bastringue,* this is traditional). A dancer at the end of a line will often clap the free hand, pattycake style, with the facing dancer on the fourth beat. One variation that approaches the ultimate in rudeness to the other dancers is for a couple to begin a swing (the next movement in the sequence) when they meet in the middle, refusing to move backward with the group.

Transitions

Most contra movements require dancers to be fairly close together. Almost any movement that follows a forward and back can be overly challenging to get into if the dancers have moved all the way back to their starting places. (The fear of being cheated out of two or three beats of a swing is what leads dancers to adopt rude variations.) The secret is to take smaller steps on the way back than on the trip forward, and (in the case of a swing) to follow the forward and back with one or two longer-than-usual steps toward the facing dancer, losing hardly any time.

Like the balance, the forward and back really ought to begin precisely on the first beat of the phrase. But because it's longer than the balance, transitions into forward and back are easier to fudge.

Timing

Always a full 8 beats. (The sole exception that comes to mind is the modern version of *Money Musk,* where the forward and back has been shortened to 4 beats. Done that way, it's really a balance, and that's what I prefer to call it.)

Star

Done by

Three or more dancers who are in a more or less circular group. Four is the usual number.

Description

The dancers extend their right or left arms toward the center of the group and make contact in one of two ways (see below). They move forward around their extended hands (clockwise in the case of a right-hand star), usually once around. Right or left hands are nearly always specified, but if not, a right-hand star is generally understood.

Wrist star or *box star:* This works with any number of dancers. Each person holds the wrist of the one directly in front of him or her as they face around the circle. For everyone's comfort, the thumb should be held against the forefinger, not used to grip the other person's wrist.

Hands-across star: There must be an even number of dancers. Each person joins right or left hands with the dancer who is directly across the center of the group. In a mixed star, the gents usually join hands above the ladies' hands. Elbows are slightly bent, and the dancers give weight (pull gently toward themselves) as they go around.

Result

After the usual once-around star, all the dancers are in their starting position.

Teaching Technique

The star is one of the easiest movements for new dancers to understand, although giving weight is an issue, particularly in hands-across stars. In a wrist star, dancers should be told to *rest* their hand on the wrist ahead of them, rather than *grasping* with the thumb.

Variations

None, apart from the question of hands across vs. wrist stars. Much ink has been spilled on the "correct" way to do stars; aside from a few dances where the context demands one or the other, it would be impossible to prescribe a universally correct way without over-stepping the bounds of one writer's authority.

In teaching and calling, however, it is suggested that you refer to the wrist hold as "right-hand star" or "left-hand star," and to the other hold as "right hands across" or "left hands across," avoiding the word *star*. This conforms to the traditional usage of several areas, and may avoid some confusion.

Transitions

Like the star itself, most transitions into and out of it are easy. The primary exception is the star followed by a move with a new neighbor. Examples are a left-hand star into a balance, or a right-hand star into an allemande left. The dancers must take care not to overshoot the mark and pass by the new neighbor before they realize what's happening. This will be especially challenging to the ladies out of a left-hand star and to the gents out of a right-hand star (assuming a duple improper setup).

Timing

For four people, 8 beats to star once around.

Pass Through

Done by

Any number of dancers, facing a similar number. (Pass through, like forward and back, may be done by two solo dancers but is rarely used that way.)

Description

Each dancer moves forward four steps, keeping to the left and passing right shoulders with the opposite dancer.

Result

Each dancer has exchanged places with the opposite dancer, and is back to back with that dancer. The movement ends at this point and must be followed by another call, such as "turn alone" or "on to the next."

Teaching Technique

The pass through is the most straightforward, figuratively and literally, of the movements in these chapters. It is presented here because it's an important building block, being the ordinary means of travel in progressive circles and an element of "right and left," and also because it may require more instruction and practice than it would appear to at first thought. Many dancers will try to turn immediately after a pass through, either individually (about-face) or in tandem (usually to the right). You'll need to forestall this by telling the dancers firmly and clearly, before they've finished passing through, what you want them to do next.

Variations

Practically none. A pass through by the left shoulder is possible but almost unheard of.

Transitions

Most transitions into and out of the pass through are easy. An exception is a circle for four people followed by a pass through: the dancers must quickly change from facing the center of the circle to facing one of the adjacent dancers, then adjust themselves so that the person they face is slightly to their right rather than directly opposite. Once the technique for doing this has been learned, the combined moves can be quite satisfying, as the dancers help to propel each other through just before releasing hands.

Timing

4 beats. In progressive circle dances, 8 beats are traditionally allowed for "pass through and on to the next."

Balance in a Wave

Done by

Any number of adjacent people who are alternately facing in opposite directions.

Description

Each dancer joins the nearest hand with the dancer on each side, if hands were not already joined. The usual hold is the same as for a hand turn, with arms bent and elbows pointing down. Each dancer stands slightly behind a line formed by all the joined hands, so that the dancers facing in one direction are offset from those facing in the opposite direction. (This formation is sometimes called an "ocean wave," partly because it resembles one and partly because it's the dominant figure of a singing square dance to the tune of Life on the Ocean Wave. Some present-day contra callers refer to it as a "wavy line.") In this position, each dancer performs a balance, either forward and back or side to side depending on local custom or the context of the routine.

Result

All dancers are in their starting positions. Choreographers use the balance in a wave to fill musical phrases or to add variety to an otherwise smooth routine.

Teaching Technique

This movement should be taught as it appears in the course of a dance party, and not during a preliminary session of instruction. This is both because it's quickly and easily grasped by the dancers, and because the "right" way to do it depends on its context.

All that's normally needed is to talk the dancers into formation and call for a balance. Ideally they will all know the basic balance; if not, even that can be instructed on the spot. The only styling point unique to the balance in a wave is that if the balance is forward and back, the dancers' arms can and should act as springs against each other.

Variations

Theoretically, any variant of the basic balance may be done in a wave. In practice, though, it's best to keep the steps fairly uniform.

Since this is a movement involving the whole minor group or even the entire set, to do it well requires teamwork.

As noted above, some dances work better with a forward and back balance, others with a sideways balance. Tradition and experimentation will tell you which are which.

Transitions

The most common transitions into a balance in a wave are from a hand turn and from a do-si-do. The hand turn flows easily into the balance; dancers simply join their other hand with the adjacent person. The do-si-do can be problematic if the dancers choose to spin; as always, they must finish by facing in their original direction just as if they had not spun.

Note that a balance in a wave, just like any other balance, must be danced precisely on the four beats of music allotted to it. The dancers must be alert enough to anticipate the move and be in formation in plenty of time.

The balance in a wave is usually followed by either a hand turn or a pass through. Neither presents any special problems.

Timing

As for the basic balance, 4 beats; 8 beats if repeated.

Ladies Chain

Done by

Two facing couples, each with the lady on the right.

Description

The two ladies move forward, joining right hands as if for a handshake. They pass each other, release hands, and approach their opposite gent. Each gent moves a step to his right, begins rotating in place to his left, and receives the approaching lady's left hand (palm down) with his hand (palm up) as if for a promenade. The gent puts his right arm around the lady's waist and she joins her right hand with his, completing the promenade position. The two dancers, side by side, pivot counterclockwise, the lady moving forward and the gent backward, until they are facing the opposite couple. (The pivot in promenade position is sometimes called a "courtesy turn.")

Result

The ladies have exchanged places; the gents are in their starting position.

Teaching Technique

Relating the unknown to the known is good teaching. The dancers will grasp the ladies chain quickly if they see how much of it is simply a promenade.

A two-part process works well in teaching the ladies chain:

1. Have facing couples assume promenade position and pivot in place until couples are facing each other again. Then the ladies will know what to do when they get to the opposite gent.
2. Have the ladies take two steps forward and turn to face their partners (the ladies are now back to back). Then have partners join left hands and go into the courtesy turn.

If Step 1 is used without Step 2, the dancers are likely to have trouble figuring out how to get side by side for the turn.

Variations

The ladies chain has been the subject of more controversy than any other movement in recent years. Dancers in every generation have modified figures to suit themselves, and today's dancers are no exception. Many people prefer to omit the courtesy turn, substituting a move in which the lady turns under the gent's arm or spins one or more times as the gent supports her by keeping his left arm raised. Any of these variations is often referred to generically as a "twirl," whether or not the lady actually spins.

The controversy stems from two facts: first, enough dancers prefer the twirl that it has become more than a variation, though not yet the standard; and second, many dancers do not enjoy twirling or being twirled. The prevailing attitude in local dance communities ranges from very conservative (twirling is frowned on by the leadership and a majority of dancers) to avant-garde (showing annoyance at twirls is frowned on).

Tension between the dancing masters and the common people is as old as dancing itself. Any solution will depend on the good will of both sides. Many leaders are suggesting that dancers use the twirl only between "mutually consenting adults." The lady, as the one who must work harder and runs the risk of getting dizzy, is generally conceded the privilege of choosing to twirl or not. She indicates her desire by raising her left arm (for a twirl) or keeping it down (for a courtesy turn) as the gent takes her left hand. A gentleman worthy of the name will respect the lady's decision.

If a twirl is indicated, the gent should back around as he would in a courtesy turn, constantly facing the lady and keeping his raised left arm steady as the lady spins beneath it. The lady should strive to master the art of spinning on the proverbial dime, to avoid colliding with ladies in other sets. As in any twirl, hands should form a ball-and-socket joint.

Transitions

Problems are more likely to arise after a ladies chain than before it. From a courtesy turn, any following move will be awkward if the couple hold on to each other too long; they should be ready to let go as the phrase ends. From a twirl, it's crucial for both dancers to think about the direction they're about to travel in and "put on the brakes" rather than letting the lady careen wildly like the top in a game of skittles.

From either ending, but especially from a twirl, the gent can quickly release the lady's left hand from his left and catch it with his right hand, ready to help direct her into the next movement (such as a circle or a forward and back).

See the next section on right and left for the special case of ladies chain preceded or followed by that movement.

Timing

8 beats (of which about 4 are allotted to the ladies crossing and 4 to the couple turn); 16 beats for a round trip. (In New England terminology, a "ladies chain" used to mean a round trip, and a single exchange must be called a "ladies half chain." Now that the half chain is frequently used as a choreographic device, it has taken the name "ladies chain," and a "chain back" must be made explicit.)

Right and Left (Through)

Done by

Two facing couples, each with the lady on the right, or two adjacent gents facing two adjacent ladies.

Description

The dancers execute a pass through. If adjacent dancers form a mixed couple, they assume promenade position (in some areas they put their arms around each other's waist instead). If they are of the same sex, they may put their arms around each other's waist or shoulders, or simply think of themselves as a couple as if their adjacent shoulders were glued together. Thus attached, they pivot counterclockwise as a couple, remaining side by side, halfway around to face the opposite pair.

Result

Each pair of adjacent dancers has exchanged places with the opposite pair. In each pair, the right-hand person is still on the right.

Teaching Technique

The right and left gets my vote for the most difficult move to teach. It's a compound movement: the dancers go straight ahead and then turn, and they turn in a way they couldn't have predicted. A common error is for the lady (or right-hand person) to turn solo to the right after the pass through.

You can avoid a deal of trouble by waiting to use the right and left until you have taught the promenade, ladies chain, and pass through. Then every part of the new move can be related to something the group already knows.

This is one move that benefits greatly from the technique of telling the dancers where they'll end up before you start to walk them through it. If they know that they're about to exchange places with the facing couple, and that the right-hand person will still be on the right, they'll be more confident and also able to recover quickly if they do go astray.

The timing of your instructions is critical; just before the dancers finish the pass through, tell them firmly to stop. Then have them take promenade position (or whatever style you're using) and hold still as you tell them which way to turn.

Variations

Apart from the different holds and non-holds used during the pivot turn, the most common variation is the replacement of the turn with a twirl. The discussion of twirls in the ladies chain applies to the right and left as well.

In some areas, dancers give a right hand to the opposite person as they cross. If this style is used, the dancers must be sure to release right hands as soon as they are abreast of their opposites. If they hold on too long, they may find themselves pulled around to face the direction they came from; this will be especially disorienting to new dancers.

Transitions

For transitions into the right and left, see the section on pass through. For transitions out of the right and left, see ladies chain.

Note that in practice, the courtesy turn in a right and left is slightly different from the one in a ladies chain. The pivot point in a right and left is typically between the two dancers, so that they travel an equal distance (one forward and one backward). In a ladies chain, the pivot point is often closer to the gent, making the lady travel farther and faster than the gent. This means that a ladies chain followed by a right and left is awkward for the lady, who must slow down considerably in order to pass through at the same speed as the gent beside her. A right and left followed by a ladies chain is smoother, as the lady must accelerate into the chain, always easier than braking.

Timing

8 beats (of which about 4 are allotted to the pass through and 4 to the couple turn); 16 beats for a round trip. (As with the ladies chain, in New England "right and left" or "right and left four" used to mean a round trip, and a single exchange must be called a "half right and left." In the 1950s, probably influenced by the various Western styles of square dancing, some New England callers began using "right and left through" to mean a single exchange, and adding the call "right and left back" when they wanted a return trip. This usage is now widespread, though a few callers prefer the old terminology. Some callers use the old call "right and left" when two ladies are facing two gents, and the modern call "right and left through" for mixed couples.)

Cast Off

Done by

Two couples, one active and one inactive.

Description

The cast off usually begins with an active couple in the center of the set, between the members of an inactive couple. They may have their hands joined in a line of four, or the active couple may be finishing a movement up the center. All four dancers face up the set, if they were not already doing so. The active couple release their joined hands. Each active person takes the nearest hand of the adjacent inactive person (if those hands were not already joined), or the two may put their near arms around each other's waist or shoulders. The active moves forward around the spot the inactive is standing on, as the inactive rotates in place to stay side by side with the active. Normally the active person goes three-quarters of the way around, beginning by facing up the set and ending by facing across.

In many dance routines the cast off is the inactives' only chance to move up the set, to compensate for the actives' downward progression and keep the entire set from drifting down the hall. In such a dance the inactive person must back around slightly, as the gent does in a ladies chain, rather than turn in place. The final adjustment upward can be made as the pair finish the cast off.

Result

Each pair of dancers is facing the opposite pair; the active person is below the inactive person. The cast off is almost always used as a means of progression – indeed, for many years it was by far the most common means of progression.

Teaching Technique

The cast off is a relatively uncomplicated movement, especially if it is done following "ones down the center and back." In this case the active people are already in motion, and there should be no question about who goes forward. From a line of four the cast off is more subtle, and dances with this transition are best saved for more experienced groups.

It's wise to freeze the action when the actives have arrived between the inactives and to tell the dancers where they should end the cast off. It often helps if you tell the inactives that they are the hinge on a gate and that the active person will be the gate, moving around them.

Variations

Whether to dance the cast off hand in hand, arm in arm, or even solo depends on local custom and the tradition and context of each dance routine. If the two dancers on each side are already holding hands, it makes sense to do a "hand cast" rather than shift awkwardly to arms around each other.

Transitions

"Ones up the center" commonly precedes the cast off. This combination is smooth in terms of body flow, but awkward in terms of timing. If the actives have taken seven or eight normal-sized steps down the center, as dancers often do, they will need to return the same distance in order to cast off. But the usual time allotted to "up the center" *and* "cast off" is a mere eight beats!

Few dancers have the presence of mind to reverse direction before the end of the first eight beats, even after the caller has urged them to do so. Most dancers lengthen their stride on the return trip, rush the return or the cast off or both, are late for the following movement, or all of the above. There's a reason why you almost never see a dance with a balance after a cast off! (The traditional way of coping with this in English country dancing is to use a walking step down the center and a skipping step on the way back.)

See "turn contra corners" at the end of this chapter for the transition from the cast off into that movement.

Timing

4 beats, often "stolen" from the time allotted to other movements (notably "up the center").

Half Figure Eight

Done by

Two couples, one active and one inactive.

Description

Each active person is standing next to an inactive person; partners are facing across the set. The actives dance diagonally toward each other and toward the inactives. They cross paths as they pass between the inactives, the gent letting the lady go in front of him. They continue crossing to the opposite side of the set, beyond the inactive who was next to their partner, and go around behind that inactive until they can again face their own partner across the set.

The inactives may stand still, but they will enjoy themselves more, and make life easier for the actives, if they "counter-dance," constantly moving out of the actives' way. As the actives dance inward and (for example) down the set, the inactives dance outward and up the set. As the actives continue out and up, around behind the inactives, the latter move in and downward to their starting point. The inactives usually face their partner throughout, while the actives "follow their noses" around their prescribed track. (Counter-dancing is common in English country dancing, from which this move is borrowed.)

Result

Partners are facing, as they were at the start. The actives have exchanged places with each other, but they have not progressed up or down the set; if they were above the inactives, they are once again above them.

Teaching Technique

This move presents no special problems. A demonstration will be helpful.

Variations

The half figure eight can be done with the actives either above or below the inactives. It can send the actives from their proper side to their improper side, or vice versa.

The full figure eight, common in English country dancing, appears to be unknown in contra dancing. It consists of two half figure eights done in succession, returning all dancers to their original places.

Transitions

As this is a hands-free movement, transitions into and out of it will be smooth as long as they don't call for any sudden reversals of body flow. A well-choreographed dance will avoid such awkwardness.

Timing

8 beats. A full figure eight would take 16 beats.

Hey

Done by

Four dancers (rarely three) in a straight line. A hey may be called to two facing couples, in which case two designated dancers will move forward to become the centers.

Description

In a hey for four, each dancer travels along a floor track that resembles a figure eight with an extra loop in the middle. The dancers will weave by each other, passing right shoulders with some and left shoulders with others, until each dancer has been to both ends of the line and has returned to his or her starting point. There are two ways to begin: either the center two dancers make the first pass or the pairs at each end start together.

Center two start. The center two dancers face each other; the end dancers face toward the middle of the hey. The centers pass (for example) right shoulders to face the opposite end people. They pass left shoulders with the ends, who move to the middle and pass right shoulders with each other. The original centers now loop to their left (counterclockwise), halfway around a circle about three feet in diameter, and come back into the hey, passing left shoulders with the end person they have not met before. As the ends move out and start to loop, the centers move into the middle to repeat the pattern in the opposite direction, meeting the same people in the same order. The ends loop to the left as the centers did, coming back in with a left shoulder pass. They pass each other in the middle by the right shoulder, pass a center by the left, and follow the next call.

All four start. Each center dancer faces an end dancer; the centers are back to back in the middle. Facing dancers pass (usually) right shoulders; the original ends move to the middle and pass left shoulders with each other. The original centers loop to their right (clockwise), halfway around a circle about three feet in diameter, and come back into the hey, passing right shoulders with the end person they have not met before. As the ends move out and start to loop, the centers move through the middle, passing left shoulders with each other, and repeat the pattern in the opposite direction, meeting the same people in the same order. The ends loop to the right as the centers did, coming back in with a right shoulder pass. They pass each other in the middle by the left shoulder, pass a center by the right, loop to the right once more, and follow the next call.

Either type of hey may begin with a left shoulder pass, in which case all the "rights" and "lefts" above are reversed.

No matter who begins a hey for four, the floor track is the same (except for right- or left-handedness): all the passes and loops are "right," except the pass in the middle which is "left" (or vice versa). A dancer leaving a hey for four by the right shoulder must loop to the right and come back in by the right shoulder.

In some routines, two of the dancers do not quite complete the hey. Often they are the original ends, who are now called upon to dance with a new neighbor. In a complete hey, they would find themselves looping away from that new neighbor at the end of the musical phrase; instead, they veer toward him or her after passing each other in the middle.

Result

Normally, all the dancers have returned to their starting point. The context of the dance will determine the facing direction of each person, and whether or not they complete the hey.

Teaching Technique

A demonstration is almost essential. But be aware that watching a hey will intimidate unseasoned dancers if they simply look at the blur of people moving back and forth. Tell those watching to follow the track of one dancer, the one whose part is identical to their own. It may help to mention in advance that each person will make a round trip, reaching both ends of the line before returning to his or her original place.

When you reach the walkthrough stage, it's good to say, "If you meet someone who looks lost, tap your own opposite shoulder on the side you want them to pass you on." The most common error in heys is to stop in one's tracks when one has run out of people to pass, then to turn around on the spot and plow back in, usually with the wrong shoulder. Remind everyone to make big loops at the ends; this will help them come back into the hey more confidently. Remind the dancers, too, that they need to weave from side to side as they go through the hey, and not barge through in a straight line.

Variations

As noted above, a hey can begin with the center two people making the first pass, or with the two end pairs passing at the same time. It can start with either the right or the left shoulder. And the dancers beginning it can be partners, neighbors, or people of the same sex.

The track on the floor is the same in each case; the difference lies in where each person starts.

Half heys and other fractional heys have become popular with choreographers in recent years. As with full heys, the details vary from one dance to another.

The hey for three, common in English and Scottish country dancing, is rarely seen in American contras. The floor track is a figure eight, without the extra loop. The center person faces one of the end people and they pass (say) right shoulders. The other end person waits four beats and then passes left shoulders with the first end person, who is now approaching him or her from the center. Each dancer, after leaving the hey and looping around the end, comes in between the other two. Because there is no pass in the very center, the circuit for each person involves a pair of right-shoulder passes at one end and a pair of left-shoulder passes at the other. The traditional timing allows 16 beats; dancers must make very large loops in order to "use up the music."

Transitions

The hey was reintroduced into contra dancing in the 1970s, after choreographers had started to pay more attention to body flow. Because of this, most transitions into and out of heys are smooth. Occasionally, a hey will be followed by a balance; as a hey for four in 16 beats is tightly timed, the dancers must move briskly in order to be on time for the balance.

Timing

For four, 16 beats. For three, 12 to 16 beats depending on the dance.

Turn Contra Corners

Done by

Three couples, an active person between two inactives all facing their partners. (Minor sets can overlap, so that each inactive person may be part of two groups.)

Description

Each dancer identifies his or her *first corner* (diagonally to the right across the set) and *second corner* (diagonally to the left). The active dancers move into the center of the set and turn each other by the right hand a little more than halfway around. They release each other and move toward their first corners, whom they turn by the left hand about once around. The actives again meet each other in the center and turn by the right hand, this time about three-quarters around. Finally, they move toward their second corners and turn them by the left hand about once around.

Result

The inactives are in their starting positions. The actives may also be in their starting positions, but are more commonly in the center of the set, facing each other without much regard to their orientation to the inactives, as the next call usually directs the actives to balance and/or swing.

Teaching Technique

Much confusion can be avoided if you make sure all the dancers have identified their first and second corners before you let anyone move. One method is to have everyone point to partner with both hands ("I know it's not polite, but do it anyway") and then tell them to spread their arms apart until they're pointing to the people flanking their partner.

Once the walkthrough is under way, try to control the dancers' speed with your voice. Give the next direction when the dancers are about to come into position to follow it, just as you would when calling to music.

Variations

In a triple minor dance, each group of three couples is separate from the others. In a duple minor dance, the sets overlap: each inactive person must dance as a "first corner" with one active couple and as a "second corner" with another.

Experienced dancers in a crowded hall will sometimes finish the left-hand turns ahead of time and spin once just before meeting their partner.

Transitions

This movement frequently follows a cast off. In a proper dance, the active gent has no trouble going from a cast off to the right-hand turn with partner, since his right hand is free. The active lady, however, usually has her right arm around the inactive lady's waist and must somehow free it in time for the first turn (obviously this transition was invented by a man!). Most seasoned female dancers have learned to loosen their right-arm hold quickly and bring their right hand down and forward in a sort of "submarine" motion; an alternative is to put the right hand on the other lady's shoulder for the cast off instead of reaching around her waist.

The inactives in a duple minor dance must use the same hand twice in succession during "turn contra corners," but there is enough time between the two turns that most dancers don't consider the movement awkward.

Timing

16 beats, which works out to about 3 beats for each right-hand turn and 5 beats for each left-hand turn. Note that this traditional timing is comfortable if the actives are to meet in the center of the set, but rushed if they are to return to their starting position.

14
Circle Dances

Circles are powerful. There's something special about a circle, be it a ring of solid matter, a ring of objects all alike, or a ring of people with joined hands. A circle symbolizes completeness, perfection, unity. Many cultures recognize this in one way or another; an impressive number reflect it in their dances. In some cities you can now attend an evening of "sacred circle dances" from around the world.

Country dancing has included circles since the beginning of its recorded history. Besides having an appeal all their own, they provide the spice of variety to a dance party. Many callers make a point of programming at least one circle dance during an evening.

The Big Circle

It's a good idea to begin a group's initial exposure to contra dancing by having them form a single circle of couples, all facing the center with hands joined. In each couple, the lady stands at the gentleman's right. If the room will not accommodate a single circle comfortably, two or more concentric circles may be formed. The instructions and calls will remain the same regardless of the number of circles.

There are many reasons for beginning with a circle:

- A circular formation, in which all positions are equal and each couple's movements identical, will give the group a feeling of solidarity. Individual dancers won't feel singled out.
- The joined hands of a circle give strong support to the individual. It's much easier to move in the right direction when one is physically connected to many other dancers, all going the same way.
- Because in a single circle there are no couple numbers or different roles to learn, a caller can get people moving to music in less time than with any other formation.
- A circle is ideal for teaching or demonstration from the floor. The leader can stand in the center or toward one side, or in smaller groups even join the circle, and still be visible to all.
- Circle dances are traditional in many regions of the continent and, as such, are part of our North American heritage. That they have stood the test of time speaks well of their constructive qualities.

- Any movement that is danced by two people can be taught in a big circle. This enables a new group to learn about half of the basic movements of contra dancing before having to deal with couple numbers or progression.
- The same length of routine employed in almost all contra dances (64 steps, about half a minute) can be used in a circle, getting the dancers accustomed to this common element.
- Most circles are mixers, changing partners for each round of the dance to avoid monotony. Dancing mixers will enable even the shyest members of a group to mingle with the crowd; it may also make it easier for some people to learn the basic moves, away from a constant partner who might be a source of embarrassment or encourage bad dancing habits.
- From a single circle, the group can be easily moved into a progressive circle formation and introduced to the concept of couple progression, a key element of the contra dance.

The Progressive Circle

The progressive circle (sometimes called a Sicilian circle from the name of a popular dance in this formation) is a hybrid between the big circle and the progressive longways that we know as the contra dance. In a progressive circle dance, the big circle is broken into smaller groups of facing dancers. Each group comprises either a couple, a trio, or a line of two couples facing a like number of people. One half of the group faces clockwise, the other counterclockwise. The couples or lines are arranged around the room like the spokes of a wheel; each half-group is back to back with half of another group.

The movements in a progressive circle are similar to those in a contra dance, and are done to tunes of the same length. In most such dances, the progression is accomplished during the last phrase of music, and is fairly straightforward: typically the couples or lines either pass through each other or promenade around each other and on to the next couple or line.

There are definite advantages to using the progressive circle in teaching contra dancing:

- In a progressive circle, the dancers can learn any of the movements that are done by two couples, without being distracted by the dancers in other groups.
- In this formation, dancers can be introduced to the concept of progression without having to remember couple numbers or to deal with neutral couples.

- As in a contra dance, partners remain together throughout but have the opportunity to dance with many different couples. This will put the dancers on familiar ground when they first try contras.

A point of caution in using progressive circles is that they work best if there are enough dancers for at least half a dozen groups. Otherwise, the curve that the dancers must follow to reach the next couple will be so sharp that they may fail to see it and become disoriented. If a large crowd is split into two concentric circles, the same caution applies to the smaller circle in the middle. With two or more circles, there is a real danger of couples passing through and going on to a new couple in the wrong circle.

In recent years there has been a revival of the four-face-four progressive dance (sometimes called "mescolanze"), which some people feel combines the best features of squares and contras. Such dances are now usually done up and down the hall, rather than in a circle; this makes better use of the floor space but requires neutral couples at the ends as in a contra. Note, though, that it is often possible for two waiting couples to dance all or part of the routine, modifying it on the fly.

Some basic routines in both big circle and progressive circle formations are given here. Many of the books listed in the Resources section contain circles, particularly the books by Amidon, Barclay, Davis, Jennings, and Rose.

Circassian Circle

(author and date unknown)

This dance, in one form or another, has probably been around for a century or two. There is no single "right" way to call it; many versions exist, from different times and places. The circles in A.1 are sometimes replaced by "all forward and back" twice, although that makes for a lot of repetition in the first half of the routine. Traditionally a 16-beat swing occupies the entire B.1 music; the do-si-do has been added to make the dance useable with groups that have trouble swinging smoothly. (Many if not most beginning dancers fall into that category, and this dance is otherwise ideal for them.)

Another version, which I find myself using frequently, keeps A.1 as given below and changes A.2 to "all forward and back" twice.

You may want to let people dance with their original partners the first time through the sequence. It can be frustrating to ask someone to dance and be separated right away by the caller. Groups that might be confused by the change in the routine, such as very young children, are probably not ready for mixers in the first place. (A few preschoolers at a family dance shouldn't keep you from using mixers, but the older folks in the circle will have to share the responsibility of steering them in the right direction.)

Some callers use this dance as a framework for improvisation, calling at least the "A" parts differently each time. At one-night stands I often improvise the opening big circle completely, but when I use a circle mixer I prefer to stick with the same sequence throughout.

Circassian Circle
(The Dance Movements)

Big circle dance

A.1	All circle left	8 beats
	All circle right	8 beats
A.2	Ladies forward and back	8 beats
	Gents forward, turn to the left, and come out	8 beats
B.1	Do-si-do corner	8 beats
	Swing corner	8 beats
B.2	Promenade corner, who becomes new partner	16 beats

Circassian Circle
(The Calls)

Beats:	1	2	3	4	5	6	7	8
Intro:	—	—	—	—	All join	hands and	circle	left
A.1:	—	—	—	—	—	— Now	circle	right
A.2:	—	—	—	—	Ladies	all go	forward and	back
	—	—	—	—	Gents	all go	forward,	now!
B.1:	—	— But	turn to your left,	—	Out to the	corner,	do-si-	do
	—	—	—	—	Swing that	corner	high and	low
B.2:	—	—	—	— And	prome-	nade, a-	round you	go
	—	—	Face the	middle,	All join	hands and	circle	left

Ted's Mixer

(Ted Sannella, 1979)

This is an enjoyable mixer, and an excellent way to present the basic movements: it contains all the commonly used moves that are done by two people. The transition from the promenade to the balance is tricky, making the dance a little too tough for a first exposure to country dancing. Even with experienced dancers, this transition must be taught carefully, perhaps with a demonstration. You may want to have the dancers identify their corners while still in the single circle, as they must find corners quickly during the dance.

The double balance in B.2 is Ted's original version. Many of today's dancers prefer a single (4-beat) balance and a 12-beat swing, which is fun to dance but tricky to call. Both versions are shown in the call chart on the facing page.

Ted's Mixer
(The Dance Movements)

Big circle dance

A.1	All forward and back	8 beats
	Forward again; ladies come back as gents "fold" to the right to face partner	8 beats
A.2	Turn partner by right hand, once and a half	8 beats
	Do-si-do partner	8 beats
B.1	Turn partner by left hand, once and a half (retain left-hand hold)	8 beats
	Promenade partner (after promenade, retain left-hand hold; ladies move forward slightly and face center while gents drop back and face wall; all join right hands with corner)	8 beats
B.2	Double balance in a ring (ladies facing in, gents out)	8 beats
	Swing the one on the right (end facing center)	8 beats

Ted's Mixer
(The Calls)

Beats:	1	2	3	4	5	6	7	8
Intro:	—	—	—	—	All join	hands, go	forward and	back
A.1:	—	—	Gents to the	right,	—	— Go	forward a-	gain
A.2:	—	—	—	—	Face your	partner,	right hand	do-si-
	—	—	—	—	Round your	partner,	do-si-	do
B.1:	—	—	—	— Hold	Turn your	partner,	left hand	round
	—	—	Ladies turn	in,	on with the	left and	prome-	nade
B.2:	—	—	Balance a-	gain	Gents reach	back and	balance,	now!
	—	—	Face the	middle,	—	— Now	swing on the	right
	—	—	—	—	All join	hands, go	forward and	back

Alternate version with longer swing:

| B.2: | — | — | Swing on the | right, new | partner | swing if it | takes all | night |
| | — | — | Face the | middle, | All join | hands, go | forward and | back |

Sanita Hill Circle

(Ed Durlacher, 1949 or earlier)

This is as easy as a progressive circle can get. I routinely use this with complete beginners, right after the initial big circle. For years I thought I'd invented the sequence, but it's in Ed Durlacher's monumental book *Honor Your Partner* (1949) and also appears on two recordings that Ed made at around that time. Many similar glossary sequences have been written and improvised; I find this one particularly satisfying.

The only trouble spot in this dance is the ending. In a crowded hall, the forward and back will be uncomfortable and a pass through from one subset to the next will take only about four steps. Making two circles of couples, one inside the other, will alleviate the crowding; but the inner circle must have enough subsets that the dancers can easily see where they are going next. Chip Hendrickson used to replace the pass through with "zig and zag" (couples move diagonally right four steps, then diagonally left four steps). This uses up the music; Chip also felt it was less confusing for new dancers than a pass through, as it allows partners to stay connected.

If you prefer, you can replace the term "opposite" with "neighbor." This makes particular sense if you plan to introduce your group to longways contras, as it points up the fact that this dance is a true contra in most respects.

Sanita Hill Circle
(The Dance Movements)

Progressive circle dance

A.1	Circle left	8 beats
	Circle right	8 beats
A.2	Do-si-do opposite	8 beats
	Do-si-do partner	8 beats
B.1	Right-hand star	8 beats
	Left-hand star	8 beats
B.2	Forward and back	8 beats
	Pass through to the next couple	8 beats

Sanita Hill Circle
(The Calls)

Beats:	1	2	3	4	5	6	7	8
Intro:	—	—	—	—	Join	hands,	circle	left
A.1:	—	—	—	—	—	— And	circle	right
A.2:	—	—	—	—	With your	opposite,	do-si-	do
	—	—	—	—	With your	partner,	do-si-	do
B.1:	—	—	—	—	Right hands	in,	right hand	star
	—	—	—	—	Change	hands,	left hand	back
	—	—	—	—Take your	partner's	hand, go	forward and	back
B.2:	—	—	—	—	Forward a-	gain and	pass	through
	—	—	—	next,	Join	hands,	circle	left
	—	—	On to the					

Sicilian Circle

(author unknown, before 1858)

This is the quintessential progressive circle; many callers use its name as a generic term for any dance in this formation. Several versions under various names appear in Elias Howe's *Complete Ball-room Hand Book* (1858); the dance is probably older than that book.

Portland Fancy is a similar dance, done by a line of two couples facing another such line. In one version the routine is identical to *Sicilian Circle* except that the circle left in A.1 usually goes all the way around and the circle to the right is omitted. There are other, more distinctive versions of *Portland Fancy*, involving "chassez" or sliding steps (which are rare in modern contra dancing). Both *Sicilian Circle* and *Portland Fancy* were used as "gathering dances" at nineteenth-century balls, either following the initial grand march or just after intermission.

The same caution as in *Sanita Hill Circle* applies to the figures in B.2.

Sicilian Circle
(The Dance Movements)

Progressive circle dance

A.1	Circle left	8 beats
	Circle right	8 beats
A.2	Right and left (over and back)	16 beats
B.1	Ladies chain (over and back)	16 beats
B.2	Forward and back	8 beats
	Pass through to the next couple	8 beats

Sicilian Circle
(The Calls)

	1	2	3	4	5	6	7	8
Beats:								
Intro:	—	—	—	—	Join	hands,	circle	left
A.1:	—	—	—	—	—	— And	circle	right
	—	—	—	With the	opposite	couple,	right and	left
A.2:	—	—	—	—	Turn as a	couple and	right and left	back
	—	—	—	—	Same two	couples,	ladies	chain
B.1:	—	—	—	—	—	—	Chain	back
	—	—	—	—	Toward that	couple, go	forward and	back
B.2:	—	—	—	—	Forward a-	gain and	pass	through
	—	—	On to the	next,	Join	hands,	circle	left

15
Whole-Set Dances

A category of country dance often overlooked by callers is the whole-set longways. Whole sets use the basic formation of the contra dance – two long lines of facing partners – but not the distinctive contra progression, in which every other couple leads the figure. Instead, as the name implies, the entire set works together, with only one couple leading. Typically the active couple begins at the top and moves to the bottom at the end of their round.

This progression is simpler, and is much more easily grasped by new dancers, than that of the true contra. Because of this simplicity, whole sets are a boon to teachers looking for material suitable for children, families, and people with disabilities. Callers specializing in one-night stands will also find whole sets invaluable.

Traditionally, couples line up for a whole set as they would for a proper contra dance, with the lady to the gent's right as the couple faces the head of the hall. In many whole-set dances, however, the lady's and gent's parts are identical, making it possible to use these routines without adaptation even if some or all of the dancers have partners of the same sex. This is true of all three dances given here, although the *Virginia Reel* will take a bit of modification or some deft teaching and calling to use in this fashion.

Some whole sets, like *Rural Felicity* and *Galopede,* are appropriate for almost any number of couples; the only restriction is that the top couple must be able to reach the foot in the allotted time. Dances that include a "strip the willow" figure, like the *Virginia Reel,* are best done with short sets – no more than about six couples. This is because the "reel" takes much more time to complete in a longer set, and that fact, combined with the greater number of couples who must all have their turn at the top, makes the dance interminable.

Additional dances of this type can be found in the books by Amidon, Barclay, Davis, Laufman, and Rose listed in the Resources section.

Rural Felicity

(author unknown, before 1858; adapted by Dudley Laufman)

This dance appears in somewhat different form in Elias Howe's *Complete Ball-room Hand Book* (1858) and Rickey Holden's *Contra Dance Book* (1956). It was simplified by Dudley Laufman, who sparked a contra dance revival among the "baby boom" generation in the 1960s (see Chapter 2). At that time he concentrated on classic contras like *Chorus Jig* and *Petronella,* but he has since shifted his primary focus to easy dances that schoolchildren and families can readily learn and enjoy.

This dance lends itself to adaptation to the needs of different groups. For example, if the dancers have trouble swinging comfortably, B.1 may be changed to "all do-si-do and swing partner." Similar dances can be improvised on the spot.

Rural Felicity
(The Dance Movements)

Longways dance, whole-set type (top couple active)

A.1	All forward and back	8 beats
	Top couple slide down to foot	8 beats
A.2	All forward and back	8 beats
	Same couple slide up to place	8 beats
B.1	All swing partners	16 beats
B.2	All but top couple form arches	
	Top couple down through the arches	8 beats
	All clap hands twice, move up one place	8 beats

Note: This dance is traditionally done to the tune of the same name, also known as Haste to the Wedding, which appears in *Fiddler's Fakebook,* p. 131, and *New England Fiddler's Repertoire,* no. 30, and is recorded on *The Hammered Dulcimer* (Front Hall FHR-302). The tune has two accented notes at the beginning of the last 8-beat phrase (halfway through the "B" part). The hand claps in B.2 should fall on those two beats.

Rural Felicity
(The Calls)

Beats:	1	2	3	4	5	6	7	8
Intro:	—	—	—	—	All join	hands, go	forward and	back
A.1:	—	—	—	—	Top	couple	slide	down
	—	—	—	—	All join	hands, go	forward and	back
A.2:	—	—	—	—	Same	couple	slide	back
	—	—	—	—	Every-	body	swing your	own
B.1:	—	—	—	— The	others	arch and	top couple	through
	—	—	—	—	Every-	body	clap your	hands with a
B.2:	One,	two,	move up	one,	All join	hands, go	forward and	back

Galopede

(author and date unknown)

This dance, well known in England, makes a good introduction to the longways formation. A beginning group will be challenged by A.1 and A.2, where the idea is to keep the lines straight as they advance, retire, and pass through each other. If you think your group will respond better to a more "connected" dance, you can change the first pass through to "cross by the right hand" and the second to "cross by the left hand." Another version, in place of the pass through, has the dancers facing a given direction join hands and make arches as they cross while their partners duck under. The arches will be made first by the gents and then by the ladies (or vice versa). For a gender-free version, announce that the line facing the clock (or other obvious landmark) will always make the arches.

The long swing in B.1 may be changed to a do-si-do and swing, or to a pair of hand or elbow turns with partner, first by the right and then by the left.

Galopede
(The Dance Movements)

Longways dance, whole-set type (top couple active)

A.1	All forward and back	8 beats
	Pass through, turn alone	8 beats
A.2	All forward and back	8 beats
	Pass through to original place, turn alone	8 beats
B.1	All swing partners	16 beats
B.2	Top couple down center to foot, others clap	16 beats
	(three quick claps and a pause, to end of phrase)	

Note: This dance is traditionally done to the tune of the same name, which appears in *Chimes of Dunkirk,* p. 14, *Fiddler's Fakebook,* p. 115, and *New England Fiddler's Repertoire,* no. 68, and is recorded on the *Chimes of Dunkirk* CD.

Galopede
(The Calls)

Beats:	1	2	3	4	5	6	7	8
Intro:	—	—	—	—	All join	hands, go	forward and	back
A.1:	—	—	Turn a-	—	Forward a-	gain and	pass	through
A.2:	—	—	round a-	lone,	Join	hands,	forward and	back
B.1:	Back to	place and	turn a-	lone,	Forward a-	gain and	pass	through
B.2:	—	—	—	—	Every-	body	swing your	own
	One, two,	three and a	one, two,	— First	couple	down and the	others	clap with a
	—	—	—	three	—	—	—	—
	—	—	one, two,	—	All join	hands, go	forward and	back

Virginia Reel

(author and date unknown)

Every caller should know how to teach and call the *Virginia Reel*. People request it more often than any other group dance – contra, square, or circle.

The key figure of the dance is known in the British Isles as "strip the willow" and is often called "the reel" by Americans. It consists of a series of hand turns or elbow swings, depending on local custom or the skill of the group (elbow swings are easier). The top couple alternates between turning partner (by the right) and the dancers in the opposite line (by the left). The amount of music required for the reel, and therefore for each round of the dance, depends on the number of couples in the set (as noted at the beginning of this chapter, short sets are advisable in any dance containing this figure).

This is one of many versions. A few other variants are given in Don Armstrong's book (see the Resources section). If you use the version given here, emphasize that only the active couple makes an arch.

If there are many same-sex couples, it may be less confusing to let the top couple turn the dancers in their own line rather than the opposite line. Many people have a tendency to do this anyway.

Note: It won't work out this perfectly every time. Over the years, I've developed a version that comes out even with the music more often than not (the older versions generally had more movements before the top couple started their turn). You can add or subtract parts of the dance to fit a different number of couples or otherwise suit your crowd; with young children you can even leave out the reel. Don't be too concerned, though, if you find yourself starting a new round in the middle of the tune. Since you'll undoubtedly be calling all the way through, the dancers won't need to rely on the music to tell them when a new part begins. Many whole-set dances are traditionally done without much regard for musical phrasing, although it's always more satisfying if you can stay with the phrase.

In some places it is, or was, traditional for the band to play different tunes for the three parts of this dance – typically a jig, a reel, and a march. (In such areas the first part includes a great number of preliminary movements, often danced by the top gent and the foot lady, then the other two "corners.") The practice requires split-second timing and close communication between caller and band.

Virginia Reel
(The Dance Movements)

Longways dance, whole-set type (top couple active)

Four to six couples (six assumed here)

A.1	All forward and back	8 beats
	Turn partner by the right hand (or elbow)	8 beats
A.2	Turn partner by the left hand (or elbow)	8 beats
	Do-si-do partner	8 beats
B.1	Top couple slide down the center (both hands joined)	8 beats
	Slide back to place	8 beats
B.2	Top couple turn partner by the right, once and a half	8 beats
	Turn #2 person in opposite line by the left once	4 beats
	Turn partner by the right in center once	4 beats
A.1	Turn #3 person in opposite line by the left once	4 beats
	Turn partner by the right in center once	4 beats
	Turn #4 person in opposite line by the left once	4 beats
	Turn partner by the right in center once	4 beats
A.2	Turn #5 person in opposite line by the left once	4 beats
	Turn partner by the right in center once	4 beats
	Turn #6 person in opposite line by the left once	4 beats
	Turn partner by the right in center halfway around (to original side of the set)	4 beats
B.1	Top couple slide back to original place	8 beats
	All face up the hall and march (top couple turn away from partner and go down the outside of their own line; the others "follow the leader")	8 beats
B.2	Top couple meet partner at foot and make an arch; others go past the arch, meet partners and come up through the arch to places	16 beats

(The calls appear on the next two pages.)

Virginia Reel
(The Calls)

Beats:	1	2	3	4	5	6	7	8
Intro:	—	—	—	—	All join	hands, go	forward and	back
A.1:	—	—	—	— Go	forward a-	gain with a	right hand	round
A.2:	—	—	—	— Now	forward a-	gain with a	left hand	round
	—	—	—	— And	forward a-	gain with a	do-si-	do
B.1:	—	—	—	— The	first	couple	slide	down
	—	—	—	—	—	— And	come on	back
B.2:	Once	and a	half a-	round, to the	partner	right with a	right hand	round
	—	— Your	partner	right,	opposite	side with a	left hand	round
	—	—	—	— The	—	— The	next one	left

Chapter 15: Whole-Set Dances

A.1:	—	— Your	partner	right,	—	— The	next one	left
	—	— Your	partner	right,	—	— The	next one	left
A.2:	Partner	— Your	partner	right,	—	— The	last one	leftyour
B.1:	—	right,	halfway	round and	slide	back to the	head of	town
	Some go	right and	some go	left,	Face	up,	everybody	march
B.2:	First couple	arch and the	rest come	through, a	All the way	down to the	bottom of the	set
	—	—	—	And	new couple	up to the	head you	do
	—	—	—	—	every-	body	forward and	back

16
Contra Dances

Once the group is comfortable with the concept of progression, which was introduced in circle form in Chapter 14, you can begin to teach contras in the standard longways formation. Seven are described in this chapter; two are proper, four are improper, and one can be danced either way.

After you and the group have mastered these dances, the world of contra dancing is yours to enjoy. There are thousands of contras available in books and magazines, on recordings, and on the Web. Not all of them are equally enjoyable – and certainly some are much more difficult than any of the material in this book – but a little judgment will produce a repertoire broad enough for many years of happy dancing.

A list of good dances not included in this book, and where they may be found, appears in the Resources section. Most of the books listed there include contras; the books by Armstrong, Gaudreau, Hinds, Hubert, Jennings, Johnson, Knox, Parkes, and Sannella are especially rich sources of material. The best source of the classic pre-revival contras is *Cracking Chestnuts* by Smukler and Millstone.

Jefferson's Reel

(Dudley Briggs, 1954; adapted by folk process)

This is a simplified version of an older contra dance entitled *Jefferson and Liberty*. It has become popular among callers who work with beginning dancers, for two primary reasons:

- It uses only two "code words" for movements, *circle* and *star* (plus the concept of movement *up* and *down* the hall); the rest of the dance is called in plain English.
- The form of progression, one couple ducking through another's arch, is easily understood and nearly foolproof.

Jefferson's Reel
(The Dance Movements)

Contra dance, duple improper (or proper)

A.1	Circle left	8 beats
	Circle right	8 beats
A.2	Right-hand star	8 beats
	Left-hand star	8 beats
B.1	Number ones separate, go down the outside	8 beats
	Turn alone and come back to place	8 beats
B.2	Ones to the center, go down four in line	4 beats
	Arch in the middle, ends come around	4 beats
	Duck through the arch and face the next	4 beats
	Join hands with them, come back to place	4 beats

(The choreographer had a "right and left" rather than the stars at A.2; but the stars, being easier for beginners, have become the most common version. They appear at A.2 in the original *Jefferson and Liberty*, which continues with "down the center, come back and cast off" at B.1 and "right and left" at B.2.)

Note that the lady's and gent's parts are identical. For this reason, the dance may be done either in proper lines (all the ladies on one side, gents on the other) or in improper lines (number one couples cross over before beginning). Many leaders prefer to have the ones cross over, on the theory that the difference between the ones' and twos' parts will be clearer. If you're working with a group consisting largely or entirely of one sex, it's less confusing to keep the lines proper.

Jefferson's Reel
(The Calls)

Beats:	1	2	3	4	5	6	7	8
Intro:	—	—	—	— With the	couple be-	low,	circle	left
A.1:	—	—	—	—	—	—	Circle	right
A.2:	—	—	—	— The	same	four,	right-hand	star
A.2:	—	—	—	—	Ones roll	— And a	left hand	back
B.1:	—	—	—	—	Turn a-	out, go	down out-	side
B.1:	—	—	—	— Come	into the	lone and the	same way	back
B.2:	—	—	Arch in the	middle,	Ends come a-	round, and	four in	line
B.2:	—	—	back to	place,	—	— And	duck on	through, join
	Hands with	them, come					circle	four

The Rose Tree

(author and date unknown)

This is a traditional English longways dance. Like American contras, it's descended from the "longways for as many as will" found in John Playford's books of the seventeenth and eighteenth centuries. Like *Jefferson's Reel,* it's a good choice for a group's first exposure to contra dancing in the longways formation. Unlike *Jefferson's,* though, it includes a swing – a long one – and the dancers must be comfortable with the swing in order to enjoy the sequence in its original form. You can modify the dance by inserting a "forward and back" at the beginning of B.2, shortening the swing to eight beats.

This dance requires more space than usual along the set, to allow everyone to swing comfortably at once. All the dancers must end the swing by backing away to their own side of the set in order to locate their new "first corner."

The Rose Tree
(The Dance Movements)

Contra dance, duple proper

A.1	First gent, second lady ("first corners") turn by the right hand (once around)	8 beats
	Same two turn by the left hand	8 beats
A.2	First lady, second gent ("second corners") turn by the right hand	8 beats
	Same two turn by the left hand	8 beats
B.1	First couple down the center; turn alone	8 beats
	Come back to place and cast off	8 beats
B.2	All swing partners	16 beats

Note: This dance is traditionally done to the tune of the same name, which appears in *Fiddler's Fakebook,* p. 235 (as Rose Tree I), and *New England Fiddler's Repertoire,* no. 67.

The Rose Tree
(The Calls)

Beats:	1	2	3	4	5	6	7	8
Intro:	—	—	—	—	—	—	—	—
A.1:	—	—	—	— First	gent, next	lady,	turn by the	right
	—	—	—	—	—	—	Back by the	left
A.2:	—	—	—	— First	lady, next	gent,	turn by the	right
	—	—	—	—	—	—	Back by the	left
B.1:	—	—	—	—	Ones	down the	center,	go!
	—	—	—	—	Turn a-	lone and	come on	back
B.2:	—	—	Cast	off,	Every-	body	swing your	own
	—	—	—	—	—	—	—	—
	—	—	—	— First	gent, next	lady,	turn by the	right

Orono Special

(Tony Parkes, 1974)

> This dance was written with a minimum of "code words"; the few that are used are ones the dancers should have learned in the big circle and progressive circle formations. This will enable the group to concentrate on understanding the contra setup and progression, without having to learn any new basic moves. ("Down the hall" and "turn as couples" are close enough to plain English that I don't consider them to be code words.)

Orono Special
(The Dance Movements)

Contra dance, duple improper

A.1	All forward and back	8 beats
	Ones do-si-do partner	8 beats
A.2	Do-si-do neighbor	8 beats
	Swing neighbor	8 beats
B.1	Down the hall go four in line	4 beats
	Turn as couples	4 beats
	Come back to place and ends close in	8 beats
B.2	Circle left	8 beats
	Circle right	8 beats

Orono Special
(The Calls)

Beats:	1	2	3	4	5	6	7	8
Intro:	—	—	—	—	All join	hands, go	forward and	back
A.1:	—	—	—	—	Ones in the	middle,	do-si-	do
A.2:	—	—	—	—	With your	neighbor	do-si-	do
A.2:	—	—	—	—	Down the	hall, go	Swing that	one
B.1:	—	—	—	As	couples,	turn and	four in	line
B.1:	—	—	—	—	Ends close	in and	come on	back
B.2:	—	—	—	—	—	—	circle	left
B.2:	—	—	—	—	—	—	Circle	right
B.2:	—	—	Back a-	way,	all join	hands, go	forward and	back

Essex Reel

(Tony Parkes, 1985)

> This is one of several contras based on an old dance entitled *The Good Girl*. It was written specifically to be easy to learn and remember, with no surprises. Nearly all the moves take 8 beats to dance, and the moves within each musical phrase complement each other.

Essex Reel
(The Dance Movements)

Contra dance, duple improper

A.1	Do-si-do neighbor	8 beats
	Swing neighbor	8 beats
A.2	Down the hall go four in line	4 beats
	Turn as couples	4 beats
	Come back to place and ends close in	8 beats
B.1	Circle left	8 beats
	Circle right	8 beats
B.2	Right-hand star	8 beats
	Left-hand star	8 beats

Essex Reel
(The Calls)

Beats:	1	2	3	4	5	6	7	8
Intro:	—	—	—	—	With your	neighbor	do-si-	do
A.1:	—	—	—	—	—	—	Swing that	one
A.2:	—	—	—	As	Down the	hall, go	four in	line
	—	—	—	—	couples,	turn and	come on	back
B.1:	—	—	—	—	Ends close	in and	circle	left
	—	—	—	—	Same	four,	Circle	right
B.2:	—	—	—	—	Change	hands,	right-hand	star
	—	—	Leave the	star,	on to the	next and	left hand	back
	—	—	—	—	—	—	do-si-	do

Newbury Reel

(Tony Parkes, 1980)

This dance is identical to *Orono Special* except that the circle four at B.2 is replaced by a ladies chain. It can serve as an introduction to the ladies chain in what will be a familiar context. Even if the dancers have encountered the ladies chain in squares or progressive circles, this will be their first experience with it in a contra, where they begin and end with neighbors and only get partners momentarily.

The call "break in the middle" should be self-explanatory, and "bend the line" nearly so. The pair of dancers at each end of the line simply pivots to face the other pair, with the end person moving forward and the center person backward. As they finish bending, the pair will probably need to adjust the size of the set by moving slightly backward in order to make room for a comfortable ladies chain.

Newbury Reel
(The Dance Movements)

Contra dance, duple improper

A.1	All forward and back	8 beats
	Ones do-si-do partner	8 beats
A.2	Do-si-do neighbor	8 beats
	Swing neighbor	8 beats
B.1	Down the hall go four in line	4 beats
	Turn as couples	4 beats
	Come back to place, break in the middle and bend the line	8 beats
B.2	Ladies chain	8 beats
	Chain back	8 beats

Newbury Reel
(The Calls)

Beats:	1	2	3	4	5	6	7	8
Intro:	—	—	—	—	All join	hands, go	forward and	back
A.1:	—	—	—	—	Ones in the	middle,	do-si-	do
A.2:	—	—	—	—	With your	neighbor	do-si-	do
	—	—	—	—	—	—	Swing that	one
B.1:	—	—	—	—	Down the	hall, go	four in	line
	—	—	—	As	couples,	turn and	come on	back
B.2:	—	—	Break in the	middle,	Bend the	line and the	ladies	chain
	—	—	—	—	—	—	Chain right	back
	—	—	Lady on the	right,	All join	hands, go	forward and	back

Flirtation Reel

(Tony Parkes, 1985)

This dance provides an easy context for introducing the hey and the gypsy. The pattern of this hey is particularly easy to remember, as the loops are to the right (the way most people instinctively turn) and all the passes are by the right shoulder except the one in the middle, which is always done with one's partner. You can make a joke of this, pointing out that in this dance's hey, "it's always right when you're not with your partner."

While the "turn alone" can be done in either direction, I encourage dancers to turn toward their neighbors so that "everyone gets a smile and no one gets a cold shoulder."

The sequence is forgiving: dancers who have trouble finishing the hey in 16 beats can extend it into the next phrase, shortening the gypsy, as they can begin the swing on time no matter where they are in the gypsy. Even if they extend the gypsy into the time allotted for the swing, they can still recover, since the timing of a swing is also flexible.

The beginning and end of the routine are taken from Ted Sannella's fine dance *Scout House Reel*.

Flirtation Reel
(The Dance Movements)

Contra dance, duple improper

(Ones between the twos, all facing down)

A.1	Down the hall go four in line	8 beats
	Turn alone and the same way back	8 beats
	(end by facing neighbor)	
A.2	Hey for four	16 beats
	(begin by passing right shoulders with neighbor)	
B.1	Gypsy with neighbor	8 beats
	Swing neighbor (end by facing across)	8 beats
B.2	All forward and back	8 beats
	Ones swing partner in the center	8 beats
	(end by facing down, ready to take the next couple down four in line)	

Flirtation Reel
(The Calls)

Beats:	1	2	3	4	5	6	7	8
Intro:	—	—	—	—	Down the	hall, go	four in	line
A.1:	—	—	—	—	Turn a-	lone and the	same way	back
A.2:	—	—	—	—	Face your	neighbor,	hey for	four
	—	—	—	—	—	—	—	—
B.1:	—	—	Face a-	cross,	Gypsy	round your	neighbor,	go!
	—	—	—	—	—	— Now	swing 'em,	too
B.2:	—	—	Face	down,	All join	hands, go	forward and	back
	—	—	—	—	Ones	swing in the	middle of the	ring
	—	—	—	—	Take the	next, go	four in	line

Chorus Jig

(author unknown, 1795 or earlier)

This is one of the very oldest contras that are still done regularly; it appears in three manuscripts, all dated 1795 (see p. 230). It's one of a handful of classic contras, sometimes termed "chestnuts," that are traditionally danced to a specific tune which is used for no other dance. The tune was originally in 6/8 time, which explains the "Jig" in its name, but at some point it got squeezed into 2/4 time.

Chorus Jig was chosen to represent the "chestnuts" in this book because it introduces "turn contra corners," a call that every contra dancer ought to know. Some leaders prefer the triple minor dance *Sackett's Harbor* for this purpose; in it the groups of three couples are isolated from each other, making things less confusing for the inactives. But the timing of "contra corners" in *Sackett's Harbor* is very tight: because the actives must return to where they began, 16 beats of music are hardly enough. And most people, given a little patience, can deal with the overlapping of subsets in *Chorus Jig*. They'll need to deal with it soon enough if they go out into the contemporary contra dance world. (The dance was originally a triple minor, and the subsets didn't overlap at all.)

Note that "down the center, come back and cast off," a common sequence in older contras, presents a timing problem (see the section on "cast off" in Chapter 13).

Chorus Jig
(The Dance Movements)

Contra dance, duple proper

A.1	Ones down the outside; turn alone	8 beats
	The same way back; meet partner in the center	8 beats
A.2	Ones down the center and turn alone	8 beats
	The same way back and cast off	8 beats
B.1	Turn contra corners	16 beats
B.2	Ones balance partner in the center	4 beats
	Ones swing partner (end by facing up)	12 beats

Note: This dance is traditionally done to the tune of the same name, which appears in *Fiddler's Fakebook,* p. 68, and *New England Fiddler's Repertoire,* no. 96, and is recorded on *New England Chestnuts.*

Chorus Jig
(The Calls)

Beats:	1	2	3	4	5	6	7	8
Intro:	—	—	—	—	Ones,	— go	down out-	side
A.1:	—	—	—	—	Turn a-	lone and the	same way	back
	—	—	—	—	Ones	down the	center,	go!
A.2:	—	—	—	—	Turn a-	lone and	come on	back
	—	—	Cast	off,	Turn	contra	corners,	go!
B.1:	Partner	right and the	corner	left,	—	— Your	partner	right and the
	Other one	left	—	—	Ones	balance	partner,	now!
B.2:	—	— And	swing 'em	too,	You swing	me and	I'll swing	you
	—	—	Face	up,	Lady on the	right, go	down out-	side

Note on sources: *Chorus Jig* appears in at least fifteen early manuscripts, three of them definitely or probably dating to 1795, according to the "Dance Figures Index: American Country Dances, 1710–1830" on a website maintained by the Colonial Music Institute (**www.danceandmusicindexes.org**). The manuscripts are:

Lucy Muzzey's commonplace book, Plainfield, Vermont

Another commonplace book, conjectured to be from New Hampshire

A third commonplace book, no location given

Commonplace books were a kind of personal notebook into which the owners copied anything they wanted to save, from quotations to recipes. That so many book owners chose to write down dance descriptions is a great boon to historians in our field.

17
Yes, We Do Squares Too

Many people are surprised to learn that squares are part of the style of dancing described in this book. The term "square dancing" has come to be associated with the western United States to such an extent that people in other parts of North America have all but forgotten that they ever had a square dance tradition.

Since about 1970, New Englanders have come to refer to their style as "contra dancing," partly to distinguish it from Western square dancing (both old-time and modern) and partly because contras are indeed currently more popular in the region than squares. But square dances are an important part of the New England tradition; during much of the twentieth century they were actually the dominant dance form.

Some New England squares are derived from the quadrille, a formal five-part square that was popular in the nineteenth century. A few older New England callers use the name "quadrille" for their squares, and many modern square dance callers refer to any phrased and prompted square as a quadrille. However, most present-day traditional callers use the term "squares" for all dances in this formation, regardless of style.

Although squares are generally easier for new dancers to understand than contras, they are more of a challenge to call. A contra dance is made up of ten or twenty identical "rounds," or repetitions of the same sequence. But a square has at least two types of sequence, the figure and the break. In addition, the caller must change the wording of the figure slightly during some of its repetitions, and most callers prefer to use a different break at the start of a square than at the end.

However, calling squares is not as hard as it may appear to be. A caller who understands contra dances and has called them successfully can usually learn the additional skills needed to call New England squares in a fairly short time.

There are other regional square dance traditions, of course. In many of them – perhaps most – the bond between dance movement and musical phrase is weaker than in New England style. Some callers may find this disorienting, while others will find it a relief.

Some Basic Principles

A square set comprises four couples, one on each side of a hollow square. The set should be small enough that the dancers can comfortably take hands in a circle without leaving their home positions; for adults this will be about eight feet across. Each couple has its back to a different wall of the room. The lady stands on the right side of each couple, the gentleman on the left. Adjacent dancers from different couples are corners: your corner is the person on the other side of you from your partner.

In a square, each dancer has a home position, to which he or she must return at the end of the dance. (This is one of the strongest points in favor of the argument that squares are easier than contras for new dancers: having a home place gives a feeling of security.) Many squares include a temporary change of partners, but original partners are always reunited in the end.

Positions are numbered as follows: The first couple has its back to the music, or to a designated "head of the hall" if the music is not clearly at one end of the room. The second couple is to the right of the first. The third couple faces the first, and the fourth couple is to the left of the first. The first and third couples, who face each other across the set, are often referred to as the head couples or heads. The second and fourth couples, who also face each other, are the side couples or sides. (When working with young children or foreign students who may have trouble understanding ordinal numbers, it's often better to refer to "couple one" than "the first couple.")

Almost every square dance has two types of segment: figures and breaks. They are described separately below.

The Figure

The figure is the main course of a square dance. It's what the dance is about; it's what makes this dance different from any other. If the dance is *Bird in the Cage,* the figure is where the "bird in the cage" part actually happens. It's even possible to call a whole square dance without any breaks, although few callers do.

The figure is almost always called four times. A figure can be led by one couple, in which case it's called once for each couple. Or it can be started by two facing couples, in which case it's called twice for the heads and twice for the sides. A third type of figure is begun by all four ladies, gents, or couples, and can be called four times using the same wording. This kind of dance is known as a "breakdown" and is traditionally the last in a set of squares.

If there is a change of partners during a square, it always happens in the figure. Typically, corners swing and promenade to either the gent's or the lady's place. Most partner-changing figures begin with either the heads or all four couples active. Very few figures combine a one-couple lead with a partner change. Such a figure must be called twice for each couple, for a total of eight times, to give everyone a chance to be active. If it were called only once for each couple (assuming a corner promenade to the gent's place), the original first lady would remain active all the way around the set, and no other lady would get to lead the figure!

Normally, only the figure of a square needs to be walked through. The breaks are almost always easier than the figure, and the dancers don't need – or want – to know them in advance. The walkthrough of a square is similar to that of a contra, with one exception: More often than not, a square figure ends with a promenade, usually preceded by a swing. Once your dancers have mastered the transition from a swing to a promenade, it's safe to omit the promenade from the walkthrough. The dancers will do the promenade without any trouble because a square is called throughout, unlike a contra, where the dancers must rely partly on body memory to get them through the sequence.

The principles of contra calling apply to square figures as well. The only new factor is the slight changes of wording as different couples lead the figure. For example, if a figure as written for the heads includes the call "Face the sides and circle four," you must remember during the second half of the dance not only to say "sides" instead of "heads," but to call "face the heads" instead of "face the sides." Fortunately, this is easier to do when you're watching real dancers than when you're practicing at home!

The Break

The break is the icing on the square dance cake, the tinsel on the tree. It can serve as a confidence builder, a change of pace, or a test of the dancers' wits. And it's the part of calling squares that gives contra callers the cold shakes!

This consternation stems from the fact that square dance breaks are traditionally not memorized, but ad-libbed by the caller. Callers are often known by the style of their breaks, and dancers will travel miles for the chance to hear an inventive caller.

The rules for using breaks are simpler than it might appear. A break is a series of calls which (with rare exceptions) are directed to all the dancers at once. There is almost always a break at the beginning of a square dance and one at the end, and more often than not there is one at the midpoint – after the second calling of the figure.

The one universal feature of breaks is that they never result in a permanent partner change. Almost as constant is the idea that the break of a dance should be less complex than the figure. This is not a hard and fast rule: a caller using a simple figure with an experienced group may make an intricate break the focus of that dance. Alas, some callers become infatuated with trickiness and begin calling breaks for their own amazement. In extreme cases, the dance ends up being more icing than cake.

The best way to approach breaks is to be systematic. If you're just starting to work with squares, learn a handful of breaks, probably not more than half a dozen at the outset. The introduction is usually simpler than the midpoint and closing breaks, and the same introduction may be used with many different dances. Other breaks can be used interchangeably; each one can serve as both the middle break and the closing break in a given dance.

The choreography of the breaks in a square should contrast with the figure, or at the least should not remind dancers of it. If the figure contains a number of stars and hand turns, for example, the break should avoid stars entirely and keep hand turns to a minimum. If, on the other hand, the figure is made up entirely of calls like ladies chain and right and left through, then stars in the break would be a welcome change.

Note that breaks are traditionally not walked through – another reason for choosing simple ones!

Singing Squares

One aspect of squares that has endeared them to many people – including diehard contra dancers – is the practice of singing the calls to the melody of popular songs. The selections range from Stephen Foster to the latest hit tunes. Singing calls didn't become popular until the 1920s or 1930s, but they hark back to the nineteenth-century custom of dancing quadrilles (formal squares) to specially composed or arranged music. Quadrille tunes and singing calls, by contrast with the jigs and reels used for contras, provide welcome variety in an evening of dancing.

Chapter 17: Yes, We Do Squares Too

Calling a singing square is deceptively easy. It would appear that all you need to do is memorize the words and sing them as you would a popular song. Not so! You're not just an entertainer; you're still a teacher and facilitator, even though you're singing at the same time. You still need to emphasize the key words of the call, and be ready to break out of your preset routine if the dancers are having trouble. This makes calling a singing square *well* a tougher job than calling other material.

Another peculiarity of singing squares is that in most of them, the calls are not prompted, but are concurrent with the action. By the time the dancers hear the call, they must be starting the movement that the call directs them to do – at least, if they are to dance in phrase with the music. This is possible only if the dancers know what the call is before the caller delivers it. And indeed, where singing squares are traditional, that's the way they're done: everyone knows what's coming and can therefore dance to the phrase, even though the caller is not prompting. (It should be added that most singing squares that have stood the test of time are rather loose-timed, so that dancers unsure of the figures can lag a beat or two behind the call without appearing to be out of phrase. They simply do an eight-beat movement in six or seven beats, and end with the phrase, ready to repeat the same technique with the next call.)

One way you can make it easier on yourself is to use singing squares only with fairly experienced groups. Seasoned dancers, of course, are less likely than beginners to have trouble with any given routine; and they will adapt more readily to concurrent calls.

* * *

A few squares that should pose no great problems for contra callers are given here, along with some samples of typical breaks. For more good squares, see the books by Butenhof, Dalsemer, Edelman, Everett, Gunzenhauser, Kraus, Linnell, Parkes, Sannella, and Sweet in the Resources section. Dalsemer, Kraus, Lyman, and Sweet are good sources of singing calls; Hinds 1997 and Sannella 2005 have large collections of breaks.

Queen's Quadrille

(Jerry Helt, about 1955)

This is probably the best known of the easier New England style squares (even though it was written by a Cincinnati caller!). It mixes the dancers well, but is within the capability of almost any group. All the movements take either 8 or 16 beats, making the figure as easy to call as it is to dance.

Note that the "corner" in B.1 is not the original corner, because the ladies are across from their home places when the call to swing is given.

Queen's Quadrille
(The Dance Movements)

Square dance figure

A.1	Head couples right and left through	8 beats
	Same ladies chain	8 beats
A.2	Side couples right and left through	8 beats
	Same ladies chain	8 beats
B.1	All circle left halfway	8 beats
	Swing corner	8 beats
B.2	Promenade to gent's place	16 beats

SEQUENCE: Twice for heads, twice for sides

Note: The second time through the figure, the order of the calls remains the same, although I prefer to call "At the head" rather than "Head couples" whenever an original side lady or gent has moved to the head. The third and fourth times through, the word "head" wherever it occurs should be replaced by "side" and vice versa. This is what "Twice for heads, twice for sides" (at the bottom of the dance movements above) means to you, the caller.

Breaks should be added at the beginning and end of the dance, and a break may be inserted between the first two figures and the last two figures. The call lines at the beginning and end of the figure should be adapted as necessary.

Queen's Quadrille
(The Calls)

Beats:	1	2	3	4	5	6	7	8
Intro:	—	—	—	—	Head	couples	right and left	through
A.1:	—	—	—	—	Same	ladies	chain a-	cross
A.2:	—	—	—	—	Side	two do a	right and left	through
	—	—	—	—	Same two	ladies	chain you	do
B.1:	—	—	halfway	round,	All join	hands and	circle	left
	—	— Go	—	— And	Swing the	corner	up and	down
B.2:	—	—	—	—	prome-	nade a-	round the	town
	—	—	—	—	—	—	—	—
	—	—	—	—	At the	head, do a	right and left	through

Buffalo Quadrille

(Ed Gilmore, before 1955)

Here's another New England style square written by an out-of-area caller, in this case a Californian. It was a favorite of the late Duke Miller of New York State, who called it to the tune O'Donnell Abhu. It should be easily handled by most contra dancers, once they know that a "four ladies chain" involves a right-hand star in the center and that the ladies go to the same gent as in a "two ladies chain." To change partners smoothly, the gents should let go with both hands after the second chain, move a step or two into the center, and begin a left-face solo turn. As his corner lady starts to move to her right around the outside, each gent can take her hands in promenade position and fall into step with her.

This figure will be trickier to call than *Queen's Quadrille* because of the four-beat movements in A.2.

Buffalo Quadrille
(The Dance Movements)

Square dance figure

A.1	All circle right halfway	8 beats
	Circle left halfway	8 beats
A.2	All balance in place (hands still joined)	4 beats
	Couples wheel around to face out	4 beats
	All balance in place (facing out, hands joined)	4 beats
	Couples wheel around to face the center	4 beats
B.1	Four ladies chain across	8 beats
	Chain back	8 beats
B.2	Take the corner, promenade to gent's place	16 beats

SEQUENCE: Four times through

Note: This figure is called the same way all four times, as all the couples are equally active.

Breaks should be added at the beginning and end of the dance, and a break may be inserted between the first two figures and the last two figures. The call lines at the beginning and end of the figure should be adapted as necessary.

Buffalo Quadrille
(The Calls)

Beats:	1	2	3	4	5	6	7	8
Intro:	—	—	—	—	Join	hands,	circle	right
A.1:	—	—	—	—	To the	left, go the	other way	back
	—	—	—	—	Stop right	there and	balance,	now!
A.2:	—	—	Wheel a-	round,	Face	out and	balance a-	gain
	—	—	Wheel a-	round,	Four	ladies	chain a-	across
B.1:	—	—	Gents roll	back,	Take the	corner,	Chain	back
	—	—	—	—	—	—	prome-	nade
B.2:	—	—	—	—	Join	hands,	circle	right

Steamboat Lancers

(re-created by Rod Linnell and Abe Kanegson, 1952)

This dance was put together by two of the Northeast's most respected callers (one from Maine, one from New York City), who named it *Do-si-do Right*. The authors later discovered that they had nearly duplicated a nineteenth-century sequence – the *Steamboat Lancers,* Figure 4 (published in *Marsden's Quadrille Guide,* 1898, and possibly earlier). Like *Queen's Quadrille,* it's composed of 8- and 16-beat movements, making it easy to call.

Steamboat Lancers
(The Dance Movements)

Square dance figure

A.1	First couple promenade outside (all the way)	16 beats
A.2	Same couple do-si-do the right-hand couple (acting as individuals)	8 beats
	Right and left through with the opposite couple	8 beats
B.1	Do-si-do the new right-hand couple	8 beats
	Right and left home with the opposite couple	8 beats
B.2	Side ladies chain (over and back)	16 beats

SEQUENCE: Once for each couple (when a side couple is active, the head ladies chain during B.2)

Breaks should be added at the beginning and end of the dance, and a break may be inserted between the first two figures and the last two figures. The call lines at the beginning and end of the figure should be adapted as necessary.

Steamboat Lancers
(The Calls)

Beats:	1	2	3	4	5	6	7	8
Intro:	—	—	—	—	First	couple	prome-	nade
A.1:	—	—	—	—	All the	way a-	round the	ring
	—	—	—	With the	right-hand	couple you	do-si-	do
A.2:	—	—	—	With the	couple a-	cross, go	right and left	through
	—	—	—	New	right-hand	couple you	do-si-	do
B.1:	—	—	—	With the	couple a-	cross, go	right and left	through
	—	—	Now you're	home, the	side two	ladies	chain a-	lone
B.2:	—	—	—	—	—	—	Chain	back
	—	—	—	—	Second	couple	prome-	nade

Deer Park Lancers

(G.T. Sheldon, around 1895; adapted by Ralph Page and others)

This is one of my favorite New England style squares. It began as Figure 1 of a lancers attributed to Prof. G.T. Sheldon in at least two dance manuals.* According to the late Ed Moody, Ralph Page thought the figure would interest his dancers, and started calling it. Several other callers modified it until it reached the form given here. (The latest change was the do-si-do, which I added in the early 1970s. If your dancers are running late, you can omit the do-si-do.)

For the dip and dive, everyone holds inside (nearest) hand with partner. The side couples make an arch while the head couples duck through, and everyone moves forward around the set, alternately going over and under, until four passes have been made. Starting and ending positions are identical.

Deer Park Lancers
(The Dance Movements)

Square dance figure

A.1	Head couples promenade outside (all the way)	16 beats
A.2	Heads face the right-hand couple; two ladies chain (over and back)	16 beats
B.1	Sides arch, dip and dive (all the way)	16 beats
B.2	Do-si-do with the same couple (as individuals)	8 beats
	Swing partner to place	8 beats

SEQUENCE:
    Once as given above
    Once with heads promenading to the left (ladies chain
      may be replaced by right and left over and back)
    Twice with sides promenading as above (heads arch
      to begin the dip and dive)

Breaks should be added at the beginning and end of the dance, and a break may be inserted between the first two figures and the last two figures. The call lines at the beginning and end of the figure should be adapted as necessary.

---

*F.L. Clendenen, *Fashionable Quadrille Call Book*, 1895; E.H. Kopp, *The American Prompter*, 1896.

Deer Park Lancers
(The Calls)

Beats:	1	2	3	4	5	6	7	8
Intro:	—	—	—	—	Heads	prome-	nade out-	side
A.1:	—	—	—	—	All the	way a-	round the	ring
	—	—	—	— With the	right-hand	couple two	ladies	chain
A.2:	—	—	—	—	—	—	Chain	back
	—	—	—	Face that	couple,	—	—	—
B.1:	—	—	—	—	sides	arch,	dip and	dive
	—	—	—	— With the	couple you	meet, do a	do-si-	do
B.2:	—	—	—	—	Swing your	partner,	home you	go
	—	—	—	—	Heads	prome-	nade to the	left

A Few Sample Breaks

Following are a few examples of breaks that can be used with any of the squares in this chapter or with similar figures. The first is about as easy as possible, both to dance and to call. It's set up here as an introduction, but can be adapted for use as a middle break or ending; simply move the "circle left" to A.1, replacing the "honors," and add a "circle right" at A.2.

Sample Break No. 1
(The Dance Movements)

Square dance break

A.1	Wait for the first call	8 beats
	Honor partner and corner	8 beats
A.2	All circle left (all the way around)	16 beats
B.1	All forward and back	8 beats
	All swing partner	8 beats
B.2	Promenade partner (once around)	16 beats

Note: The "honors" in A.1 are a good way to begin calling a square, especially if there is no musical introduction.

The bracketed words on the last line are the first call of *Queen's Quadrille.* Substitute the first call of the figure you are calling.

Sample Break No. 1
(The Calls)

Beats:	1	2	3	4	5	6	7	8
Intro:	—	—	—	—	—	—	—	—
A.1:	Bow to your	corner	—	—	Bow to your	partner	—	—And
A.2:	—	—	—	—	All join	hands and	circle	left
B.1:	—	—	—	—	All the	way a-	round the	set
	—	—	—	—	Every-	body	forward and	back
B.2:	—	—	—	—And	Swing your	partner,	partner	swing
	—	—	—	—	prome-	nade, go	round the	ring
	—	—	—	—	—	—	—	—
	—	—	—	—	[Head	couples	right and left	through]

Sample Break No. 2
(The Dance Movements)

Square dance break

A.1	Circle left halfway	8 beats
	Circle right halfway	8 beats
A.2	Allemande left corner	8 beats
	Do-si-do partner	8 beats
B.1	Gents left-hand star	8 beats
	Swing partner	8 beats
B.2	Promenade partner (once around)	16 beats

Note: The bracketed words on the last line are the first call of *Queen's Quadrille*. Substitute the first call of the figure you are calling, or an appropriate ending call (see Breaks 3 and 4).

Sample Break No. 2
(The Calls)

Beats:	1	2	3	4	5	6	7	8
Intro:	—	—	—	—	Join	hands,	circle	left
A.1:	—	—	—	—	To the	right, go the	other way	back
A.2:	—	—	—	—	On the	corner,	allemande	left
	—	—	—	—	Do-si-	do your	partners	all
	—	—	—	— Four	gents	left	hand	star
B.1:	Once a-	round and	get back	home,	Swing your	partner,	swing your	own
	—	—	When you're	through,	Prome-	nade, go	two by	two
B.2:	—	—	—	—	—	—	—	—
	—	—	—	—	[Head	couples	right and left	through]

Sample Break No. 3
(The Dance Movements)

Square dance break

A.1	Circle left (all the way around)	16 beats
A.2	Do-si-do corner	8 beats
	Turn partner by the left hand, twice around	8 beats
B.1	Ladies right-hand star	8 beats
	Left-hand star	8 beats
B.2	Balance and swing partner	16 beats

Note: The bracketed words on the last line are a suggested ending call. If you use this break as an introduction or in the middle of a dance, substitute the first line of your figure (see Breaks 1 and 2).

Sample Break No. 3
(The Calls)

Beats:	1	2	3	4	5	6	7	8
Intro:	—	—	—	—	Join	hands,	circle	left
A.1:	—	—	—	—	All the	way a-	round the	set
	—	—	—	—	On the	corner	do-si-	do
A.2:	—	—	Come back	home,	Turn a	left hand	round your	own
	Twice a-	round but	not too	far,	Ladies	in with a	right-hand	star
B.1:	—	—	Get back	home, you	Change	hands, a	left hand	back
	—	—	—	—	balance	and you	swing your	own
B.2:	—	—	—	— [And	bow	to your	partners	all]

Sample Break No. 4
(The Dance Movements)

Square dance break

A.1	Circle left halfway	8 beats
	Circle right halfway	8 beats
A.2	Ladies forward and back	8 beats
	Gents right-hand star once around (pass partner)	8 beats
B.1	Allemande left corner	8 beats
	Swing partner	8 beats
B.2	Promenade partner (once around)	16 beats

Note: The bracketed words on the last line are a suggested ending call. If you use this break as an introduction or in the middle of a dance, substitute the first line of your figure (see Breaks 1 and 2).

Sample Break No. 4
(The Calls)

Beats:	1	2	3	4	5	6	7	8
Intro:	—	—	—	—	Join	hands,	circle	left
A.1:	—	—	—	—	To the	right, go the	other way	back
A.2:	—	—	—	—	Four	ladies	forward and	back
	—	—	—	—	Four	gents	right-hand	star
B.1:	Allemande	left and	Pass your	partner,	Look for the	corner,	allemande	left
	—	—	come back	home,	Swing your	partner,	swing your	own
B.2:	—	—	When you're	through,	Prome-	nade, go	two by	two
	—	—	—	—	—	—	—	—
	—	—	—	— [And	bow	to your	partners	all]

Glossary

This glossary includes most of the terms a contra dance caller is likely to encounter; not all of them are used in this book.

Many terms used in the definitions are themselves defined at their proper place. Cross-references are printed in bold type only if they are substituting for a definition, or if turning to them is likely to be more helpful than the reader may suspect. Browsing, and checking for possible cross-references, is strongly encouraged.

Entries marked with an asterisk (*) are treated more fully in Chapters 11 through 13. To save space, some important points made in those chapters are not mentioned here.

"A"	The first part of a square or contra dance tune, normally 16 beats (8 measures) in length.
A.1, A.2	The first and second playing of the "A" part of a tune.
AABB	The standard pattern of most tunes used for square and contra dancing.
Above	Toward the head of a contra line.
Across	Toward the opposite side of a contra line.
Active	A person or couple that initiates a figure. In a contra, normally every other couple or every third couple, starting with the top couple.
Alamo ring	A closed circle of dancers alternately facing in opposite directions, like a **wave** bent back on itself. The term dates from 1949, during the transition from traditional Western to modern square dancing, and is generally accepted by those New England style callers who use the formation.
Allemande	A commonly used call for a hand turn. "Allemande right" is equivalent to "Turn by the right hand" or "Right hand round."
Along	Toward the head or foot of a contra line.
Alternate	Sometimes used as a synonym for **improper**.

253

Arch	Two adjacent dancers join nearest hands and raise them to let other dancers go through. A few dances, mostly whole-set longways, call for the arching dancers to face each other and join both hands.
Around	In a progressive circle, toward the next subset (clockwise or counterclockwise); corresponds to **along** in a contra line.
Around your own	Partners meeting in a grand right and left do a right-hand turn halfway around to reverse direction.
"B"	The second part of a square or contra dance tune, normally 16 beats (8 measures) in length.
B.1, B.2	The first and second playing of the "B" part of a tune.
Balance*	Dance forward or to the (usually right) side for two beats, then return to place in two beats.
Balance four in line	The traditional call for a balance in a wave of four people (until recently the most common number by far).
Balance in a wave*	A balance done by any number of people alternately facing in opposite directions.
Ballroom hold	The customary position for swinging in New England style: gent's right arm around lady's back, lady's left arm resting on gent's right arm, lady's right hand holding gent's left hand (or those two hands pressing each other's arm near the elbow).
Barn dance	Has meant different things in various times and places, but the most common definition is probably an evening with a more or less rustic flavor that includes several types of dancing, typically the local form of square or other group dancing alternating with the currently popular style of freestyle couple dancing. Among present-day callers, the term is often used to mean an event at which the guests are not regular dancers and do not expect any particular form of square or contra dancing. See **One-night stand**.
Basic	A dance movement with a name to which dancers have been taught to respond.
Basket	A circle of dancers with arms interlaced, either in front or in back. Each dancer holds the hands of the next-but-one on both sides. Typically, dancers in a basket are

	expected to move to the left (clockwise), using the buzz step.
Beat	The fundamental unit of choreography. Movements are classified by the number of musical beats (downbeats) it takes to dance them. Normally, dancers will take one step on each beat.
Becket formation	A duple contra dance setup in which partners are adjacent on the same side and each couple faces another couple across the set.
Below	Toward the foot of a contra line.
Bend the line	The centermost dancers in a line release hands, and each half of the line pivots to face the other half.
Big circle	A circle of couples, all facing the center, each with the lady on the gent's right.
Bottom	The foot of a contra line or other longways set.
Box the gnat	Two facing dancers join right hands and exchange places, the lady going under the gent's arm. The term, common in modern square dancing, is often used loosely by traditional callers to mean any kind of twirl to swap.
Break	In a square, a sequence called between figures as a change of pace. Typically it is easier than the figure and involves the whole set; it never involves a partner change.
Breakdown	(1) A lively dance tune in 2/4 meter, similar to a reel but with less clearly defined phrasing. (2) A square dance figure in which all four couples are active, traditionally the third change in a set of squares.
Break to a line	From a circle, one active dancer releases a handhold and leads the others into a straight line. Commonly used in squares with the active gents breaking and forming two facing lines of four.
Bull-by-the-tail	A colloquial name for the **straight-arm hold.**
Buzz step	The usual footwork for a New England swing. On the downbeat, each dancer steps forward solidly on the right foot; on the upbeat or just after it, each dancer steps lightly on the left foot just behind the right foot.

California twirl	Two dancers, side by side, join near hands, raise them, and move into each other's place, the lady going under the gent's arm. They end side by side, facing in the opposite direction.
Call	As a noun, can mean an entire dance number, one line of a number, or a single basic.
Cast	To move away from one's partner in an arc, usually going around and behind an inactive dancer. The term, common in English dancing, is fairly rare in American contra dancing but used occasionally by callers familiar with English terminology.
Cast off*	To move around an inactive dancer to a new position below him or her. Often the active and inactive dancers will hold hands or put arms behind each other's backs or waists, and the inactive will turn in place as the active moves forward.
Center	(1) The area between the two lines of a contra set or inside a square. See **Down**. (2) The dancer or dancers in the middle of a line of three or four.
Chain	See **Gents chain, Ladies chain.**
Change	As a noun, can mean a single call line, one round of a contra dance, the figure of a square dance, or an entire square (figures and breaks) done as one of a set of two or three. Used in English dancing to mean one hand or shoulder pass in a hey or "rights and lefts."
Chassez	Same as **Slide**.
Chestnut	A dance, usually a contra, that has lasted a long time in the popular repertoire. Many chestnuts are traditionally danced to their own tune. Compare **Classic**.
Circle*	As a noun, three or more dancers with hands joined to form a closed ring. As a verb, to travel to the left or right in such a ring. Circles traditionally move to the left (clockwise) if not otherwise specified.
Circle contra	Another name for a **progressive circle**.
Circle to a line	Same as **Break to a line** except that the initial circle is included. More a choreographic term than an actual call.

Classic	A dance that has stood the test of time, or a more recent one thought to be an especially good example of its type. Compare **Chestnut.**
Club dancing	See **Modern square dancing.**
Community dance	(1) An event or a series of events at which the public is welcome but a majority of people attending know how to dance (as distinguished from a modern square dance club or a one-night stand). (2) Used by some callers to mean a one-night stand as distinguished from an ongoing dance series.
Concept	A variation on a basic that the dancers will be able to associate with that basic once they have learned it. Four ladies chain is a concept of ladies chain.
Contra	Colloquially, a contra dance. Sometimes used without "a" or "the," to mean contra dancing or contra dance music in general.
Contra corners	The two people flanking one's partner. See **First corners, Second corners, Turn contra corners.**
Contra dance	(1) A dance, done in a longways set, in which the set is divided into groups of two or three couples. In each group, one couple is active and progresses down the set; the others are inactive and progress up the set. (2) An evening of such dances, often mixed with other dance types (see **Contra dancing**).
Contra dancing	As commonly used today, the entire activity that involves dancing contras, circles, and traditional squares (especially New England style squares, but increasingly including other styles).
Contra formation	A longways set, divided into groups of two or three couples for a contra dance. See **Duple, Triple, Proper, Improper.**
Corner	In a square or big circle, the lady clockwise from a gent or the gent counterclockwise from a lady. "Corner" is used by some callers to mean "neighbor" in a contra; this usage is not recommended, as "corner" already has a specific meaning in the longways formation (see **Contra corners, First corners, Second corners**).
Country dancing	Can mean the activity that includes square and contra dancing; can also mean English group social dancing

	(traditional or historical) or country-and-western dancing.
Couple	(1) The two people who are dancing as partners at a given moment (see **Partner** for more discussion). (2) Any two dancers playing opposite sex roles who are working together, as in a neighbor promenade.
Courtesy turn	A left-face pivot done by two dancers in New England promenade position, usually to complete a ladies chain or right and left.
Cross over	(1) Of the active couples, to exchange places with partner (from proper to improper) before the music starts. (2) Of a neutral couple, to exchange places with partner (from proper to improper at the head, vice versa at the foot) in preparation for rejoining the action. (3) Occasionally used as a synonym for **pass through,** especially when done by two facing individuals.
Cross through	To cross paths with another active dancer as both dancers go between two inactives (as in the first part of a half figure eight).
Cross trail (through)	Facing couples pass through, then the dancers in each couple cross paths. Formerly common in modern square dancing, this call turns up occasionally in contras.
Dance	As a noun, can mean a dance routine, one number played by the band, a set of two or three numbers (usually squares) done with the same partner, or an entire event of dancing.
Dance-walk	A name, common in England, for the basic country dance step.
Dead couples	Another term for **neutral couples.** Sometimes considered to be in poor taste.
Demanding	Requiring alertness and brisk movement in order to complete a move or sequence in the allotted time.
Dip	Same as **Duck.**
Dip and dive	To go alternately over and under other couples, making an arch and ducking through by turns.
Dive	Same as **Duck.**

Dominant figure	A distinctive movement (or combination of movements), often not callable using standard basics, that appears in only one dance (until choreographers begin "quoting" it). Examples are the Petronella turn and the Rory O'More balance. Compare **Glossary dance.**
Do-si-do*	In New England style, two people pass right shoulders and dance around each other back to back, returning to place. In Southern and Western traditions, any of several figures in which dancers do a series of hand turns with partner and corner (or opposite).
Double progression	A form of contra dance in which each couple moves two places up or down the set, rather than the usual one place, in each round. Neutral couples typically wait only part of a round.
Down	Toward the foot of a contra line. "Down the outside and back" is a common call to the active couples in contra dancing, as is "Down the center (or inside) and back."
Duck	To go under an arch.
Duple or **Duple minor**	A contra dance in which the set is divided into groups of two couples, one active and one inactive.
Ends	(1) The head and foot of a contra set. (2) The dancers at the ends of a line, as in "Ends close in."
End effects	The problems presented at the ends of the line by a contra routine in which each couple dances with the couples above and below them in the same round. No couple will be neutral for an entire round, as they will always be needed by the adjacent couple for at least part of the action. The amount of dancing the neutral couples must do, and the best time for them to cross over, vary from dance to dance.
Ends close in	From a line, the people at the ends move toward each other and join their free hands to form a circle.
Ends turn in	From a line of four, the people at the ends move toward each other, join their free hands, release the hands of the center people, and duck through an arch made by the center people.
English country dancing	The direct ancestor of contra dancing; similar in many ways, often done by the same people. Includes

	both **traditional** and **historical** dances, each with its own protocol.
Equal dance	A routine in which (1) all the couples do the same thing or (2) the couples are in motion an equal amount of time.
Evening	Used in this book to mean an event featuring contra dancing, to avoid the ambiguity of the word "dance."
Figure	Can mean a basic movement or a sequence of such basics. In a square, the sequence that gives a dance number its identity, as distinguished from the breaks.
Figure eight	Two active dancers trace a figure eight around two inactives, by crossing through the center and going behind the inactives, then repeating all that to original places. Only half of this English basic is commonly used in contra dancing; see **Half figure eight.**
First corners	Two dancers in opposite lines who are diagonally to each other's right, as the first gent and second lady in a duple proper contra.
First couple	(1) In a contra, the couple nearest the music in each minor set. Primarily an English term until recently; now used by many callers in preference to "active couple." (2) In a whole-set longways, the couple nearest the music at the beginning of each round. (3) In a square, the couple with its back to the music at the beginning of the dance.
Foot	The end of a contra line farthest from the music.
Forgiving	Of a routine or a portion of one, able to be negotiated adequately through regrouping in spite of lapses on the part of one or more dancers in a set.
Forward and back*	Dancers, usually in facing lines or a circle, move three steps toward each other and close the free foot, then repeat the same footwork backward.
Four ladies chain	In a square, the four ladies make a right-hand star and move across the set to their opposite gent, who takes their hands for a courtesy turn (or twirl) as in a normal (two) ladies chain. In a progressive circle with two facing lines of four, the ladies go to the gent diagonally opposite.
Fourth couple	In a square, the couple to the left of the first couple.

Glossary 261

Fudge To break stride or cut corners in moving from one place to another, either to recover from a lapse of mind or to compensate for an awkward transition in the routine.

Gent The member of a couple who stands on the left side to begin the dance (in a contra, to the left as the couple faces the music) and traditionally leads the other member through certain movements. A man or a woman may play the part of a gent.

Gents chain Used but not defined in nineteenth-century call books, this movement is usually interpreted now as a left-hand pass for the gents. Each gent takes promenade position with the opposite lady and moves forward (clockwise) around her as she turns in place. The motion is a mirror image of the ladies chain. Increasingly, the promenade position is also done in mirror image; that is, the lady's left arm goes around the gent's waist, rather than his right arm around her waist.

Gents' line The left-hand side of a contra set as the dancers face up; the side to the caller's right. See **Proper; Improper.**

Give and take Two facing dancers move toward each other and join both hands (or free hands if they are holding someone next to them), then one designated dancer pulls the other toward the designated dancer's starting place. The other offers resistance at first, then goes along freely. Usually followed by a swing. Named by Larry Jennings, who envisioned a 4-beat movement; dancers seem to prefer 8 beats, and Larry acknowledged that fact in his book named for this movement.

Give weight To offer resistance to another dancer, usually by pulling away slightly.

Glossary dance A routine formed of common basics, with no **dominant figure** to distinguish it from other routines.

Grand right and left Along a line or around a circle or square, facing dancers join right hands briefly as if for a handshake, then pass by each other to join left hands with the one they meet. They continue moving forward, taking right and left hands alternately with the people they meet, until the next call is given.

Grand square From a square formation, two couples (say the sides) face partners while the others continue to face across the set. Each dancer moves in a small square, one-quarter the size of the set, around his or her corner. The footwork is three steps on each side of the square, then turn a quarter on the fourth beat. The heads start by going forward, the sides backward; all are facing in throughout (toward either partner or opposite). The movement is almost always done twice, the second time with the heads' and sides' roles reversed.

Group Often used to mean a subset, especially in a progressive circle.

Gypsy* Two dancers, keeping right (or left) shoulders adjacent, dance around each other while maintaining eye contact. This English movement was recently introduced into contra dancing.

Half figure eight* Two active dancers cross paths between two standing inactives, then each active moves around and behind an inactive to end in the other active's place.

Half promenade Two facing couples, keeping to the right, promenade into each other's place by crossing the set and then wheeling to the left to face the other couple again.

Half right and left An old name for a single occurrence of "right and left" or "right and left through." In New England, "right and left" used to mean a round trip.

Half sashay Two dancers, side by side, exchange places without a raised-arm twirl; either they side-step past each other or the lady spins in front of the gent as he side-steps (the latter is usually called "rollaway"). Used primarily in old-time Western and modern squares; appears in a few contras with no special name (one choreographer has suggested "roll to swap").

Hand turn* Two facing dancers join right (or left) hands chest-high, wrists straight and elbows bent, and move around each other, giving weight.

Hands across The standard English name and style for a star: each pair of dancers who are across the center of the star from each other join right (or left) hands, a little higher than for a handshake. They bend their elbows slightly and give weight. For further discussion, see Chapter 13 under "Star."

Hands four (or six) A traditional wording for the request to join hands in circles of four (or six) people, starting at the head of a contra line, for the purpose of identifying the "ones" or active couples.

Head The end of the hall where the music is, or the end of a contra line nearest the music.

Head couples or **Heads** The first and third couples in a square.

Heel and toe Each dancer extends a foot to the side, heel on the floor and toe raised, then touches the same toe next to the other foot. This footwork, done once or twice, appears in a few contra dances done to polka music.

Hey* Three or four dancers, starting from a straight line, weave past each other until all have been to both ends of the line and have returned to their starting point. Which dancers begin the hey, which way they face, and which shoulders they pass all depend on the specific dance. The hey disappeared from contra dances early in the nineteenth century, but was revived in the 1970s. Full and fractional heys are now quite common in contra choreography.

Historical Of English country dances, revived from books or manuscripts of the seventeenth and eighteenth centuries or recently choreographed in the same (usually elegant) style. Compare **Traditional.**

Hoedown Same as **Breakdown** (definition 1).

Honor To acknowledge one's partner or corner, especially in a square. Traditionally the ladies curtsy and the gents bow, but many present-day dancers simply nod toward each other.

Hornpipe A type of dance tune in 2/4 or 4/4 meter, often with longer phrases than a reel. English and Irish hornpipes are usually in slow tempo and are not used for square and contra dancing.

Improper Of a couple, having the lady in the gent's line and vice versa; of a dance, starting with the active couples so crossed. Compare **Proper.**

Inactive A person or couple that does not initiate a figure. See **Active.**

Inside	Same as **Center** (definition 1). See **Down**.
Jig	A type of dance tune in 6/8 meter. Jigs could originally be in other meters, such as 2/4.
Key figure	Same as **Dominant figure**.
Ladies chain*	The ladies in two facing couples join right hands briefly as they pass by each other. Each lady then joins left hands with the opposite gent, who either takes New England promenade position with her for a courtesy turn or raises his left arm to support her as she twirls around him. Couples are again facing each other; ladies have exchanged places.
Ladies grand chain	Same as **Four ladies chain**.
Ladies half chain	An older name for a ladies chain with no return. "Ladies chain" in New England used to mean a round trip.
Ladies' line	The right-hand side of a contra set as the dancers face up; the side to the caller's left. See **Proper; Improper**.
Lady	The member of a couple who stands on the right side to begin the dance (in a contra, to the right as the couple faces the music) and traditionally is led by the other member through certain movements. A woman or a man may play the part of a lady.
Left hands across	See **Hands across**.
Line	During a dance: Three or more adjacent dancers, usually facing in the same direction, with near hands joined. In setting up a dance: One of the two lines forming a contra set (see **Gents' line, Ladies' line**). If the dancers are alternately facing in opposite directions, it is less ambiguous to refer to the formation as a **wave** or **wavy line**.
Longways	(1) A formation of dancers in two parallel lines, usually with partners in opposite lines facing each other to start the dance. (2) Any dance done in this formation, whether a whole-set longways or a progressive longways (contra dance).
Mad Robin	The individuals of two couples dance the floor track of a do-si-do (or a reverse do-si-do) with their neighbors while facing their partners and maintaining eye contact with partners as much as possible. A recent addition to contra dancing, borrowed from the English country

	dance of that name. The term is something of a misnomer, as in the English dance only two dancers move while the other two stand still.
March	A type of dance tune in 4/4 meter, characterized by longer phrases, and longer and fewer notes, than jigs and reels.
Medley	Two or more contra dances done in succession without a pause.
Mescolanze	A progressive dance done by lines of two couples facing similar lines; may be done in a circle or straight up and down the hall.
Meter	The rhythm of a tune, determined by the number of beats in a measure and by their value. The usual meters in square and contra dancing are 2/4, 4/4, and 6/8. Sometimes incorrectly called **tempo.**
Minor set	A group of two or three couples within a contra set, who will dance most or all of one round together.
Mixer	A dance in which every dancer receives a new partner during each round and original partners are not reunited (except by accident if the set is small enough).
Modern square dancing	A style of square dancing characterized by a large number of basic movements, formal dress and organization, almost total lack of physical connection and giving weight, loose musical phrasing, the use of recorded music, and relatively few and short swings (walk-around or buzz-step). Often called "modern Western" because it evolved from traditional Western style; often abbreviated "MWSD," particularly in Internet usage. Also called "club dancing" or "club style." Some traditionalists prefer the latter term to avoid confusion with **Western square dancing** (definition 1).
Movement	A short series of steps that the dancers do in response to a single call; the smallest unit of country dance choreography. A movement may be an accepted **basic** (such as "do-si-do") that is taught by rote, or it may be so close to plain English (such as "ends close in") that it needs no special teaching.
Neighbor	The person of opposite sex in a minor set who is not one's partner. A relatively recent term, probably dating

from around 1970; the older term was "the one below," as calls were directed to the active couples.

Neutral couples The couples at the head and foot of a contra dance set who have no couple to form a minor set with and must wait one round (part of a round in a double progression dance) before dancing again. In some newer contras, the couples at the ends must dance portions of the routine, often not contiguous (see **End effects**).

New England style A style of square and contra dancing characterized by strong physical connection, the practice of giving weight, strict musical phrasing, the use of live music, relatively few basic movements, informal dress and organization, and many relatively long buzz-step swings.

Ocean wave A name, common in modern square dancing, for a wave; may derive from the appearance of a wave or from the singing square *Life on the Ocean Wave,* in which the formation became popular.

One-night stand An event featuring square dancing or other forms of country dancing, often including ballroom dancing and/or games, geared to people who are unfamiliar with country dancing and do not intend to take it up as a hobby. The term is sometimes considered to be in poor taste, but no other term is universally understood. See **Barn dance.**

Ones A colloquial name for the first couple in a minor set, used especially in calling.

Opposite The dancer directly opposite one, when that dancer is not one's partner. Used mainly in squares and progressive circles.

Other way back An old call directing the active dancers to turn as a couple after going down the center.

Outside The area directly behind the standing dancers who form the boundaries of a set. See **Down.**

Partner (1) In a contra dance or progressive circle, the person with whom one has chosen to dance that number, no matter where he or she may be. (2) In a mixer or a square, the person with whom one is dancing a given round, often the lady to a gent's right or the gent to a

Glossary 267

	lady's left. Often the person a dancer is directed to swing becomes his or her next partner.
Pass through*	Two facing couples or lines exchange places, each dancer passing the opposite by the right shoulder. They end back to back with the other couple or line.
Pass through to a wave	Two facing couples begin a pass through. As the couples meet, the ladies (assuming "normal" couples) join left hands and turn one-quarter to become the centers of a wave; the gents move in an arc, forward and to their right, and give right hand to the nearest lady (who started beside them) to become the ends of the wave. Borrowed from modern square dancing, where it is called "Pass the ocean."
Patter	Words in a call that are not strictly necessary, but help the caller maintain the rhythm of the dance. They may come before a meaningful call and warn the dancers of it (leading patter) or after such a call and serve chiefly to entertain (trailing patter).
Petronella turn	Four dancers in a circle each move one place to the right in 4 steps, spinning to their own right as they go. A dancer who faced north before the move is facing west after it. Formerly done only in the dance *Petronella,* this movement has appeared in many recently written contras.
Phrase	A group of beats that is felt to belong together as a subset of a tune. In country dance music, phrases are generally considered to be either 8 or 16 beats long.
Phrasing	The practice of making the movements of a dance coincide with the phrases of the tune to which it is danced. Phrasing is fundamental to New England style, but used sporadically or neglected in some other styles of country dancing.
Pick up two	From a circle, one active dancer releases a handhold and adds a standing couple to the circle. Commonly used in squares.
Piece count	A measure of a dance's difficulty, based on the number of movements or combinations of movements that the dancers will perceive as separate parts to be remembered.

Progression (1) A change in the relative positions of the couples in a contra dance or progressive circle, combined with (or preparing for) a regrouping of couples into new subgroups. In a contra, the first (or active) couple in each minor set moves down the line and the other (inactive) couple or couples move up. (2) A change of partners in a square or mixer.

Progressive circle A formation composed of a number of subsets or "groups" forming a circle around the hall, each group made up of a couple or a line of three or four people facing a similar couple or line. Each half-group remains together throughout the dance, meeting and dancing with other half-groups.

Progressive longways A technical term for what is known in New England style as a contra dance, as opposed to a **whole-set longways.**

Promenade* To move as a couple, along a line or around a circle or square, in promenade position. Promenades are traditionally to the right (counterclockwise) if not otherwise specified.

Promenade position Two dancers side by side, lady to the gent's right, hands joined in one of the following ways: (1) Left hands in front of gent's chest, right hands at lady's right hip with gent's right arm around lady's waist. The usual New England practice. (2) Left hands in front of gent's chest, right hands above lady's right shoulder with gent's arm around lady's shoulders. (3) Hands joined in front, right hands (in front of lady's waist) above left hands (in front of gent's waist). (4) Gent's right arm around lady's waist, lady's left hand on gent's right shoulder, lady's right arm and gent's left arm free.

Prompt As a noun, a call given before the musical phrase to which it applies (the standard practice in contra dancing). As a verb, to deliver calls in this manner.

Proper Of a couple, having the lady and the gent in their own lines; of a dance, starting with all the couples that way. Compare **Improper.**

Quadrille (1) A formal square dance of the nineteenth century, in five or six parts. (2) Loosely, any square done in phrase with the music like a contra.

Reel	(1) A type of dance tune in 2/4 meter, characterized by short phrases and a continuous flow of short notes. (2) A common American name for **strip the willow.** (3) In Scottish country dancing, a **hey.**
Rhythm	In country dance usage, the basic downbeat to which the dancers step. To call in rhythm with the music is to make the spoken words coincide with the musical downbeats and upbeats.
Right and left*	(1) Two facing couples exchange places by doing a pass through and a courtesy turn or similar pivot (or twirl with left hands joined) to face the other couple again. (2) Two ladies exchange places with two gents as above, except that each same-sex pair pivots counterclockwise without touching or with arms behind each other's backs.
Right and left through	Same as **Right and left** (definition 1). Apparently a term from the Western and/or Southwestern square dance traditions that has found its way into New England style.
Right hands across	See **Hands across.**
Rights and lefts	Same as **Square through,** except that the dancers do not necessarily pull straight by after giving the last hand.
Rollaway	See **Half sashay.**
Roll to swap	See **Half sashay.**
Rory O'More	Also called "Rory O'More balance" or "Rory O'More spin." Dancers in a **wavy line** balance to their own right and left (4 beats), then either slide or spin to their own right (4 beats), passing the person they were holding right hands with and taking left hands with him or her. They then balance to their own left and right (starting toward the same person) and slide or spin to their left, regaining their original place. Formerly done only in the dance *Rory O'More,* this movement has appeared in many recently written contras.
Round	Used in this book to mean the amount of dancing done to one playing of a tune. In a contra, corresponds to the routine or sequence. In a square, one round can be either a figure or a break.
Routine	A dance as envisioned by its choreographer. A contra dance routine is the combination of movements done to

	one playing of the tune. A square dance routine can mean either the figure of the dance or the complete sequence of figures and breaks from the start to the finish of the music.
Same way back	An old call directing the active dancers to turn individually after going down the center.
Sashay	Same as **Slide.**
Second corners	Two dancers in opposite lines who are diagonally to each other's left, as the first lady and second gent in a duple proper contra.
Second couple	In a contra, the couple below the first couple in each minor set. In a square, the couple to the right of the first couple.
Sequence	In a contra dance, a synonym for **routine** or **round.** In a square, the number of figures and breaks in a dance and the order of their arrangement. Also used by square dance callers to mean the order of the couples in the square: A set with couples in normal order is "in sequence"; if either the heads or sides have exchanged places, the set is "out of sequence."
Set	As a noun, can mean a group of dances done with the same partner, or a group of dancers arranged in a specific formation (see the various types of dance). As a verb, an English dance term meaning to balance.
Shadow	A dancer playing the same role as one's partner (active or inactive, lady or gent) in an adjoining minor set. When partners in a duple are on the same side of the set, one's shadow is adjacent in that line. In calling, sometimes referred to as "special person" or "trail buddy," though "shadow" appears to have become the standard term.
Sicilian circle	Originally, a specific dance in progressive circle formation; often used as a generic term for any dance in this formation.
Side couples or **Sides**	The second and fourth couples in a square.
Slide	To dance sideways by leading with one foot and closing the other foot to it. Traditionally called "chassez" (pronounced "shassay," French for "chase") or "sashay" (a corruption of the French term).

Southern square	(1) A square or progressive circle dance in a style traditional in the Appalachian and Ozark Mountains, characterized by fast tempo, many dominant-figure dances, sparing use of patter, and frequent but short walk-around swings. (2) Loosely, a square danced to Southern music, particularly such a square in an evolving style that is a blend of New England, traditional Western, and modern "Western" figures.
Spin	A solo turn, in place or while traveling. Sometimes used erroneously by non-dancers or new dancers to mean **swing**.
Square formation	A set of four couples, one on each side of a square about eight feet across, all facing the center. In each couple, the lady is on the gent's right.
Square through	Four dancers move around the perimeter of a small square, alternately giving right and left hands in passing. This movement, common in English dancing under the name "circular hey with hands," was introduced into modern square dancing in 1957. It appears in several recent contras, sometimes as **rights and lefts.** Note that in the modern square dance context, the dancers pull straight by after giving the last hand and finish facing away from the foursome.
Star*	Three or more dancers move around a hub formed by their extended right (or left) hands. Each dancer normally holds the wrist of the one ahead; see **Hands across** for an alternative style.
Star through	Two facing dancers join hands (gent's right, lady's left) and exchange places, the lady going under the gent's arm. During the movement, the gent turns a quarter to his right, the lady a quarter to her left; the dancers end side by side, lady on the right. This movement was introduced into modern square dancing in 1960 and has found its way into a few contras.
Step, the	The basic country dance step is a modified walk. Dancers lead with their upper bodies, keeping weight forward and emphasizing the backward thrust of their feet. The only other steps commonly used in contra dancing are the **buzz step** and the **balance.**

Story line	The flow of physical movement and social interaction from beginning to end of a dance routine.
Straight-arm hold	One possible position in swinging: each dancer straightens right arm and puts right hand on the other's right shoulder, with left hands joined underneath. Not recommended for New England style or other situations requiring compact sets.
Strip the willow	The first couple in a whole-set longways alternately turns partner (usually by the right hand or arm) and successive dancers in the opposite line (usually by the left). A British term; the word "reel" is sometimes substituted in American usage.
Subset	A generic term for a minor set in a contra dance or a similar group in a progressive circle.
Swing*	Two facing dancers, offset slightly to their own left, take **ballroom, unisex,** or **straight-arm hold** and rotate clockwise as a unit. The **buzz step** is usual in New England style; walk-around swings are common in other styles and may be used in contras by beginning, tired, injured, or otherwise handicapped dancers.
Tempo	The speed at which the music is played (as distinguished from **timing**). Sometimes used incorrectly to mean **meter.**
Third couple	In a triple minor contra, the couple farthest from the music in each minor set. In a square, the couple facing the music.
Threes	A colloquial name for the third couple in a minor set, used especially in calling.
Timing	The number of musical beats allowed by the choreographer or the caller for the dancers to execute a movement (as distinguished from **tempo**).
Top	The head of a contra line or other longways set.
Top couple	The couple at the head of a longways set. Not a synonym for "first" or "active couple" in a contra.
Traditional	(1) Commonly used as a general term for all styles of square and contra dancing other than modern "Western." (2) Of English country dances, collected in the field

Glossary

during the twentieth century or choreographed in the same (usually robust) style. Compare **Historical.**

Triple or **triple minor** A contra dance in which the set is divided into groups of three couples, one active and two inactive. Compare **Triplet.**

Triplet A whole-set dance for three couples, using New England style and terminology (the formation is borrowed from English country dancing). Popularized in the late twentieth century by Ted Sannella. Compare **Triple.**

Turn (1) Same as **Hand turn.** (2) Any individual or couple movement to the right or left, in place or along a floor track. "Turn alone" and "Turn as a couple" are common calls following movements such as "Down the center."

Turn contra corners* Active dancers turn partner by the right hand, **first corner** by the left, partner by the right, **second corner** by the left.

Turn under A generic term used in the first edition of this book for the family of moves now known as **twirl to swap.**

Twirl A generic term for any move in which the lady spins as she goes under the gent's raised arm, his hand supporting hers. Substituting a twirl for a courtesy turn to complete a ladies chain or right and left is an increasingly common practice.

Twirl to swap* A generic term for any move in which the lady goes under the gent's raised arm. Specific moves include box the gnat, California twirl, and star through; callers in styles other than modern square dancing sometimes refer to all these moves loosely as "box the gnat."

Twos A colloquial name for the second couple in a minor set, used especially in calling.

Undemanding Able to be completed by an average set of dancers in the allotted time.

Unequal dance A routine in which the active couples are in motion significantly more of the time than the inactive couples.

Unforgiving Requiring all the dancers in a set to stay alert in order to complete a figure successfully; difficult to negotiate by regrouping if one or more dancers are out of position.

Unisex hold One of two possible positions in swinging: (1) Each dancer puts right arm around the other's back or waist and rests left arm on the other's right arm. (2) Each dancer puts right arm around the other's waist, with left hands joined underneath.

Up Toward the head of a contra line.

Walk See **Step.**

Walkthrough One round of a contra or similar dance, or one figure of a square, done without music and generally not in rhythm or up to tempo, as a means of instructing the dancers.

Waltz position Sometimes used loosely to mean the **ballroom hold** of the country dance swing – loosely because in a waltz, partners are not as offset to the side as in swinging.

Wave or **Wavy line** A line of three or more dancers alternately facing in opposite directions, so that adjacent dancers have either two right or two left hands joined.

Weight See **Give weight.**

Western square dancing (1) A style of square dancing characterized by relatively fast tempo, many dominant-figure dances, liberal use of patter, and infrequent, short, walk-around swings. Also known as "old Western," "cowboy." (2) Same as **Modern square dancing.**

Wheel around A generic term for a pivot as a couple, whether or not it is done in promenade position. In a mixed couple, the lady moves forward and the gent backward, making the pivot left-face (counterclockwise) if the lady is on the gent's right.

Whole-set longways A dance in which the longways set is not divided into minor sets. Only the couple at the head of the set is active; they may or may not interact directly with the other couples during their turn.

Resources

Contra dancing, since about 1970, has become a large and widespread enough hobby to encourage many people to produce books, recordings, and other resources such as newsletters and directories. Numerous annual events are held in addition to the weekly and monthly dances that form the backbone of the activity. This section lists a few of these publications and events, together with the organizations that make them possible. Like all such lists, these are incomplete; the chief criteria for inclusion were helpfulness to the reader and current availability. Some out-of-print items were judged too important to omit; other callers, libraries, used-book dealers, and online auction sites may have copies. Web addresses are given for major publishers and retailers, as well as for individual items whose producers are not listed elsewhere.

GOOD DANCES NOT IN THIS BOOK

These lists are not exhaustive, but will provide a beginning caller with a more than adequate repertoire of proven material. Only books judged above average in usefulness are listed as references.

Contras

Baby Rose	G&T
Becket Reel	DaW, EC, Knox, ZC, StN
British Sorrow	CC, CM, Knox, ZC, StN
Broken Sixpence	CM, DaW, Knox
Centrifugal Hey	DD2, G&T, StN
Delphiniums and Daisies	G&T
Fairfield Fancy	Knox, ZC
Good Friday	G&T
Great Escape	G&T, SoS
Hey Fever	SD
Hull's Victory (Ch)	CC, CM, DaW, EC, Knox, ZC
Judah Jig	G&T, StN
Lady of the Lake (Ch)	CC, CM, DaW, ZC
Lady Walpole's Reel (Ch)	CC, CM, EC, Knox, ZC
Mary Cay's Reel	G&T

275

Money Musk (Ch)	CC, CM, EC, Knox, ZC
Nova Scotian or The Maritimer	CM, DaW, EC, Knox, ZC
Petronella (Ch)	CC, CM, DaW, EC, Knox, ZC
Queen Victoria	CC, CM, Knox, ZC
Reunion	DD2, G&T, StN
Rory O'More (Ch)	CC, CM, DaW, Knox, ZC
Sackett's Harbor (Ch)	CC, CM, EC, Knox, ZC
Scout House Reel	B&S, Knox, ZC
Shadrack's Delight	CM, DaW, Knox, SD, ZC
Summer of '84	DD2, G&T
Symmetrical Force	DaW, ZC
Three Thirty-Three	G&T
Triskaidekaphobia	G&T
Turning Point	DD3, G&T
Weave the Line	DaW, G&T
Yankee Reel	B&S, EC, Knox, ZC

Dances labeled (Ch) are in the category often called "chestnuts." They are traditionally done to their own tune, which usually has the same name as the dance (the tune for *Sackett's Harbor* is called Steamboat Quickstep). The tunes for all these dances are printed in *New England Fiddler's Repertoire* (except Lady of the Lake, which is in *The Portland Collection*) and have been recorded on the CD *New England Chestnuts, Volumes 1 and 2*.

Big Circles

Atlantic Mixer	ZC
Ice Cream in the Sink	ZC
La Bastringue	ZC
Sibyl's Roundabout	ZC

Progressive Circles or Lines

Balance the Star	ZC
Contrarotation	CM, ZC
Etna Star	ZC
Fireman's Dance	CM, DaW
First Bloom	ZC
New Floor's Revenge	ZC
Ted's Portland Fancy	ZC

Squares

This list is confined to squares that can be called in the same style as contras; for the most part they are printed like contras in the references given. No singing squares are listed here, as their choice depends heavily on the caller's taste and their success on the caller's personality. For a good selection of singing squares, see the books by Dalsemer, Kraus, Lyman, and especially Sweet.

Beaver Lake Jig	B&S
Do-si-do and Face the Sides	B&S
Duck Through and Swing	SD
Fluid Drive	B&S
Gents and Corners	B&S
Head Couples Separate	SD
Labor Day Quadrille	StN, WS
Merry Mix-Up	StN
Parisian Star	SD
Quadrille Joyeux	B&S
Reel Your Partner	B&S, WS
Roger's Grand Chain	B&S
Separate and Do-si-do	SD
Sheehan's Reel	B&S, WS
Six Pass Through	StN
Star Breakdown	SD

References for the lists above:

B&S	Sannella, *Balance and Swing*
CC	Smukler & Millstone, *Cracking Chestnuts*
CM	Armstrong, *Caller/Teacher Manual for Contras*
DaW	Pittman et al, *Dance a While*
DD2 (3)	Hubert, *Dizzy Dances, Volume II (III)*
EC	Page, *An Elegant Collection of Contras and Squares*
G&T	Jennings, *Give-and-Take*
Knox	Knox, ed., *Contras as Ralph Page Called Them*
SD	Parkes, *Shadrack's Delight*
SoS	Parkes, *Son of Shadrack*
StN	Sannella, *Swing the Next*
WS	Edelman, *Square Dance Caller's Workshop*
ZC	Jennings, *Zesty Contras*

ALL-PURPOSE TUNES

The tunes listed here will fit any 64-beat dance routine. For the most part, they are not associated with a particular dance. Feel free to experiment with different matches of dance and tune. (Meter is 2/4 unless otherwise noted.)

Sheet Music

Angus Campbell	FF
La Bastringue	FF, NEFR
Blackberry Quadrille (6/8)	NEFR
Bonaparte Crossing the Rhine (4/4)	FF
Brisk Young Lads (6/8)	NEFR
Calliope House (6/8)	PC
Coleraine (6/8)	FF, NEFR
Come Dance and Sing	FF, NEFR
Durang's Hornpipe	PC
Earl of Mansfield	NEFR
Fair Jenny's Jig (6/8)	PC
Far from Home	PC
Farewell to Whiskey	FF, NEFR
Fireman's Reel	NEFR
Fisher's Hornpipe	FF, NEFR
Flowers of Edinburgh	FF, NEFR
Gaspé Reel	FF, NEFR
Girl with the Blue Dress On	PC2
Glise à Sherbrooke	NEFR, PC
Growling Old Man and Woman	FF, NEFR
Haste to the Wedding (6/8)	FF, NEFR
Irishman's Heart to the Ladies (6/8)	PC
Jimmy Allen	NEFR
Joys of Quebec	FF
Kitty McGee (6/8)	FF, NEFR, PC
Lady in the Boat (6/8)	FF, NEFR
Lanigan's Ball (6/8)	NEFR
Larry O'Gaff (6/8)	FF, NEFR
Maggie Brown's Favorite (6/8)	FF, NEFR
Mason's Apron	FF, NEFR, PC
Meeting of the Waters (4/4)	NEFR, PC2
Miller's Reel	FF, NEFR, PC
Mug of Brown Ale (6/8)	PC

O'Donnell Abhu (4/4)	NEFR
Off She Goes (6/8)	FF, NEFR
Old Grey Cat	PC
Out on the Ocean (6/8)	PC
Paddy on the Railroad	FF, NEFR
Pete's March (4/4)	PC2
Pointe-au-Pic, Reel de	PC2
Rakes of Mallow	NEFR
Road to Boston	NEFR, PC2
Rock Valley Jig (6/8)	PC2
Ross's Reel #4	FF, NEFR
Saint Anne's Reel	FF, NEFR
Shandon Bells (6/8)	NEFR
Silver Spire	PC2
Smash the Windows (6/8)	FF, NEFR
Swinging on a Gate	FF, NEFR
Top of Cork Road (6/8)	NEFR, PC
White Cockade	FF, NEFR
Woodchopper's Reel	FF, NEFR

References for the list above:

FF	*Fiddler's Fakebook*
NEFR	*New England Fiddler's Repertoire*
PC	*Portland Collection*
PC2	*Portland Collection, Volume 2*

Recordings

See the main Recordings section, below, for labels and album numbers where they are not given here.

Brisk Young Lads medley (6/8)	Canterbury Country Dance Orch.
Coleraine (6/8)	Canterbury Country Dance Orch.
Fairy Toddler Jig medley (6/8)	Kitchen Junket
Firemen's Reel medley	Farewell to the Hollow
Flowers of Edinburgh medley	The Hammered Dulcimer
Foxy Mary medley	High Clouds
French Fries and Gravy medley (6/8)	Starry Nights and Candlelight
Glise à Sherbrooke	Folk Dancer 6
Growling Old Man and Woman	Kitchen Junket
Lad O'Beirne's medley (6/8)	Heatin' Up the Hall

Lamplighter's Hornpipe medley	New England Chestnuts
Liza Constable's Reel medley	ONE:Two
Miss Thornton's medley	Turning of the Tide
Quindaro Hornpipe medley	Pure Quill
Reel de Montreal medley	The Hammered Dulcimer Returns!
Reel de Ti-Jean & St. Anne's Reel	Folk Dancer 41
Saint Anne's Reel	When the Work's All Done
Saint Lawrence Jig (6/8)	Folk Dancer 1
Walker Street Reel medley	Maritime Dance Party
Woodchopper's Reel medley	Kitchen Junket
Wright's Quickstep (6/8)	Folk Dancer 6
York County Hornpipe medley	Maritime Dance Party

BOOKS

These books do not include a substantial amount of music unless specifically noted. Companion recordings are available for several books. Some older titles are out of print at this writing; copies may be available in libraries, through dealers (storefront and online), and through print-on-demand services.

Dozens of contra dance choreographers have published booklets of new routines; only a handful are mentioned here, and the omission of a title implies no slight. An increasing number of composers are also putting their material online; see below under "Websites" for sources of links to them. As with websites, so with books: the bibliographies in those listed here will lead you to others.

Amidon, Peter and Mary Alice. *Jump Jim Joe: Great Singing Games for Children.* Brattleboro, VT: New England Dancing Masters, 1991. Contains 20 dance-like games from African- and Anglo-American traditions, with music.

Amidon, Peter, Mary Cay Brass, and Andy Davis, eds. *Chimes of Dunkirk: Great Dances for Children.* Brattleboro, VT: New England Dancing Masters, 1991. Ideal for its purpose, with lots of easy circles and whole-set longways (20 dances, 9 tunes). A companion recording is available, as is a video on teaching the dances.

Armstrong, Don. *The Caller/Teacher Manual for Contras.* Los Angeles: Sets in Order, 1973. Call charts for 100 dances, with descriptions for 49 of them. Aimed at modern-style callers who know squares but not contras; has much good information for traditional callers.

Barclay, Les, and Ian Jones. *Community Dances Manual, Revised Edition.* London: English Folk Dance and Song Society, 2005. Based on

Douglas Kennedy's classic booklets; contains about 130 dances and 140 tunes. Many of the dances are circles and whole-set longways easy enough for use in schools and with mixed groups.

Butenhof, Ed. *Dance Parties for Beginners.* Macks Creek, MO: Lloyd Shaw Foundation, 1990. A manual for conducting one-night stands, aimed at modern square dance callers; has many easy squares, longways, and novelty dances (98 in all).

Campbell, Calvin, Ken Kernan, and Bob Howell. *Dancing for Busy People.* Castle Rock, CO: Calvin Campbell, 2003. More than 400 squares, contras, mixers, and other group dances for general recreational use. The authors are experts in calling one-night stands as well as ongoing programs at just above entry level. **www.d4bp.com**

Dalsemer, Bob. *Smoke on the Water: Square Dance Classics.* Baltimore: Traditional Caller Productions, [1989]. Ten singing squares, with music. Available from Hanhurst/Palomino. **www.dosado.com**

Dalsemer, Bob. *When the Work's All Done: A Square Dance Party for Beginners and Old Hands.* Baltimore: Traditional Caller Productions, [1990]. Nine easy squares (singing and patter) and a circle mixer, with music. Available from Hanhurst/Palomino. **www.dosado.com**

Dart, Mary McNab. "Contra Dance Choreography: A Reflection of Social Change." Ph.D. dissertation, University of Indiana, 1992. A thoughtful analysis of the contra dance scene in the 1970s and 1980s. Can be read online, free of charge, at the CDSS website. **www.cdss.org**

Davis, Andy, Peter Amidon, and Mary Alice Amidon. *Down in the Valley: More Great Singing Games for Children, Schools & Communities.* Brattleboro, VT: New England Dancing Masters, 2000. Similar to *Jump Jim Joe;* 25 more dance-like games, with music.

Davis, Andy, Peter Amidon, and Mary Cay Brass. *Listen to the Mockingbird: More Great Dances for Children, Schools & Communities.* Brattleboro, VT: New England Dancing Masters, 1997. Similar to *Chimes of Dunkirk;* 24 dances with music, mostly longways and circles. Includes several all-purpose tunes.

Davis, Andy, Peter Amidon, Mary Alice Amidon, and Mary Cay Brass. *Sashay the Donut: Even More Dances for Just About Anyone.* Brattleboro, VT: New England Dancing Masters, 2007. Has 24 dances, mostly whole-set longways and circles, with a few squares and contras. The authors work extensively in school and family settings and have tested this material thoroughly.

Eastern Cooperative Recreation School (ECRS). *Of Play and Playfulness: Materials, Methods, and Snacks at Ten.* ECRS, 1990. A wealth of folk and folk-based material: games, dances (including a section on wheelchair dancing), songs, dramatics, storytelling, puppetry, crafts. Much good general philosophy as well. Can be read free on the ECRS website, which also offers hard copies for sale. **www.ecrs.org**

Edelman, Larry. *Square Dance Caller's Workshop.* Baltimore: The author, 1991. Similar to this book; emphasis on squares, with several examples from each regional tradition.

Everett, Bert. *Fifty Canadian Square Dances.* Toronto: Can-Ed Media, 1977, 1983. Complete call charts, including breaks, for 50 prompted and patter squares; valuable for contra callers wanting to branch out.

Fix, Penn. *Contra Dancing in the Northwest.* [Spokane, WA:] The author, 1991. Observations on contra history in the author's area, advice on dance organizing and etiquette, and 33 original dances with 14 tunes.

Gaudreau, Herbie. *Modern Contra Dancing.* Sandusky, OH: Square Dance Magazine, 1971. Calls for 50 dances by the pioneer of "all-moving" contra choreography.

Gunzenhauser, Margot. *The Square Dance and Contra Dance Handbook.* Jefferson, NC: McFarland & Co., 1996. A worthy successor to the comprehensive square dance books of the 1950s. Has 90 dances and 35 tunes, plus much good general information. Aimed at schoolteachers but valuable to anyone interested in the subject. Includes the most complete resource section I have ever seen, both in its scope and in the length of its annotations. Of course, it stops at 1996, but the information in the recommended material is timeless.

Hamilton, Bruce. *Notes on Teaching Country Dance.* Haydenville, MA: Country Dance and Song Society, 2005. A booklet of excellent thoughts on teaching, ranging from overall philosophy to specific suggestions. Aimed at English and Scottish country dance teachers, but literally 90 percent of it applies to contra callers as well.

Hendrickson, Charles Cyril. *Colonial Social Dancing for Children.* Sandy Hook, CT: The Hendrickson Group, 1995. Contains 23 dances in Colonial style. Aimed at elementary and middle-school children; for several dances, variants are given that don't require partners to touch.

Hill, Becky, and Sue Rosen. *The Rosen Hill Collection.* Cleveland Heights, OH: Dance Gypsy Publications, 2005. Contains 53 dances, mostly contras; includes a few favorites from Hill's earlier books.

Hinds, Tom. *Calling New England Squares*. Faber, VA: The author, 2005. A small book, but packed with information. Deals with timing, teaching, programming, and analyzing and adapting material. Includes 23 figures and breaks, some original.

Hinds, Tom. *Teaching the Pre-dance Lesson* and *Contra Dance Programming*. Faber, VA: The author, 1998 and 2007. Two in a series of booklets by this highly regarded dance leader on various aspects of the caller's work.

Hinds, Tom. *Dance All Night* (3 volumes); *Dance All Day Too!*; *Dances from a Confused Caller's PDA*. Arlington or Faber, VA: The author, 1989, 1991, 1992, 1995, 2005. The author's original routines for contras and squares (at least 30 in each book).

Hinds, Tom. *Give Me a Break!* Faber, VA: The author, 1997. Contains 64 "breaks" or chorus figures for New England squares, with tips on how to choose and use them.

Hoffman, Erik. *Old-Time Dance Calling for Weddings, Parties and One-Night Stands*. Oakland, CA: Know Nothing Press, 2001. Just what the title says, from a caller with long experience working with dancers and non-dancers. Over a dozen dances, plus a helpful annotated bibliography. The author has also published three collections of original contras. **www.erikhoffman.com**

Holden, Rickey. *The Contra Dance Book*. Newark, NJ: American Squares, 1956. Reprinted 1997 by Anglo-American Dance Service, Lovendegem, Belgium. The best collection of its time: 91 contras and 18 progressive circles from the period 1850–1953.

Hubert, Gene. *Dizzy Dances: Volume II* and *More Dizzy Dances: Volume III*. [Greensboro, NC:] The author, 1986 and 1990. Original contras, squares, and circle mixers (book totals of 27 and 43) in a fast-moving, "everybody active" style.

Hutson, James, and Jeffrey Spero, eds. *(Southern) California Twirls*. Brief but well-documented histories of the contra dance communities of San Diego, Los Angeles, and Santa Barbara, plus 45 dances.

Jennings, Larry. *Give-and-Take*. Cambridge, MA: New England Folk Festival Association, 2004. Contains 628 dances in shorthand notation, plus several essays. Some of the choreographic theorizing may not be of interest to everyone, but Larry's views are always thought-provoking.

Jennings, Larry. *Zesty Contras*. Cambridge, MA: New England Folk Festival Association, 1983. About 500 dances, old and new, in shorthand notation, with the author's thoughts on modern choreography and dance organizing.

Jennings, Larry, Dan Pearl, and Ted Sannella. *The Contra Connection & Basically for Callers.* Haydenville, MA: Country Dance and Song Society, 2001. A series of articles by three Boston-area leaders on various aspects of calling and dance organizing.

Johnson, Eric Orace, ed.; Michael Fuerst, dance ed. *Midwest Folklore and Other Dances.* Champaign, IL: Orace E. Johnson Memorial Trust, 1995. This tribute to a well-loved Illinois dancer, caller, organizer, and choreographer contains 112 dances, mostly contras, by composers with Midwest connections.

Kaynor, David A. *Calling Contra Dances for Beginners by Beginners.* Montague Center, MA: The author, 1991. Emphasizes human relations; argues for a casual, do-it-yourself approach to calling and playing the music. Includes 16 easy dances. **www.davidkaynor.com**

Keller, Kate Van Winkle, and Ralph Sweet. *A Choice Selection of American Country Dances of the Revolutionary Era.* New York: Country Dance and Song Society, 1975. Thirty dances from old manuscripts, with tunes and glossary.

Kitch, Jim. *To Live Is to Dance.* Bala Cynwyd, PA: The author, 1995. The author is known for writing dances that are innovative but smooth-flowing. Here are 29 of them, mostly contras.

Knox, Roger, ed. *Contras as Ralph Page Called Them.* Ithaca, NY: The editor, 1990. Over 220 contras and 31 New England style squares, taken from *Northern Junket* magazine and a dance camp syllabus. The best single source of contras danced before the 1970s revival. This book is unfortunately out of print; the dances can be harvested from the online scans of the *Junket* (see "Periodicals").

Kraus, Richard. *Square Dances of Today and How to Teach and Call Them.* New York: A.S. Barnes or Ronald Press, 1950. On-demand reprint from University Microfilms, Ann Arbor, MI (but used copies are readily available). One of the best collections of easy to intermediate patter and singing squares; 55 dances, with music.

Laufman, Dudley, and Jacqueline Laufman. *Traditional Barn Dances with Calls and Fiddling.* Champaign, IL: Human Kinetics, 2009. Instructions and music for 53 easy longways, square, and circle dances. Includes two CDs and a DVD (see "Recordings").

Linnell, Rod, and Louise Winston. *Square Dances from a Yankee Caller's Clipboard.* Norwell, MA: The New England Square Dance Caller,

1974. Reprinted 2002 by New England Folk Festival Association. About 50 squares and 7 contras, some in rough draft form; a fascinating glimpse of a choreographic genius at work. Includes "Rod's Quads" (eight-couple squares), probably Linnell's best-known dances.

Lyman, Frank, Jr. *One Hundred and One Singing Calls.* Woodbury, NJ: American Squares, 1951. Just what the title says. This was the prevailing style in New England before the contra revival. Interesting contributions from Ralph Page in his prime.

MacPherson, Pat, ed. *Dancing in Schools.* Haydenville, MA: Country Dance and Song Society, 2001. A series of essays on teaching contras and similar dances to children.

MacPherson, Pat, ed. *Family and Community Dances.* Haydenville, MA: Country Dance and Song Society, 1999. Essays on organizing and programming a family dance by several experts in the field. Has an extensive list of resources.

Melamed, Lanie. *All Join Hands: Connecting People through Folk Dance.* Montreal: The author, 1977. About 50 dances (circles, squares, contras, including some international folk dances) and a good theoretical and practical discussion of dance leadership.

Mills, Bob. *All Mixed Up: A Guide to Sound Production for Folk and Dance Music.* Second edition. Princeton, NJ: The author, 1996. Everything you need to know about choosing and operating a sound system. Includes a pull-out "quick reference" card. This is the book I wish had been available when I started calling.

Morningstar, Glen, Jr. *Dance the Winter Away.* Highland, MI: The author, 2005. Has 37 contras and 3 progressive circles, each written for a specific teaching need, all with an eye to traditional style and smooth flow.

Morrison, James. *Twenty-Four Early American Country Dances, Cotillions and Reels.* New York: Country Dance and Song Society, 1976. Eighteenth-century dances in their original form; includes music and a glossary of terms.

Page, Ralph. *An Elegant Collection of Contras and Squares.* Denver: Lloyd Shaw Foundation, 1984. Page's working repertoire at the end of his career (47 contras, 12 squares); some tunes.

Page, Ralph. *Heritage Dances of Early America.* Colorado Springs: Lloyd Shaw Foundation, 1976. Twenty-five contras from around 1800, translated into modern terminology; some tunes.

Page, Ralph. *The Ralph Page Book of Contras*. London: English Folk Dance and Song Society, 1969. Traditional contra dances along with some from the 1950s and 1960s (22 in all), with tunes.

Parkes, Tony. *Shadrack's Delight* and *Son of Shadrack*. Bedford, MA: Hands Four Books, 1988 and 1993. Original square, circle, and contra dances (more than 40 in each volume) by the author of this book.

Pimentel, Joseph. *The Cardinal Collection*. Columbus, OH: The author, 2004. Has 34 dances by the author and his friends; includes some updated versions of traditional contras.

Pittman, Anne M., Marlys S. Waller, and Cathy L. Dark. *Dance a While: A Handbook for Folk, Square, Contra, and Social Dance*. Tenth edition. San Francisco: Benjamin Cummings (a division of Pearson Higher Education), 2009. The standard college text on recreational dance; includes 35 contras and about 50 squares, plus many international folk dances and novelty dances. **www.pearsonhighered.com**

Roodman, Gary M. *Calculated Figures*. Binghamton, NY: The author, 1987. A dozen dances, mostly in New England style, with music; an elegant presentation of carefully constructed material. The author has produced nine volumes of original dances, mainly in English style.

Rose, Marian. *Step Lively* (3 volumes). Vancouver, BC, Canada: The author, 1998 on. Book-and-CD sets of wonderful material for schools, families, and community gatherings. Volume 1 has 20 all-purpose dances, Volume 2 has 30 traditional and contemporary Canadian dances, Volume 3 has 28 dances and singing games for younger children. Dances with their own tune have sheet music. The author is a full-time folk dance teacher and gives many useful tips learned from long experience. **www.marianrose.com**

Rosenberg, Paul. *Peel the Banana!* Albany, NY: The author, 2003; revised 2006. A book-and-CD set with 18 easy dances for school and community use. Book has printed music, directions, and calls; CD has called tracks. Music, by George Wilson and Peter Davis, is excellent. **www.homespun.biz**

Sannella, Ted. *Balance and Swing*. New York: Country Dance and Song Society, 1982. Contains 55 squares, contras, and triplets, mostly by the author, with copious notes; includes music for every dance, a glossary, and an excellent account of Boston-area dance history.

Sannella, Ted. *Calling Traditional New England Squares*. Haydenville, MA: Country Dance and Song Society, 2005. This booklet is worth several times its price; it contains the thoughts and advice of a master caller on many aspects of the subject, including the improvisation of breaks.

Price includes a CD of Ted calling 14 squares (with two examples of his signature "Merry-Go-Round"), recorded live at dance camps and weekends.

Sannella, Ted. *Swing the Next.* Northampton, MA: Country Dance and Song Society, 1996. Contains 80 squares, contras, and other dances, mostly by Ted, along with his always valuable thoughts on various aspects of dancing and calling. Music is included for every dance.

Smukler, David, and David Millstone. *Cracking Chestnuts: The Living Tradition of Classic American Contra Dances.* Haydenville, MA: Country Dance and Song Society, 2008. These contras were the backbone of the activity until around 1970 and still offer much enjoyment. Two callers who love them describe 17 in detail (including printed music) and give the calls for another 20. Includes teaching guidelines and several essays.

Spalding, Susan Eike, and Jane Harris Woodside, eds. *Communities in Motion: Dance, Community, and Tradition in America's Southeast and Beyond.* Westport, CT: Greenwood Press, 1995. Scholarly essays on squares, contras, clogging, and other forms including Native American and African-American dance. Required reading for anyone interested in traditional dance history and sociology.

Stix, Peter, ed. *Contra-butions.* Minneapolis: The editor, 1992. New dances and tunes from the upper Midwest. Two later volumes (1995, 1997) include dances by Ted Hodapp and Carol Ormand.

Sweet, Ralph, and Nils Fredland. *On the Beat with Ralph Sweet.* Haydenville, MA: Country Dance and Song Society, 2010. The life's work of a master caller. Directions, calls, and music for 90 patter and singing squares, all of which contra dancers and callers will enjoy.

Tolman, Beth, and Ralph Page. *The Country Dance Book.* Weston, VT: The Countryman Press and Farrar & Rinehart, New York, 1937. Reprinted by A.S. Barnes, New York; reprinted 1976 by Stephen Greene Press, Brattleboro, VT. The bible of the 1940s contra revival; over 70 dances, plus a wealth of historical and anecdotal information. All editions are out of print, but used copies are easy to find.

TUNE BOOKS

Brody, David. *The Fiddler's Fakebook.* New York: Oak Publications, 1983. A monumental collection: over 400 tunes from Northern, Southern, and Celtic traditions. Carefully transcribed from recordings.

Holenko, John. *Contra Dance Encyclopedia.* Pacific, MO: Mel Bay, 2009. Has 134 tunes, some pre-assembled into medleys, plus a section on how to play danceable music on various instruments. Title is misleading: the book contains no dance information other than a brief and not very accurate description of contra dancing.

Kennedy, Peter. *The Fiddler's Tune Book* and *The Second Fiddler's Tune Book.* London: English Folk Dance and Song Society, 1951 and 1954. Reprinted by Hargail Music Press. Reprinted in one volume (with chord symbols) by Dave Mallinson Publications; distributed by Mel Bay. Each book has 100 jigs, reels, hornpipes, polkas, and waltzes. Most tunes are useable for contras; many are easy to play.

McQuillen, Bob. *Bob's Note Books* (12 volumes and counting). Peterborough, NH: The author, 1982 on. About 100 tunes in each book, all by the author, who is renowned for his happy jigs and reels and haunting waltzes.

Miller, Randy, and Jack Perron. *The New England Fiddler's Repertoire.* East Alstead, NH: Fiddlecase Books, 1983. The best current collection of contra dance music as played in the Northeast: 168 time-tested tunes.

Miller, Randy, and Jack Perron. *The Fiddlecase Book of Polkas.* East Alstead, NH: Fiddlecase Books, 1978. Over 100 tunes in 2/4 and 4/4 time, many useable for squares and contras.

Reiner, David, and Peter Anick. *Old-Time Fiddling Across America.* Pacific, MO: Mel Bay, 1989. Contains 66 tunes in various regional styles; discusses the differences between those styles.

Sky, Patrick, ed. *Ryan's Mammoth Collection.* Pacific, MO: Mel Bay, 1995. A reprint of an 1883 classic, this was the Northeastern fiddler's bible until Brody, Miller/Perron, and Songer/Curley came along. Many musicians know it as Cole's *One Thousand Fiddle Tunes.*

Sloanaker, Jack, and Tony Parkes. *Square Dance Chord Book and Tune Locator.* Plymouth, VT: F&W Records, 1979. No tunes, just 500 chord charts for tunes common in New England (many tune books omit chords). Cross-reference to books and records containing the melodies is dated but interesting.

Songer, Sue, and Clyde Curley. *The Portland Collection: Contra Dance Music in the Pacific Northwest.* Two volumes. Portland, OR: The authors, 1997 and 2005. Here's proof of contra dancing's spread and universal appeal: a tune collection compiled by Oregon musicians has been adopted as a performance book by the New England Folk Festival Orchestra. These volumes are masterfully put together and include many fine tunes that have become standards in recent years. Some "chestnuts" are absent by design, as they're readily available in other books. Containing 318 and 322 tunes respectively, each volume includes extensive commentary and a resource list. Companion recordings are available. **www.theportlandcollection.com**

Sweet, Ralph. *The Fifer's Delight.* Hazardville, CT: The author, 1964, 1981. Begins with a graded series of pieces for fife; includes many good square and contra dance tunes (300 tunes in all). A book of harmony parts is available: *The Fifer's Delightful Companion* by Carol Greenfield (1988). **www.sweetheartflute.com**

RECORDINGS

There are many fine recordings of dance music intended for listening. Preference in this list has been given to recordings with at least some selections long enough for dancing (generally at least 7 to 9 rounds, though some tracks are much longer). Companion books are available for several titles. Recordings are on CD unless otherwise noted.

This list is also biased toward fairly traditional tune choices and playing styles. Many present-day bands draw inspiration from jazz, rock, and other genres; readers are encouraged to explore any "fusion" styles that appeal to them. Some of the websites mentioned at the end of the Resources section have longer lists of dance recordings than could be included here.

Any Jig or Reel. Becky Tracy, Keith Murphy, and Andy Davis. New England Dancing Masters. Three fine musicians play nine medleys for dances that don't require specific tunes. Also includes three waltzes.

Calling Traditional New England Squares. This booklet-and-CD set is described under "Books" (see Sannella).

Canterbury Country Dance Orchestra. F&W 8. This was Dudley Laufman's band. One of the first recordings of the current revival, and still inspiring. CD reissue includes tracks from two LPs, plus two five-minute tracks made for CDSS and originally issued as a single.

Chimes of Dunkirk: Great Dances for Children. Peter and Mary Alice Amidon. New England Dancing Masters. Companion to the book; includes music for several circles and whole-set longways, plus two all-purpose medleys (jigs, reels) for squares or contras.

Contra Music: The Sound of New England. Great Meadow Music. A bargain-priced sampler of tracks from the catalog of this company, which specializes in contra dance music. Some are dance length; all are worth listening to.

Contra Roots and Branches. Great Meadow Music. Co-produced by CDSS. Compiled to illustrate the spread of contra dance music; features 14 bands from across North America.

Domino. This CD by the French-Canadian band of the same name includes two terrific ten-minute tracks suitable for contras: Le Galant (jigs) and Le Tricentenaire (reels).

Down in the Valley. Andy Davis and the Amidon family. New England Dancing Masters. A companion to the book; has 25 singing games.

F&W String Band. F&W 1 (LP). Perhaps the first album of the current revival; has been widely imitated. One side is all dance-length tunes.

Farewell to the Hollow. New England Tradition. Whistler's Music 9860. Jigs, reels, marches, and waltzes played "straight" by some of the best-loved musicians in the Northeast.

Folk Dancer Records. Solid versions of old standard jigs and reels, played long enough for contras. The original releases were mostly on 78 rpm discs; most titles have been reissued on CD and are available from the Kentucky Dance Foundation. **www.folkdancer.org**

Full Swing. Mary Cay Brass and friends with Susan Kevra. Great Meadow Music. Several dance-length tracks for squares and contras, including three with calls by Kevra. Includes 24-page booklet of instructions and calls.

Grand Right & Left. The Rhythm Rollers. Topnotch contra dance musicians from both coasts; features Bob McQuillen at the piano.

The Hammered Dulcimer. Bill Spence with Fennig's All-Star String Band. Front Hall FHR-302. Joyful jigs and reels with the title instrument, fiddle, and banjo sharing the lead. **www.andysfronthall.com**

The Hammered Dulcimer Returns! Bill Spence with Fennig's All-Star String Band. Front Hall FHR-041. More up-tempo jigs and reels with the contrasting textures of fiddle and hammered dulcimer.

Heatin' Up the Hall. Yankee Ingenuity. Varrick 038. Several high-energy jig and reel medleys; one old-time Western square with calls by Tony Parkes.

Jump Jim Joe. Peter and Mary Alice Amidon. New England Dancing Masters. A companion to the book; includes 20 dance-like games. Ideal for children too young for squares and contras; fun for all ages.

Kitchen Junket. Yankee Ingenuity with Tony Parkes. Alcazar 200 (double-length cassette). Ten jig and reel medleys (each 7x32 measures), with and without calls for New England squares. Especially valuable for its 30 breaks; each one is different. Originally issued on two LPs; used copies are fairly easy to find.

Let's Square Dance! Richard Kraus. RCA Victor (issued on LP, 45, and 78). Five albums, graded for school use; each includes a circle, a longways, and several squares, all with calls, plus an instrumental tune. Some of the patter is sexist by today's standards, but Kraus's style and energy are worth copying. Out of print, but worth searching for in schools and libraries; used copies appear frequently on eBay.

Listen to the Mockingbird. New England Dancing Masters. A companion to the book. An all-star band from Vermont and western Massachusetts plays five medleys in various styles (10x32 measures each) plus several specialized tunes and three squares with calls by Andy Davis.

Live at the Guiding Star Grange. Wild Asparagus. This two-CD set is the first collection of dance-length tracks by this western Massachusetts group, for many years the premier touring contra dance band.

Lloyd Shaw Foundation contra records. An extensive series of recordings, originally issued on 45 rpm discs, with calls on one side and the same music without calls on the other. Good for the "training wheels" method of learning to call. Now available on custom-compiled CDs or as MP3 downloads. **www.lloydshaw.org**

Maritime Dance Party. Gerry Robichaud. Alcazar 201/202 (double cassette; includes an album of old-time Western squares with calls by Sandy Bradley). Jigs, reels, and a waltz (all dance-length) by an excellent Canadian-American fiddler with full backup. Originally released on LP; all versions are out of print but worth searching for.

New England Chestnuts, Volumes 1 and 2. Rodney and Randy Miller and friends. Alcazar 203/204 (two LPs or double cassette). Reissued in a two-CD album by Great Meadow Music. All the standard pre-revival contra dance tunes; would be indispensable even if the playing were ordinary, but it's superb.

ONE:Two. Old New England. This trio, Bob McQuillen's current band, plays in a solidly traditional New England style. They now have four CDs; this second volume is my favorite for its dance-length tracks.

Peel the Banana! This book-and-CD set is described under "Books" (see Rosenberg).

Pure Quill. Rodney Miller and Bob McQuillen. Great Meadow Music. These musicians have become New England institutions. Brilliant fiddling and solid piano playing combine to produce inspiring dance music.

Ralph Page Calls Contras and Squares. RPMC 1 (cassette). Produced in Ralph's memory by NEFFA; made from early commercial recordings and more recent tapes from dance camps. A must for students of contra dance history.

Sashay the Donut. New England Dancing Masters. A companion to the book, this CD has several all-purpose tracks of jigs and reels in addition to dances that require special tunes.

Shadrack's Delight. Tony Parkes. Hands Four HF 101. Short samples, with calls, of all the dances in the companion book. A few squares are complete, to illustrate the use of breaks. Music is licensed from F&W Records (Canterbury Country Dance Orchestra and F&W String Band). Can be used as a guide to matching tunes with dances.

Shindig in the Barn. Ralph Sweet's All-Stars. A dozen singing squares called by a master, backed by well-known contra dance musicians.

Smoke on the Water. Bob Dalsemer and friends. Rousing renditions of singing squares of the 1940s and 1950s. Available with or without calls, on CD or MP3, from Hanhurst/Palomino. **www.dosado.com**

Starry Nights and Candlelight (formerly titled We *Love Contra Dances*). Pat Spaeth, Phil Williams, and Vivian Williams. Voyager VRCD 333. Several jig and reel medleys, made expressly for dancing. Fiddle and accordion dominate. **voyagerrecords.com**

Step Lively. These book-and-CD sets are described under "Books" (see Rose).

Total Warm-Up. Shelley Kristen. My favorite warm-up CD of several I've bought; has 20 exercises that let you ease into your full singing or speaking voice. **www.singingvoicelessons.com**

Traditional Barn Dances with Calls and Fiddling. Described under "Books" (see Laufman), this set includes two CDs with called and instrumental tracks, as well as a DVD.

Turning of the Tide. Fresh Fish. KME-2. Excellent playing of jigs and reels, tight and high-powered. The state of the art in contra dance music.

When the Work's All Done. Bob Dalsemer and friends. Easy singing and patter squares, well called and played. See *Smoke on the Water,* above, for format and ordering information.

VIDEOS

Chimes of Dunkirk: Teaching Dance to Children. A companion to New England Dancing Masters' book and CD of the same name, this hour-

Resources 293

long video includes 17 dances from the book, with scenes of children dancing them interspersed with teaching tips.

Contra Connections. Includes *Paid to Eat Ice Cream,* described below, along with *What's Not to Like?,* a documentary by David Millstone about his own monthly community dance in Norwich, Vermont.*

Contra Dance Training for Beginning Dancers. This teaching series, produced by the Atlanta-based Chattahoochee Country Dancers, is available on a high-resolution DVD or as free downloads on YouTube. Links to the YouTube version are at **www.contradance.org** (click on the "What is contra dancing?" tab) and **www.cdss.org** (under "Resources and References").

The Other Way Back: Dancing with Dudley. A documentary on Dudley Laufman, the caller whose charisma inspired hundreds of young people to take up dancing, playing, and calling in the 1960s and '70s. Half a century later, Dudley is still going strong.*

Paid to Eat Ice Cream. A documentary on Bob McQuillen, a well-loved New Hampshire dance musician, whose career spans more than 60 years. Includes video clips and still photos of square and contra dancing in the 1940s, '50s, and '60s.*

Sweet Talk. An interview with Ralph Sweet, who became first a modern square dance caller and then an elder statesman of the traditional square and contra dance scene. Includes audio and video clips from the square dance boom of the 1950s.*

Together in Time: A Story of New England Contra Music and Dance. A 27-minute documentary touching on contra history and showing several present-day dance venues. Distributed by Great Meadow Music.

*Produced by David Millstone, a New England caller whose love for the dance and its people is manifest in the care he puts into his films.

COMPUTER SOFTWARE

Digital Music Magician. Turns a laptop computer into a virtual MP3 player, with large, easy-to-see controls. Lets the user manage a library of audio files and cue cards. Similar programs are made for DJs; this one is designed for callers. **www.dosado.com/software.default.htm**

GoldWave. A digital audio recorder and editor. **www.goldwave.com**

Wave Repair. A progam specifically for cleaning up WAV files made from vinyl records. **www.waverepair.com**

ORGANIZATIONS

Callerlab. 200 SW 30th St., Suite 104, Topeka, KS 66611. The professional association of modern square dance callers; has a committee for community and traditional dance; allows subscriber memberships. **www.callerlab.org**

Contralab. An association of contra callers working primarily within the modern square dance movement. **www.contralab.net**

Country Dance and Song Society. 132 Main St., P.O. Box 338, Haydenville, MA 01039. National in scope, covers all traditional styles of square and contra dancing as well as folk music and English dancing. Functions as a clearinghouse of dance information; sponsors camps; publishes and sells books and recordings. Many local dance groups are affiliated with CDSS; its *Group Directory,* essential for travelers, lists all known groups whether affiliated or not. **www.cdss.org**

Eastern Cooperative Recreation School. A long-established group that has helped keep folk recreation alive between revivals. Deals with folk and square dancing, singing, games, crafts, informal dramatics. Sponsors summer and winter weeks and year-round weekends. Excellent for dance leaders interested in broadening their scope. Website has a resource list covering many art forms. **www.ecrs.org**

English Folk Dance and Song Society. Cecil Sharp House, 2 Regent's Park Rd., London NW1 7AY, England. The original English group from which CDSS was born. Covers American as well as English styles. Like CDSS, has many local affiliates and a sales division. **www.efdss.org**

Folk Arts Center of New England. 10 Franklin St., Stoneham, MA 02180. Serves as a liaison between the folk community and the world at large; deals primarily with international folk dance but co-sponsors a few contra dance events. Gives some grants aimed at developing dance musicians. A good source of information on material suitable for children and families. **www.facone.org**

Lloyd Shaw Foundation. In memory of the educator whose name is linked with the revival of the Western square dance, works to preserve and promote all forms of American group dancing, old and new. Sponsors camps (for all) and university workshops (for intensive teacher training); produces and sells dance items. The LSF Archives, now part of the Carson-Brierly Dance Library at the University of Denver, may be the largest square dance–related collection in the world. **www.lloydshaw.org**

New England Folk Festival Association. P.O. Box 2789, Acton, MA 01720. Co-founded by Ralph Page, NEFFA exists primarily to run its annual festival (see "Events," below) but sponsors many other events and gives grants to still others. Has a Ralph Page Memorial Committee with an annual event of its own. **www.neffa.org**

New Hampshire Library of Traditional Music & Dance. Milne Special Collections & Archives, Dimond Library, University of New Hampshire, Durham, NH 03824. The personal collection of Ralph Page, augmented by gifts and bequests from other callers and dancers, is the largest and most valuable research library in the East devoted to Anglo-American dance. Also covers folk song and international dance to some extent. Now includes the CDSS archives. **www.library.unh.edu/special/index.php/category/folk-music-dance**

Traditional Square & Contra Dance in Denmark. Smakkegaardsvej 102, st. th., DK-2820 Gentofte, Denmark. Active mostly within Denmark, but a good source of information about contra dancing and traditional square dancing across Europe. **www.tscdd.dk**

RETAILERS

Anglo-American Dance Shop. Resedastraat 8, B9920 Lovendegem, Belgium. Probably the largest dealer of contra dance material in Europe; has an extensive selection of CDs and books. Website is in English and has links to many traditional dance groups in Europe. **www.aads.be**

Community Dance Project. C/o Marian Rose, Box 56078, First Avenue, Vancouver, BC, Canada V5L 5E2. Books and recordings of traditional dances for school and community use. **www.marianrose.com**

Contracopia. An online-only dealer in CDs of contra dance music. Searches can be made by musical style as well as by artist name. Has audio samples; maintains an affiliate program. **www.contracopia.net**

Country Dance and Song Society. 132 Main St., P.O. Box 338, Haydenville, MA 01039. Exhaustive selection of dance books, tune books, and recordings. Specializes in English and American country dance, morris and sword dance, and traditional folk song. **www.cdss.org**

Folk Arts Center of New England. 10 Franklin St., Stoneham, MA 02180. Folk dance recordings, primarily international but some square and contra. **www.facone.org**

Folk Dancer Record Center. 6290 Olin Road, Brandenburg, KY 40108. A service of the Kentucky Dance Foundation; the current producer and distributor of Michael Herman's classic folk, square, and contra dance recordings; has reissued most titles on CD. Also sells vintage dance records on other labels. **www.folkdancer.org**

Great Meadow Music. Produces and sells CDs of contra dance music; has reissued some important older recordings. Has audio samples; gives discounts to contra performers. **www.greatmeadowmusic.com**

Hands Four Books. P.O. Box 641, Bedford, MA 01730. The publisher of this and other books and recordings on contras and squares, primarily for callers. **www.hands4.com**

Hanhurst's Music Review Service/Palomino Records. 2818 Highway 44 East, Shepherdsville, KY 40165. A well-known source of modern square dance recordings; stocks a few traditional items and is the current distributor of Bob Dalsemer's material. Also sells sound systems, components, parts, and accessories. **www.dosado.com**

Lloyd Shaw Foundation, Sales Division. Contra, square, folk, and novelty dance recordings; books; curriculum kits. **www.lloydshaw.org**

New England Dancing Masters. 41 West Street, Brattleboro, VT 05301. Books and recordings of dances and singing games for school and community use. **www.dancingmasters.com**

EVENTS

This is a selective listing, with preference given to well-established events. Dancers and musicians with little or no experience are welcome at most events, but read the literature or website carefully (better yet, ask someone who's been there) to get an idea of the atmosphere. Events marked with an asterisk (*) are primarily devoted to folk song and/or instrumental music, but have had a substantial amount of dancing in recent years.

Ashokan. Summer weeks and year-round holiday weekends in southern New York State. Fiddle and Dance, P.O. Box 49, Saugerties, NY 12477. **www.ashokan.org**

Augusta. A summer dance week and a week-long callers' intensive workshop as part of a large and varied folk arts curriculum, all held in central West Virginia. Augusta Heritage Center, Davis & Elkins College, 100 Campus Drive, Elkins, WV 26241. **www.augustaheritage.com**

Bay Area Country Dance Society. Sponsors several weeks and weekends in California. **www.bacds.org**

Berea. Christmas Country Dance School, a winter week in central Kentucky. Emphasis on dance leadership. Berea College CCDS, CPO 2159, Berea, KY 40404. www.berea.edu/peh/dance/ccds/default.asp

Brasstown. A winter dance week and other dance events as part of a huge and varied folk arts curriculum, held in western North Carolina. John C. Campbell Folk School, 1 Folk School Road, Brasstown, NC 28902. www.folkschool.org

Champlain Valley Folk Festival.* A summer weekend in northern Vermont. P.O. Box 172, Burlington, VT 05402. www.cvfest.org

Clearwater's Hudson River Revival.* A spring weekend in southern New York State. www.clearwater.org

Country Dance and Song Society. Sponsors several summer weeks at Pinewoods (Massachusetts), plus one each at Ogontz (New Hampshire) and Timber Ridge (West Virginia). Several weeks include calling or leadership workshops. CDSS, 132 Main St., P.O. Box 338, Haydenville, MA 01039. www.cdss.org

Dance Flurry. A winter weekend near Albany (New York). P.O. Box 448, Latham, NY 12110. www.danceflurry.org

Downeast Country Dance Festival. A spring weekend near Portland (Maine). 455 East Pond Rd., Nobleboro, ME 04555. www.starleft.org/decdf/

Festival of American Fiddle Tunes.* A summer week in Washington State. Emphasis on dance music. Centrum, P.O. Box 1158, Port Townsend, WA 98368. www.centrum.org/fiddle/

Harvest Moon Dance Festival. A fall weekend in Santa Barbara (California). Santa Barbara Country Dance Society, P.O. Box 21904, Santa Barbara, CA 93121. www.sbcds.org/hm/

Lady of the Lake. Weeks and weekends in Idaho. www.ladyofthelake.org

Mainewoods. Summer weeks in Maine. Emphasis on international folk dance; usually a contra caller on staff. www.mainewoodsdancecamp.org

Michigan Dance Heritage. Sponsors spring and fall weekends in Michigan. http://mdh-online.org

New England Folk Festival. A spring weekend in Massachusetts that features contras and squares, international folk dance, ethnic food, crafts, sales area. NEFFA, P.O. Box 2789, Acton, MA 01720. www.neffa.org

Northwest Folklife Festival.* A spring weekend in Seattle (Washington). 305 Harrison St., Seattle, WA 98109. www.nwfolklife.org

Old Songs Festival.* A spring weekend near Albany (New York). Old Songs, P.O. Box 466, Voorheesville, NY 12186. **www.oldsongs.org**

Philadelphia Folk Festival.* A summer weekend in Pennsylvania. 7113 Emlen Street, Philadelphia, PA 19119. **www.pfs.org**

Pinewoods – See Country Dance and Song Society. (Scottish and international folk dancers also use the camp; see **www.pinewoods.org** for more information.)

Ralph Page Dance Legacy Weekend. Held in January at the University of New Hampshire, this is the closest thing in existence to a contra dance leaders' conference, with workshops for callers, musicians, and dancers. The syllabi from past years, some of which are online at **http://www.library.unh.edu/special/index.php/ralph-page-dance-legacy-weekend**, are a treasure trove of material. **www.neffa.org**

Tropical Dance Vacation. Another sign of the growth of contra dancing: George Marshall, the caller for Wild Asparagus, sponsors dance weeks in Hawaii and St. Croix. **www.tropicaldancevacation.com**

PERIODICALS

Most of the groups listed above under "Organizations" publish their own magazines or newsletters. The trend is toward making them available online only, though some can still be obtained in paper form. Some groups send their publications only to members; others sell them separately or allow "subscriber" memberships, usually at a reduced rate.

One magazine, no longer published, deserves special mention:

Northern Junket. Ralph Page's inimitable blend of dance information and Yankee humor. Every issue included directions (and often music) for at least one contra dance, one square dance, and one international folk dance. Published from 1949 to 1984; scanned pages of all issues are now accessible online through the University of New Hampshire. **http://www.izaak.unh.edu/dlp/NorthernJunket/pages/**

MAILING LISTS

Increasing numbers of dancers, callers, musicians, organizers, and sound technicians are using electronic mailing lists to stay in touch and exchange information. Only those of broad general interest are mentioned here; there are also numerous local and regional lists.

Shared Weight. Has separate lists for callers, musicians, and organizers. The primary focus of the callers' list has been on helping newer callers. **www.sharedweight.net**

Trad-Dance-Callers. A place for callers of all experience levels to "talk shop." All styles of traditional square and contra dancing are represented, with a few modern square dance and English country dance leaders. **http://groups.yahoo.com/group/trad-dance-callers/**

WEBSITES

In addition to the websites maintained by the publishers, retailers, and organizations listed above, there are a few sites that exist solely for the sake of collecting and imparting information. Those listed below are well-established and have links to many more sites.

Contra Dance Links. Attempts to list all the contra dance series in the world, with links to those maintaining active websites. Has dance schedules, band and caller listings, and an extensive Resources page including links to more than 300 essays on contra dancing and related forms, plus newspaper articles and blogs, and a list of 1,000 CDs of contra dance music. **www.contradancelinks.com**

The Dance Gypsy. An interactive calendar of events devoted to contra dancing and similar dance forms. Searches can be made by date, location, caller, or musicians. Originally limited to New England, this site now attempts to cover the entire United States and Canada (and beyond). **www.thedancegypsy.com**

Internet Resources for Contra Dance Callers. A short but interesting page; its unique value is a set of links to handouts from several respected leaders' contra calling workshops. **www.quiteapair.us/calling/**

Michael Dyck's Contradance Index. A monumental work: attempts to list, by title and author, every contra dance ever published. Cites the source (book or website) of each dance; if the source is a website, the citation is a live link. As of October 2010, the dance count is 6,375! **www.ibiblio.org/contradance/index/**

Index

See also the discussion of various terms in the Glossary, which is not indexed.

A
"A" part of tune, 25, 46, 79, 159
Accordion
   as core of band, 132
Acoustics of hall, 10, 108, 110
Active couples, 20, 22
Adolescents, 115–16
   and same-sex couples, 119
   at family dances, 139
Adult education programs, 126–27
Advanced dances, defined, 72
Affinity groups, 11
   and one-night stands, 128
   and series, 130
African-American dance, 15
Age of dancers, as programming factor, 66
Alcohol, 128, 135, 145
   as programming factor, 66
Allemande. *See* Hand turn
Ambiguity in dance routines, 71
Amplifiers, 96–97
   and impedance matching, 98
Anticipation, 51
   of balances, 164
   of circle, 169
Armstrong, Don, 47, 210

B
"B" part of tune, 25, 46, 79, 159
Balance
   and modern square dancers, 123
   difficulty of, 138
   discussed in depth, 162–64
   transition from hey, 189
   transition from star, 173
   transition to do-si-do, 164
   transition to hand turn, 155
   transition to swing, 164
   transitions from other moves, 164
Balance in a wave
   discussed in depth, 176–77
   transition from do-si-do, 151, 177
   transition from hand turn, 177

Balance of sexes, as programming factor, 66
Ballroom hold for swing, 156
"Bars" of music, 46, 80
Basic movements, 59, 149
   as difficulty factor, 72
   discussed in depth. *See under names of basic moves*
Beats of music, 26, 40, 46, 80
Becket formation, 22, 123
Beginning dancers, 42, 59, 68
   and duration of dance, 43
   at series, 137–38
   reaction time of, 40
Big circle dances
   Circassian Circle, 196
   discussed in depth, 193–94
   Ted's Mixer, 198
Big circle, as teaching format, 149, 167, 193
Body language
   between dancers, 144
   with musicians, 85
Body memory, 55, 58
"Booking ahead", 144
Books, how to use, 45–47
Boredom, avoiding, 69
Box the gnat, 165
Breakdown (type of square), 233
Breaking into calling, 8–10
Breaks. *See* Square dance breaks
Breathing, 36
Briggs, Dudley, 216
Brundage, Al, 16
"Bull-by-the-tail" swing, 158
Burchenal, Elizabeth, 15
Buzz step, 15
   discussed in depth, 156
   teaching to jigs, 83

C
Cables, loudspeaker, 102
Cables, microphone, 100
California twirl, 165

301

Called recordings, 5, 7, 8, 10
Caller, defined, 3
Caller/Teacher Manual for Contras (Armstrong), 47
Calls
  fitting to music, 33–36, 39–41
    with jigs, 83
  sound balance vs. music, 108
Camps, children's, 113, 116
Cardioid microphones, 99, 100
Cards, index, 45, 75
Care of media, 93
Cassette tapes, 91
  care of, 93
Cast off, 22
  discussed in depth, 183–84
  transition to turn contra corners, 191
Change of partners, in squares, 233
Change of roles, 23
Changing tunes, 87–88
  and diminishing calls, 42
  and duration of dance, 87
Children, 113–14, 232
  and same-sex couples, 119
  and whole-set longways, 205
Choosing material, 70–74
Choosing tunes, 79–84
Choreography, 17
Circle (basic move)
  discussed in depth, 168–69
  transition from swing, 158
  transition to pass through, 174
  transitions from, 169
Circle dances
  Circassian Circle, 196
  discussed in depth, 193–95
  programming of, 68
  Sanita Hill Circle, 200
  Sicilian Circle, 202
  Ted's Mixer, 198
Classes
  and recorded music, 90
  in adult education programs, 126–27
  pros and cons of, 56–57
Cleanup of hall, 135

Clothing, 146
Club square dancing. *See* Modern square dancing
Community dance. *See* Series
Compact discs (CDs), 90
  care of, 93
Complete Ball-room Hand Book (Howe), 202, 206
Computer files of music, 91
Conflicts, scheduling, 133
Contra corners. *See* Turn contra corners
Contra dance, defined, 13
Contra Dance Book (Holden), 206
Contra dances
  Chorus Jig, 228
  discussed in depth, 215
  Essex Reel, 222
  Flirtation Reel, 226
  Jefferson's Reel, 216
    walkthrough of, 53–55
  Menotomy Reel, 78
  Newbury Reel, 224
  Ocean View Reel, 78
  Orono Special, 220
  Rose Tree, 218
Contra dancing
  as generic term, 17, 231
  compared with modern square dancing, 17
Contra formation, 19–22
Contredanse, 14
Core group, 11, 130
Counter-dancing, 185
Country dance, 14
Couple dances, in history, 15
Couple numbers, in equal dances, 20
Couple status of dancers, as programming factor, 66
Courses. *See* Classes
Courtesy, 143–45
Courtesy turn, 161
  defined, 178
  vs. twirl, 17
Cracking Chestnuts (Smukler & Millstone), 215
Cross at head and foot, 23, 24

Index

Crowd size
   and progressive circles, 66, 195
   as programming factor, 66
Crowding, as programming factor, 66

D

"Dance camp romance", 74
Dancing masters, 15
Dancing space, 10, 131
Dancing style, 50–52
   in classes, 126
Dancing, as prerequisite for calling, 6–7
Decorations, 129, 136
Demanding sequences, 73
Demonstrations, 57–58
   for foreign students, 118
   of hey, 58, 188
   of swing, 158
Diction, 37
Difficulty level
   of evening, 64, 67
   of guest set, 63
   of one-night stands, 128
   of routines, judging, 72–74
   of series, 69
Dimensions of set, 20
Diminishing calls, 41–42
Disabilities, 117
   and whole-set longways, 205
Discouragement, 12
Dividing sets, 43
Door-sitters, 136
Do-si-do
   discussed in depth, 150–51
   transition from balance, 164
   transition to balance in a wave, 151, 177
   transition to hand turn, 151
   use in teaching gypsy, 152
Double progression, 22, 124
Down four in line, as means of progression, 22
Downbeat, 26, 80
   of jigs, 82
   of marches, 81
   of reels, 80
Dress for dancing, 146

Duple formation, 20, 190
Duration of dance, 42–44
   and recorded music, 92
   and tune changes, 87
Durlacher, Ed, 200

E

Eastern Cooperative Recreation School, 118
Easy dances, defined, 72
E-mail, 134
Ending calls, 44
Ending the music, 88
Energy level, 67
English as a second language, 118
English country dancing, 14, 52, 184, 185–86, 189
English Dancing Master (Playford), 14
Equal dances, 16, 17, 19
   couple numbers in, 20
Equalization (sound), 108
   and feedback, 109
Etiquette, 143–46
Evening dance, programming, 64–68
Excitement level, 43, 67
Experience level of dancers, as programming factor, 66
Experienced dancers
   and duration of dance, 43
   reaction time of, 40, 41
Eye contact
   with musicians, 85

F

Facing twirl, 165
Family dances, 138–39
Father-daughter dances, 114
Fatigue, of dancers, 43
Feedback (sound), 38, 100, 103, 107, 109
Female voices, equalization of, 108
Fiddle
   as core of band, 132
   equalization of, 108
Figure eight, 186
"Flavors" of tunes, 86
   and tune changes, 88
Flexibility, in programming, 65–67

Floor surface, as programming factor, 66
Floor, care of, 136
Flow (choreography), 70
Flyers, 134
Folk dances, international, 139, 169
Food, 135
Ford, Henry, 15
Foreign students, 118, 232
Forgiving sequences, 73
Forward and back
    discussed in depth, 170–71
    transition from swing, 158
    transition to swing, 170
    transitions into, 171
Foster, Stephen, 234
Four-face-four dances, 20, 195
Freezing the action, 53, 54, 61
Frontier whirl, 165
Fudging, 164
    in cast off, 183
    in half promenade, 160

G

Gaudreau, Herbie, 16, 22, 123
Gender balance, as programming factor, 66
Gender-free dancing, 118–21
Gilmore, Ed, 16, 238
Gimmick method of composing, 77
Give-and-Take (Jennings), 46, 261
Giving weight, 51, 138
    in circle, 168
    in hand turn, 154
    in swing, 157
Glossary dances, 76
Golden Rule, 143
Grapevine step, 169
Graphic equalizer, 109
Guest sets, 9
    planning for, 63
Guitar
    as core of band, 132
    equalization of, 108
Gypsy, discussed in depth, 152–53

H

Half figure eight, discussed in depth, 185–86
Half promenade, 160, 161
Half right and left, 182
Hall acoustics, 10, 108, 110
Hall rental, 130–31
Hall size and shape, as programming factor, 66
Hand turn
    discussed in depth, 154–55
    transition from balance, 155
    transition from do-si-do, 151
    transition from star, 173
    transition from swing, 158
    transition to balance in a wave, 177
Handicapped dancers, 117
    and whole-set longways, 205
Hands-across star, 172
"Hands four", 20
Hash, 18, 50
Hay on floor, 129, 136
Helping words, 38, 41
Helt, Jerry, 236
Hendrickson, Chip, 200
Hey
    discussed in depth, 187–89
    teaching, 58
    transition to balance, 189
High school, 115–16
Hiring musicians, 131–33
History, 6, 14–18
Holden, Rickey, 206
Hornpipes, 81
Howe, Elias, 202, 206
Hybrid twirl, 165

I

Impedance matching, 98
Improper formation, 14, 20
Inactive couples, 20, 43
    at one-night stands, 128
Index cards, 45, 75
Instruction session, 56, 137–38
    publicity for, 137
Instrumentation, 132
Intermediate dances, defined, 72
Intermission, as programming factor, 67
International folk dances, 139, 169

Introduction, musical, 87
Introductory calls, 33–36
Irish music, 15

J

Jennings, Larry, 46, 53, 73, 261
Jigs, 82–84
   teaching buzz step to, 83
"Jingle Bells" analogy, 25, 30, 33, 34
Junior high school, 115

K

Kanegson, Abe, 240
Karaoke machines, 104
Key words of call, 39
   timing of, 41

L

Ladies chain
   and same-sex couples, 121
   discussed in depth, 178–80
   etiquette of, 144
   transition from right and left, 182
   transition from swing, 158
   transition to right and left, 182
Laufman, Dudley, 17, 206
Learning to call, 6–8
Left-foot balance, 163
Length of set, 43
Level. *See* Difficulty level; Energy level; Excitement level; Experience level
LGBT community, 119
Line array loudspeakers, 101–2
Linnell, Rod, 240
Liquor, 128, 135, 145
   as programming factor, 66
List of dance titles, making, 75
Live music
   advantages of, 84
   working with, 84–89
Lloyd Shaw Foundation, 118
Locations for dancing, 10, 131
Log of programs, 69
Loudspeakers, 100–102
   and impedance matching, 98
   line array, 101–2
   placement, 105–7

M

Mailing list, 134
Marches, 81–82
Marker couple, 44
Measures of music, 46, 80
Medleys, 18, 43
Memorization, 45
   ease of, 70
Mental fatigue, of dancers, 42, 67
Mescolanze formation, 20, 195
Meter of tunes, 79
   of hornpipes, 81
   of jigs, 82
   of marches, 81
   of reels, 80
Microphone technique, 38
Microphones, 98–100
   and impedance matching, 98
   and sound check, 111
   unidirectional, 38, 99, 107
   wireless, 57, 99
Middle school, 115
Miller, Duke, 238
Millstone, David, 215
Minidiscs (MDs), 91
Minor set, 20
Mistakes by callers, 12, 37, 45
   in writing dances, 77
Mistakes by dancers
   at end of line, 23
   caller's attitude toward, 60
   circling too far, 42
   in gypsy, 152
   in hey, 188
   in pass through, 174
   in right and left, 181
   in stars, 173
   in walkthroughs, 56, 58, 59
Mixers, 66, 68, 194
Modern square dancers, calling contras to, 121–24
Modern square dancing, 76, 117
   and recorded music, 84
   compared with contra dancing, 17
Modifying dances
   for older adults, 117
   for same-sex couples, 121
   for special education, 118

Money, 4
  and musicians, 133
  collecting, 136
Monitors, 102
  placement, 107
Moody, Ed, 242
MP3 files, 91
Multi-caller dance, 11
Music
  ending, 88
  fitting calls to, 33–36, 39–41
    with jigs, 83
  sound balance vs. calls, 108
  starting, 86
  structure of, 25–31
  working with, 79–93
Musicians
  and sound check, 110
  hiring, 131–33
  working with, 84–89
Muzzey, Lucy, 230

N

Neighbor, 13
Neutral couples, 24
New dances, writing, 76–78
Newsletters, 134
Non-English-speaking dancers, 118
Notation, 45–47
Number of couples, 19, 23–24
  limiting, 19, 43

O

Ocean wave, 176
Older adults, 117
  and duration of dance, 43
  and same-sex couples, 119
Older material, 78
Olson, Al, 73
One-night stands, 127–29
  for new callers, 11
"Ones", 20, 22
Open mike dance, 10
Organizing material, 75–76
Original dances, writing, 76–78
Outdoor dances, and care of media, 93

P

PA systems. *See* Sound equipment
Pacing of evening, 52, 67–68
  at one-night stands, 129
Page, Ralph, 12, 16, 87, 242
Partner change in squares, 233
Pass through
  as part of right and left, 181
  discussed in depth, 174–75
  transition from circle, 174
Patter, 15, 38
Phrasing, 30–31
  vs. timing, 30
Piano, as core of band, 132
Piece count, 73
Piper, Ralph, 163
Pitch of voice, 36, 39
Playford, John, 14, 218
Playlists, 92
Popular music, 115, 116
Positive approach, 60
Posts in hall, as programming factor, 66
Posture, 50
Potluck suppers, 135
Practicing, 8, 33
Praise
  for band, 88
  for dancers, 61
Press releases, 134
Program planning
  for evening dance, 64–68
  for guest set, 63
  for series, 68
Progression, 22
Progressive circle dances
  and crowd size, 66, 195
  discussed in depth, 194–95
  Portland Fancy, 202
  Sanita Hill Circle, 200
  Sicilian Circle, 202
Progressive circle, as teaching format, 167, 194
Projection of voice, 36

Promenade
 as analogy in teaching ladies
  chain, 178
 discussed in depth, 160–61
 modifying, 121
 omitting from walkthrough, in
  squares, 233
 positions for, 121, 161
 transition from swing, 158, 161
Prompted calls
 defined, 33
 timing of, 39
Proper formation, 20
Proximity effect, 38, 99
Public service announcements, 134
Publicity, 133–35
 for instruction session, 137
Puritans, 14

Q

Quadrilles, 231, 234
Quotation within routines, 74

R

Radio publicity, 134
Reaction time of dancers, 40, 41
Reading calls, 45, 75
Reasons for calling, 3
Recorded calls, 5, 7, 8, 10
Recorded music, 89–93
 formats, 90
 practicing with, 7, 8, 33
 sound systems for, 103
 strengths of, 90
 with no intro, 33
Recording
 for self-criticism, 8, 36, 37, 39
 in field, 7, 8
Record-keeping, 67, 69
Records, vinyl, 91
 care of, 93
Recovering from mistakes, 60
Reels, 80–81
Refreshments, 135
Repetition
 at a series, 68
 in classes, 127
 of walkthrough, 55
 to undo mistakes, 59

Retirement-age dancers, 117
Reverb, on amplifier, 110
Rhythm, 26
 calling in, 36
Ricciotti, Chris, 120
Right and left (through)
 difficulty of, 138
 discussed in depth, 181–82
 modifying, 121
 teaching, 60, 61
 transition from ladies chain, 182
 transition to ladies chain, 182
Right and left four, 182
Roughness, in hand turn, 155

S

Same-sex couples, 118–21
Sannella, Ted, 73, 198, 226, 273
Scheduling a series, 133
Schools, dancing in, 113, 125
Scottish country dancing, 189
Scottish music, 15
Senior citizens, 117
Senior high school, 116
Series
 difficulty level of, 69
 programming, 68
 running, 130–38
 starting, 10–11
Setup of hall, 135
Sheldon, G.T., 242
Shoes, 146
Shorthand, 75
Shyness, 4, 115, 116, 194
Sicilian circle (formation). *See*
 Progressive circle
Side-by-side twirl, 165
Signaling the band, 88
Singing squares, 234–35
 as contra tunes, 82
Single file promenade, 161
Size of crowd
 and progressive circles, 66, 195
 as programming factor, 66
Size of set. *See* Dimensions of set;
 Number of couples
Smukler, David, 215
Social networking, 135
Software for playing music, 91, 92

Solo moves, and older adults, 117
Sorting material, 65, 75
  by difficulty level, 72
Sorting tunes, 86
Soul-searching, 3–6
Sound check, 107, 108, 110–11
Sound columns, 102
Sound equipment, 95–111
  care of, 111
  low-cost, 104
  used, 104
  who brings, 133
Spaces for dancing, 10, 131
Speakers. *See* Loudspeakers
Special education, 117
Spinning
  after hand turns, 155, 191
  in do-si-do, 150, 151
  in do-si-do to a wave, 177
Square dance breaks
  discussed in depth, 233–34
  examples, 244–51
Square dance figures
  Buffalo Quadrille, 238
  Deer Park Lancers, 242
  discussed in depth, 232–33
  Queen's Quadrille, 236
  Steamboat Lancers, 240
Square dances, 13, 19
  and tune changes, 87
  and tune structure, 25
  choosing recordings for, 92
  length of, for band, 87
Square dancing
  as generic term, 16, 17
  as national fad, 16
Square formation, discussed in depth, 232
Stage fright, 12
Standardization, 18
Star
  discussed in depth, 172–73
  transition into balance, 173
  transition into hand turn, 173
Star through, 165
Starting the music, 86
Step, basic, 138, 146
  and modern square dancers, 123

Story line, 71
Straight-arm swing, 158
Style, 50–52
  in classes, 126
Summer camp, dancing at, 113, 116
Swing
  and modern square dancers, 122
  as means of progression, 22, 122, 157
  difficulty of, 138
  discussed in depth, 156–59
  transition from balance, 164
  transition from forward and back, 171
  transitions from, 158, 161
  two-hand, 121
  unisex, 121, 156
    transitions from, 159
Swing dancing, 158

T

Talent, 4
Tapes, cassette, 91
  care of, 93
Teacher, choosing a volunteer, 137
Teaching, 49–61
  at series, 137–38
  of buzz step, 157
  progression, 22
Teenagers, 115–16
  and same-sex couples, 119
  at family dances, 139
Tempo, 25, 81
  and older adults, 117
  setting, 86
  signaling band for, 88
  vs. timing, 27
"Threes", 22
Timing, 26
  as difficulty factor, 73
  of basic moves, table, 28–29
  of calls, 39–41
  of walkthrough, 53
  vs. phrasing, 30
  vs. tempo, 27
Tone controls. *See* Equalization
Traditionalists, 17
"Training wheels" method, 8

Index *309*

Transitions, 51. *See also under names of basic moves*
  as difficulty factor, 72
Triple formation, 20, 22, 24, 190
Tune changes, 87–88
  and diminishing calls, 42
  and duration of dance, 87
Tune list, 86
Tune structure, 25–26, 79
  and phrasing, 30
Tunes, choosing, 79–84
Turn contra corners
  discussed in depth, 190–91
  transition from cast off, 191
Turntables, 91, 93, 104
Twirl
  in modern square dance swing, 122
  vs. courtesy turn, 17, 161, 166, 179, 182
Twirl to swap
  discussed in depth, 165–66
Two-hand swing, 121
"Twos", 20, 22

U

Undemanding sequences, 73
Unequal dances, 19
  and duration of dance, 43
  at one-night stands, 128
Unforgiving sequences, 73
Unidirectional microphones, 38, 99, 107
Unisex swing, 121, 156
  transitions from, 159
Up the center, transition to cast off, 184
Upbeat, 26, 80, 132
  of jigs, 82
  of marches, 81
  of reels, 80
Used sound equipment, 104

V

Variety
  in programming, 64–65, 69
  with recorded music, 90

Vinyl records, 91
  care of, 93
Voice
  care of, 37
  diction, 37
  equalization of, 108
  pitch of, 36
  projection, 36
  technique, 36–39
  volume of, 39
Volume
  of voice, 39
  setting, 107
  signaling band for, 88

W

Walkthroughs, 52–56
  and reading vs. memory, 45
  how many, 55–56
  of hey, 188
  of squares, 233
  of turn contra corners, 190
  sample, 53–55
WAV files, 91
Wave. *See* Balance in a wave
Wavy line, 176
Weather, as programming factor, 67
Web-based publicity, 135
Weight. *See* Giving weight
"Western" squares. *See* Modern square dancing
Wheel around, vs. twirl, 166
Whole-set longways dances, 13
  discussed in depth, 205
  Galopede, 208
  Rural Felicity, 206
  Virginia Reel, 13, 210
Wind instruments, 132
Wireless microphones, 57, 99
Women's voices, equalization of, 108
Word of mouth, 133, 135
Wrist star, 172
Writing new dances, 76–78

Z

Zesty Contras (Jennings), 46, 53

www.ingramcontent.com/pod-product-compliance
Lightning Source LLC
Chambersburg PA
CBHW021833220426
43663CB00005B/228